p 12

See p 172

D1598795

A
PEDAGOGY
FOR
LIBERATION

A PEDAGOGY FOR LIBERATION

DIALOGUES ON TRANSFORMING EDUCATION

Ira Shor
&
Paulo Freire

BERGIN & GARVEY
New York • Westport, Connecticut • London

Library of Congress Cataloging-in-Publication Data

Shor, Ira, 1945-
  A pedagogy for liberation.

Bibliography: p. 189
  Includes index.
  1. Education—United States—Aims and objectives.
2. Teaching. 3. Discussion. 4. Dialogues.
I. Freire, Paulo, 1921-   . II. Title.
LB41.S554 1987   370′.973   86-17184
ISBN 0-89789-104-X
ISBN 0-89789-105-8 (pbk.)

Library of Congress Catalog Card Number: 86-17184
ISBN: 0-89789-104-X
      0-89789-105-8 (pbk.)

First published in 1987

Bergin & Garvey, One Madison Avenue, New York, NY 10010
An imprint of Greenwood Publishing Group, Inc.

Printed in the United States of America

The paper used in this book complies with the
Permanent Paper Standard issued by the National
Information Standards Organization (Z39.48-1984).

10 9 8 7 6

Early in the century, the millowners had planned schools as places which preached the culture of the townspeople to make millworkers docile and receptive. Through several decades, each new generation replaced its parents in the mill, in spite of increased schooling . . . The school is not a neutral objective arena; it is an institution which has the goal of changing people's values, skills, and knowledge bases.

—Shirley Brice Heath, *Ways With Words* (1983)

There is in the gap between our highly idealistic goals for schooling in our society and the differentiated opportunities condoned and supported in schools a monstrous hypocrisy . . . We will only begin to get evidence of the potential power of pedagogy when we dare to risk and support markedly deviant classroom procedures.

—John I. Goodlad, *A Place Called School* (1983)

Among schools there was one important difference, which followed from a single variable only: the social class of the student body. If the school principally served poor adolescents, its character, if not its structure, varied from sister schools for the more affluent. It got so I could say with some justification to school principals, Tell me about the incomes of your students' families and I'll describe to you your school.

—Theodore R. Sizer, *Horace's Compromise* (1984)

There is, I think, no point in the philosophy of progressive education which is sounder than its emphasis upon the importance of the participation of the learner in the formation of the purposes which direct his activities in the learning process, just as there is no defect in traditional education greater than its failure to secure the active co-operation of the pupil in construction of the purposes involved in his studying. But the meaning of purposes and ends is not self-evident and self-explanatory.

—John Dewey, *Experience and Education* (1938)

CONTENTS

PREFACE AND ACKNOWLEDGEMENTS

Ira proposed this dialogue-book in February 1984, when Paulo was at the University of Massachusetts, Amherst. Paulo liked the idea of a long discussion on the questions teachers ask most about liberating education. He wanted to begin right away on what he named our "talking book."

We met again in 1984 for a week in Ann Arbor in March, and for another week in New York in May, to review the questions we would speak about. Then, in July, we got together in Vancouver, where Paulo held a seminar at the University of British Columbia. In Vancouver, we spoke over seven days, in three-hour sessions each time, taping the conversations. Ira took the tapes home to New York for the winter and edited them into a transcript. We met again in Amherst in February and March 1985, to edit the transcript and to do more taping. After that, Ira drafted several revised transcripts and circulated them to readers. We met twice more in Massachusetts, in July 1985, and then again in February 1986, to complete the manuscript, which will also be published in Portuguese in Brazil.

We'd like to thank some people who helped make this book with us. In Vancouver, Paz Buttedahl graciously accommodated our taping needs while the seminar she organized with Paulo was in session. Yom-Tov Shamash from the University of British Columbia rescued us with tapes, a professional recorder, and nightly copying of the tapes we finished. Herb Perr from Hunter College was faithfully our tech man and audience for each taping. Ya-Ya Andrade helped us with Portuguese translations during our Vancouver sessions. Also, Cynthia Brown, Nan Elsasser, Patricia Irvine, Arthur Maglin, Bertell Ollman, and Rachel Martin read drafts of the transcript and gave us most helpful criticisms. Michael Coffey's intelligent copy-editing of the manuscript improved it as well. Special thanks to Arthur Maglin for originally suggesting this kind of book. Lastly, the Research Foundation of the City University of New York generously supported the completion of this book with a grant.

IRA SHOR
PAULO FREIRE

New York City
Sao Paulo

A
PEDAGOGY
FOR
LIBERATION

The Dream of Liberating Education

A "Talking Book": A Dialogue on Dialogue

Ira We want to say first what our "talking book" will be. We will discuss questions teachers have asked most often about 'liberating' or transformative education. Paulo says the word 'liberating' and I refer to the pedagogy as 'liberatory,' so we'll be using both terms equally.

I collected an agenda of issues raised by teachers interested in social change and liberating classrooms, real issues teachers face in re-creating school and society. Those questions cover a lot of ground: What is liberatory learning? How do teachers transform themselves into liberatory educators? How do they begin the transformation of the students? What are the fears, risks and rewards of transformation? What is 'dialogical' teaching? How should teachers speak in liberatory classrooms? Does a liberating course have rigor, authority and structure? Are teachers and students equal in a liberatory program? How does liberatory education relate to political transformation in the larger society? Does this process apply to courses other than literacy and communications? How can you teach subject matter in a dialogue method? How do liberating teachers use tests and texts? What do we mean by 'empowerment'? Can we apply a pedagogy from the Third

World to the First World? How do themes of race, sex, and class fit into the liberatory process?

These issues have appeared often in our sessions with practicing teachers. They will be the points in our discussions. We don't have all the answers and don't know all the questions that should be asked. We still make mistakes when we teach and we have some classes that don't work well. But, Paulo has devoted his life to these issues and I spent the last fifteen years testing liberatory methods and studying transformative pedagogy. So, we are determined to share what we know and continue here a dialogue underway in many places about the theory and practice of dialogic pedagogy.

Most of us who work in classrooms know that teaching is very demanding. It's also a very practical activity, even though everything in the classroom is the tip of a theoretical iceberg. However, teachers are more interested in practice than in theory. While every practice has a theory and vice versa, most of the research on education is not helpful in the helter-skelter hours of the real classroom. Further, too much of the ideology or philosophy of education comes at teachers in a language foreign to them. Teachers face too many classes, too many students, and too much administrative control, so the need for something that works in class stands out stronger than the apparent need for theory. Still, the troubling failures of the school system call out for new ideas. Even overworked teachers are curious about alternatives. They want to know how to use them in the classroom, can dialogics make a difference in the classroom, can it speak the language of their real situation.

I hear teachers in different places asking similar questions about liberatory alternatives. This is good if only because many teachers are facing the same issues at the same moment. If they and we can engage in a dialogue through this book, starting with problems and materials of wide recognition, grounded in the urgent reality of teaching, our "talking book" will be useful.

Some months ago I suggested to Paulo that we have a dialogue and he thought it would be a good thing to do.

Paulo   I think the idea of talking a book and not just writing a book is valuable. Different aspects make this spoken book interesting to me. The question is whether we are able to bring into this dialogue the possible readers of this conversation. That will depend on the dynamism of our discussion. Another interesting aspect is that such a book can be serious without being pedantic. We can rigorously approach the ideas, the facts, the problems, but always in a light style, almost with a dancelike quality, an unarmed style.

Ira   I hope we find a dancing style. So, let's take turns being poetic and comic and profound.

What will help us stay in touch with reality is beginning with questions teachers have already been asking. Our own experiences and those of other teachers are enwrapped in what we say. This is not an archival study of education. Neither are we answering questions nobody asked. Maybe we can capture the real life dramas in what we learned in and out of the classroom. There is nothing more compelling than the facts of real life. For me, the primary goal is for theory to embrace everyday living.

This problem of merging critical thought with daily life is always a challenge. Perhaps nowhere is it more important than in teaching, which is a human experience full of unpredictable moments. When I write an education book at home by myself, I am closed off from an audience and I wonder if my words are meaningful. If I hear from others that my book reads as if I were speaking to them, I know I found the voice I wanted.

Paulo   Another highly important aspect of doing a spoken book is that dialogue is itself creative and re-creative. That is, in the last analysis you are re-creating yourself in dialogue to a greater extent than when you are solitarily writing, seated in your office, or in a small library. And from the human perspective, the need for dialogue is so great, that when the writer is alone in the library, facing the blank sheets in front of him or her, the writer needs at least mentally to reach the possible readers of the book even if there is no chance that he or she will ever meet them. The writer needs to get to know, to interact with, the distant readers, who probably will read the book when he or she is no longer in existence. Here, in our case, we are facing uncountable, unknown readers, facing them symbolically, but we are one in front of another, you and I. In a sense, I am already your reader and in a sense you are already my reader.

While we are each other's reader as we talk, the readers of our own oral words and not yet of our written words, what happens here is that we each stimulate the other to think, and to re-think the former's thought. In this, I think, rests another fundamental dimension of the richness in an exchange like this one. This mutual possibility to read ourselves before writing can make our writings better, because in this interaction we can change ourselves in the very moment of the dialogue. In the last analysis, dialogue is not just "Good morning, how are you?" Dialogue belongs to the nature of human beings, as beings of communication. Dialogue seals the act of knowing, which is never individual, even though it has its individual dimension.

I am sure that in this experience, by trying to answer some of the questions we have received in different moments and spaces in the country, we are also trying to re-know what we thought we knew at the moment in which we tried to answer some years before. And our discussion will be more important for the possible readers of this spoken book if in different moments of it, even when we keep some silence, which the readers have almost to guess at—"in that moment Paulo stayed silent"—we are able to challenge the readers and not just give answers to them. If we are able to make our readers uneasy, fill them with some uncertainty, then the book will be important. If we can do that, then the book will have rigor. We will be rigorous.

Rigor and Motivation in a Liberating Course

Paulo   I think that many people are absolutely mistaken, naive, concerning the meaning of *rigor*. I feel rigorous if I challenge *you* to be rigorous. Rigor is something which exists in history, made in history. Because of that, what is rigorous today may not be tomorrow.

Ira   You mean that rigor is not something permanent or universal. It is a way of knowing rooted in the time and conditions of the knower?

Paulo   Yes, rigor is not universal. What is universal is the need to be rigorous.

Ira   Rigor is a desire to know, a search for an answer, a critical method of learning. Maybe rigor is also a communication which challenges the other to take part, or includes the other in an active search. Perhaps this is why so much formal education in classrooms fails to motivate students. The students are not included in the search, in the activity of rigor. They are told the answers to memorize. Knowledge is handed to them like a corpse of information—a dead 'body of knowledge'—not a living connection to their reality. Hour after deadly hour and year after dull year, learning is just a chore imposed on students by the droning voice of the official syllabus.

Paulo   You mentioned motivation. I think it is an interesting issue. I never, never could understand the process of motivation outside of practice, before practice. It is as if first I needed to be motivated and then I could get into action! Do you see? That is a very anti-dialectical way of understanding motivation. Motivation takes part *in* the action.

It is a moment of the very action itself. That is, you become motivated to the extent that you are acting, and not before acting. This idea applies to our book as well as to the classroom. This book will be good if at the very moment in which the possible reader is reading, he or she is able to feel motivated because of the act of reading, and not because he or she read about motivation. Nevertheless, we are responsible for that, also. It means we have to work seriously in this book to make it more than a conversation.

Ira   I'd emphasize that motivation has to be inside the action of study itself, inside the students' recognition of the importance of knowing to them. We can figure out what schooling sounds like to students from inside their ears. Teachers and administrators and counselors are constantly lecturing them on how important schooling is or what it will give them some time in the distant future. All this promoting of school only reveals its failure to motivate with the materials being studied.

It's not possible to assume motivation from the students in my classes when I begin teaching. The problem of motivation is at the heart of the teaching crisis now in the States, which has brought out a grand parade of offical reports in the past three years.[1] The current predicament is as you said, Paulo. The dominant curriculum treats motivation as outside the action of study. Tests, discipline, punishment, rewards, the promise of future jobs, are considered motivating devices, alienated from the act of learning now. In the same way, one definition of 'literacy' is 'basic skills' separate from serious materials of study, separate from issues of critical value to students. First learn the skills, and then you can get a real education! First get a real education and then you can get a good job! The best thing is always the thing you are not doing. No wonder students are non-cooperative.

Paulo   I am asked often about how to motivate students. Why don't you say more about that in your situation.

Ira   A big crisis now in the U.S. is student resistance to the official curriculum. Another way of putting it is that teachers and administrators are refusing to change the curriculum that alienates students. In response, students are refusing to perform inside official curricula. The official pedagogy is motivating students against intellectual work. This power struggle in curriculum has led to a stalemate in schools and colleges, which various official bodies have mis-defined as student 'mediocrity.' I call it a 'performance strike' by students who refuse to study under current social conditions. No small part of the equation is the shabbiness of many schools, the overcrowded rooms, and the fact that the business world won't reward hard work with good-paying, important jobs. The job market has few rewards for high achievement. Unemployment is high and entry-level wages are low. The great mass of students are destined for cheap-labor jobs, so they decide that it's a fool's game to play by rules not benefiting them and made by someone else.

The problem of motivation hangs over the schools like a rain cloud. We all know that unmotivated students in school can be very motivated outside. Commercial culture manipulates their buying habits. They also find open spaces outside school and home to build their subjective culture of sex, friendship, sports, drugs, music, and so on. When students want something badly, they move heaven and earth to get it. They find cheap cars and bargain auto insurance, a part-time job at Christmas, how to wheel and deal for a discount stereo system or a new guitar or a concert ticket, or how to get a bad grade erased at the college, or how to get into closed courses or into a civil service exam. These contexts engage their shrewdness. Such student interest in everyday subjects has led me to use themes from daily life for critical inquiry, where I ask students to write their own small books. I also bring in readings so that a tension develops between two kinds of discourse, their self-designed texts and pre-printed texts, which gives the course linguistic dynamism at several levels, official texts versus the unofficial texts written by the students.

So, when I begin teaching a course, I can't take student motivation for granted. I try to find the profile of motivation—motivation *for* what and *against* what, their existing knowledge and cognitive skills. I can find this out only by carefully observing what students say, write, and do. But first, I must establish an atmosphere where students agree to say, write, and do what is authentic to them. To help them say more, I restrain my own voice in the early going, to give their voices room. It's easy for the verbal density of an over trained intellectual to silence the verbal expression of undertrained students. By saying as little as necessary in the early going, I get some serious exercises and dialogue underway where the students are as active as I am. This makes the starting point of their education in the classroom also the starting point of my education.

What matters most to me in the beginning is how much and how fast I can learn about the students. For me, this is an experimental moment. I try exercises which educate me and the students at the same time, short-term reading, writing, thinking and debating experiences, and I keep my course plans small and loose. I fly by the seat of my pants a lot without a fully architected course plan or reading list to reassure me with familiar order. I want to learn with them what their real cognitive and affective levels are, what their authentic language sounds like, what degree of alienation they bring to critical study, what their living conditions are, as groundings for dialogue and inquiry. Students are motivated out of the learning process when the course fully pre-exists in the mind of the teacher, in the syllabus or reading list or state requirements. Do you see the corpse here? The learning already happened someplace else. The teacher merely implements a curriculum built elsewhere, merely reports conclusions reached someplace else. The student is supposed to memorize the report.

There is a lot of pressure to teach this traditional way, first because it is familiar and already 'worked out,' even if it doesn't 'work' in class. Second, by deviating from the standard syllabus you can get known as a rebel or radical or 'flake,' and be subjected to anything from petty harassment to firing.

How can I motivate students unless they act with me? Inventing a course in-progress with the students is both exciting and anxiety-producing. I feel anxious in the middle of such a creative process, wondering if all the threads will come together, but I know this openness is required to overcome the student alienation which is the biggest learning problem in school. How can a teacher learn to do this kind of teaching? By doing it. Unfortunately, academic departments and education schools discourage teachers from experimenting, and we see very few models in the teachers who taught us while we were in school.

Modeling a Critical Theory of Knowing

Paulo Do you know, Ira, I think that all these things you are saying at this moment are linked to a very, very serious epistemological question. I am convinced that the deficient comprehension of what we can call *the gnosiological cycle* is related to the misunderstandings we are talking about. By 'gnosiological cycle' I mean the distinct moments in the way we learn. The cycle of knowing has separate phases related to each other, and by seeing these moments we can understand better what happens when we try to teach or to learn.

For example, if we observe the gnosiological cycle of knowledge, we can discern that there are only two moments in the cycle, not more than two, two moments that are dialectically related. The first moment of the cycle, or one of the cycle's moments, is the one of *production*, the production of new knowledge, something new. The other moment is the one during which the produced knowledge is known or perceived. One moment is the production of new knowledge and the second is one in which you know the existing knowledge. What happens generally is that we dichotomize these two moments; we make them separate. Knowledge is produced in a place far from the students, who are asked only to memorize what the teacher says. Consequently, we reduce the act of *knowing* the existing knowledge into a mere *transference* of the existing knowledge. And the teacher becomes just the specialist in transfering knowledge. Then, he or she loses some of the necessary, the indispensable qualities which are demanded in the production of knowledge, as well as in knowing the existing knowledge. Some of those qualities are, for example, action, critical reflection, curiosity, demanding inquiry, uneasiness, uncertainty—all these virtues are indispensable to the cognitive subject, to the person who learns!

Ira   Skepticism and scrutiny, being passionately involved in learning...the motivation of knowing you are opening up new terrain. The teacher needs to model an active, skeptical learner in the classroom who invites students to be curious and critical...and creative.

Paulo   Exactly! And another question is that when we separate *producing* knowledge from *knowing* the existing knowledge, schools become easily spaces for selling knowledge which corresponds to capitalist ideology.

Ira   You mean that schools are set up as delivery systems to market official ideas and not to develop critical thinking?

Paulo   Precisely, yes! Delivering services means you are sabotaging and separating what needs to be integrated.

Ira   Critical education has to integrate the students and the teachers into a mutual creation and re-creation of knowledge. Knowledge is now produced at some distance from the classroom, by researchers and scholars and textbook writers and official curriculum committees, but it is not created and re-created by students and teachers in their classrooms.

Paulo   And there is another thing told to teachers, that teaching has *nothing* to do with researching, with the *production* of knowledge. Because of that, there is the myth that if you are a teacher who does no kind of research, you lose prestige. As if leading a seminar one semester in existing knowledge about biology or chemistry or philosophy is of no matter, as if you were not a kind of researcher. When I think of spending three hours with a group of students discussing the political nature of education, or the educational nature of politics, if I think that this is *not* researching, then I do not understand anything! That is, I am *reknowing* what I thought I knew, with students who are beginning to know about these issues. But this kind of dichotomy between teaching and research also explains the dichotomy I have already talked about between the two moments in the cycle of knowing, producing knowledge, and knowing knowledge.

Ira   Another part of the problem is the political hierarchy of knowledge. Some knowledge is given more value than others. Some knowledge can't get recognized for its value unless it takes a traditional shape in one discipline or another. For example, technology is more important to big business and to the military than is the humanities, so scientific research gets more money than the liberal arts. Pro-corporate research is handsomely funded while peace studies or feminist research or socialist scholarship are marginalized. Also, knowledge produced inside a university counts more than knowledge produced by independent scholars outside.

Even more, if I say that one research I do is listening to students, some colleagues ask, Are you a linguist? There are important studies on language in daily life, like the works of Hoggart, Bisseret or Heath.[2] I research the spoken and written words of the students to learn what they know, what they want, and how they live. Their speeches and writings are privileged access to their consciousnesses. I examine the words and themes most important to them so I will have reality-materials for the class studies. The worst thing is to be in classrooms where students are silent or where they speak and write in the phony, defensive language they invent for teachers and other authorities. We teachers spend many desperate hours in front of silent students who stare back at us unmoved. We also spend countless classes listening to student repeats of our own teacherly language. If I don't hear or read their authentic thought-language, I feel frustrated because I can't begin research into their themes and levels of development.

This kind of grounded research has little market value in the academy. It's unfortunate because grounded intelligence is one thing teachers need to animate students. It is the base information for reinventing knowledge in the classroom. This research-teaching has a high practical value. It educates the teacher in designing a curriculum which is intrinsically motivating. It also closes the professional distance between the teacher and the students.

The first researcher, then, in the classsroom, is the teacher who investigates his or her students. This is one basic task of the liberatory classroom, but by itself it is only preparatory because the research process must animate students to study themselves, the course texts, and their own language and reality. I think this kind of classroom can produce *unsupervised or unofficial knowledge*. This would challenge the schools' marketing of official ideology. We will not sound like the textbooks, syllabi, and mainstream media swarming over the students. I try to sound natural instead of professorial, critical instead of disapproving, enthusiastic instead of ceremonial. Critical inquiry can produce a literature from the grass-roots, a parallel education or parallel classroom in contention with the official ones. Teaching like this can produce dissenting knowledge and alternate ways of using knowledge.

Education is much more controllable if the teacher follows the standard curriculum and if the students act as if only the teacher's words count. If teachers or students exercised the power to remake knowledge in the classroom, then they would be asserting their power to remake society. The structure of official knowledge is also the structure of social authority. That is why the syllabus, the reading list, and the didactic lecture predominate as the educational forms for containing teachers and students inside the official consensus. The lecture-based, passive curriculum is not simply poor pedagogical practice. It is the teaching model most compatible with promoting the dominant authority in society and with disempowering students.

Remaking Knowledge and Power: The Politics of Reading

Paulo   You are right about the politics of the official curriculum. And above all, in the classroom, if the teacher quotes from research texts, then it must be the most important knowledge. For me, one of the serious problems we have to face is knowing how to confront a strong and old tradition of transfering knowledge. Even the students have difficulty understanding a teacher who does not make a transference of knowledge. The students do not believe the liberating teacher who does not shove information down their throats. Look, of course we are not against intellectual discipline. It is absolutely indispensable. How should it be possible for someone to have an intellectual exercise if he or she does not create serious discipline for studying? Yes, we need that. We need to read seriously, but above all we need to learn what it really means to read!

I say that reading is not just *to walk on the words*, and it is not *flying* over the words either. Reading is re-writing what we are reading. Reading is to discover the connections between the text and the context of the text, and also how to connect the text/context with my context, the context of the reader. And what happens is that many times we read authors who died one hundred years ago and we know nothing about his or her time. And often we know very little about our own time!

So, I am very much for demanding intellectual seriousness to know the text and context. But for me, what is important, what is indispensable, is to be critical. Criticism creates the necessary intellectual discipline, asking questions to the reading, to the writing, to the book, to the text. We should not submit to the text or be submissive in front of the text. The thing is to fight with the text, even though loving it, no? To engage in a conflict with the text. In the last analysis, it is a very, very, very demanding operation. The question then is not just to impose on the students quantities of chapters from books, but to demand that students confront seriously the texts.

Nevertheless, if you appeal to the students to assume a critical posture as readers, as ones who re-write the text being read, you risk the students not accepting your invitation, and their intellectual production declines. The invitation for students to re-write the text rather than to simply swallow it may invite the students to think that your own intellectual rigor is weak. The students might think that you are not rigorous because you asked them to critically read and re-write a single text instead of imposing on them the obligation of reading 300 books in a semester!

Ira   There is that risk. Students are used to the transfer-of-knowledge. The official curriculum asks them to submit to texts, lectures, and tests, to habituate them to submitting to authority. Students are very good at resisting the demands of authority, but they can also reject the nontraditional classroom. Some do it with silent disregard; some actively resist; some are simply out to lunch. The problem is to ease a transition gradually away from the old habits. When I listen intently to students early in the term, I learn how dominated they are by the old ways of schooling. This lets me know what kind of transition pedagogy I have to introduce. Each group of students presents a new profile of resistances and openings which I discover by researching them while the course is underway, through the dialogue and exercises. I make some concessions to the old learning habits, to reduce the level of resistance and anxiety. I assign some readings, some papers, just enough bones from the old skeleton to make us all feel at home.

There are some other problems of transition from the transfer-of-knowledge. Teachers often come into class and ask students to write essays about a book, an article in a journal, or about an academic or social question. The students frequently ask, Do you want *my* opinion? Teachers respond, Of course, you should write what you think. Students then produce largely dull and error-filled papers. They don't write with real depth, in general. Many teachers already consider themselves frustrated in their desire to get students thinking critically. One problem is that the material brought in by the teacher is disorienting to students. It is often in academic language, an English they don't use. It is often written about subjects irrelevant to their experiences, and it is even out-of-sync with the perceptual pace of mass culture, an electronic and speeded milieu. Even worse, the social relations of the classroom are alienating and silencing. That cold distance between students and the teacher keeps the students far from the material. The way in which the class arrives at a printed text and the nature of the text itself need examination. We must reinvent reading in the context of what prevents serious reading.

The Myth of Value-Free Learning

Paulo   There are also teachers who ask the students not to illuminate the intimacy of the book, the soul of the text, in order to talk about it from the student point of view. But on the contrary they just ask the students to describe the text. They often ask students to describe a second object, society itself. The students are only to describe what they see in a text or in society, and nothing more because teachers say it is not for scientists to interpret, but just to describe. Of course, they will go further and say it is not for scientists to even think to change reality, but just to describe it. In this kind of ideological understanding of the act of knowing, that is what they call the 'neutrality' or the 'objectivity' of science.

Ira   This myth of value-free inquiry is common in my culture, but it also coexists with an acceptance of the partisan nature of knowledge. Political forces in the U.S. use scientific research to support their demands or policies. But, in schools and colleges, science, engineering, technology, business and many social science courses generally present knowledge as value-free, free of ideology or politics. If not value-free, then these subjects are presented from an establishment point of view. Students are trained to be workers and professionals who leave politics to the offical policy-makers at the top. These falsely neutral curricula train students to observe things without judging, to see the world from the official consensus, to carry out orders without questioning, as if the given society is fixed and fine. Their courses emphasize techniques, not critical contact with reality. This prevents political analysis of the forces that make curricula as well as skyscrapers. A scientist, a professional, keeps his or her nose clean by staying out of politics, by not asking critical questions about your superior's decisions or about the impact of your work.

Paulo And the more you put gloves on our hands in order to avoid contamination with reality, the better a scientist you are, from this point of view of course, but not from mine.

In liberating education, we do not propose mere techniques for gaining literacy or expertise or professional skills or even critical thought. The methods of dialogical education draw us into the intimacy of the society, the *raison d'etre* of every object of study. Through critical dialogue about a text or a moment of society, we try to reveal it, unveil it, see its reasons for being like it is, the political and historical context of the material. This for me is an act of knowing, not a mere transfer-of-knowledge or a mere technique for learning the alphabet. The liberating course 'illuminates' reality in the context of developing serious intellectual work.

Ira I like that idea, Paulo, to 'illuminate' reality. And I also agree that liberating education is not a manual of clever techniques, but is rather a critical perspective on school and society, learning for social transformation.

Paulo Besides being an act of knowing, education is also a political act. That is why no pedagogy is neutral.

Ira They all have a form and a content that relate to power in society, that construct one kind of society or another, and they all have social relations in the classroom that confirm or challenge domination?

Paulo Yes. I think, for example, that the dominant ideology 'lives' inside us and also controls society outside. If this domination inside and outside was complete, definitive, we could never think of social transformation. But, transformation is possible because consciousness is not a mirror of reality, not a mere reflection, but is *reflexive and reflective* of reality.

As conscious human beings, we can discover *how* we are conditioned by the dominant ideology. We can gain distance on our moment of existence. Therefore, we can learn how to become free through a political struggle in society. We can struggle to become free precisely because we can know we are not free! That is why we can think of transformation.

Ira   I like the irony of consciousness that makes liberation possible. By studying our lack of freedom we can learn how to become free. This is the dialectic of the liberatory class. It's one place where we think critically about the forces interfering with our critical thought. So, liberatory classes illuminate the conditions we're in to help overcome those conditions, offering students a critical distance on society in place of an uncritical immersion in the status quo, to think of changing it.

Paulo   This is our invitation to the students.

Notes

[1] The premier report of the 1983 reform crisis in U.S. education was *A Nation at Risk* (National Commission on Excellence in Education, Washington, 1983). It was issued with great fanfare by the Reagan White House. Following this media event, many official reports appeared. Among the most important were:
—*Action for Excellence* (Education Commission of the States, Denver, 1983)
—*Making the Grade* (Twentieth Century Fund, New York, 1983)
—*Academic Preparation for College* (The College Board, New York, 1983)
—*America's Competitive Challenge* (Business-Higher Education Forum, Washington, 1983)
—*Educating Americans for the 21st Century* (National Science Board, Washington, 1983)
—*High Schools and the Changing Workplace* (National Academy of Science, Washington, 1984).
A stalking horse for this official eruption was Mortimer Adler's *The Paideia Proposal* (New York, 1982), which proposed the top-down reimposition of traditional academic subjects. Many scholarly studies appeared in these years on the sad state of teaching and schooling: C. Emily Feistritzer's Carnegie report *The Condition of Teaching* (1983), Richard Richardson's *Literacy in the Open Access College* (1983), a Teacher's College research team report by Sedlak, Wheeler, Pullin, and Cusick called *Classroom Perspectives on High School Reform* (1985), and Powell, Cohen and Farrar's *The Shopping Mall High School* (1985). Diane Ravitch issued her historical study of schooling called *A Troubled Crusade* (1983) and then became a leader of the traditionalist party pushing 'excellence in education.' Her collaborator in *Against Mediocrity* (1984) and co-founder of the National Network for Excellence in Education was Chester Finn, who left academe in 1985 to become Assistant Secretary of Education in the Reagan Administration.
There was also a liberal undercurrent to the conservative tide. Taking exception to the official panaceas for reform were Ernest Boyer in *High School* (1983), John Goodlad in *A Place Called School* (1983), Theodore Sizer in *Horace's Compromise* (1984), and Linda Darling-Hammond in *Beyond the Commission Reports* (1984). Goodlad's study was the most progressive and the most ig-

nored, but the California Commission on the Teaching Profession included Goodlad, and produced a more sensible state plan for reform, *Who Will Teach Our Children?* (1985) Two other reports pulling the debate in a liberal direction were *Involvement in Learning* (National Institute of Education, 1984) and *Integrity in the College Curriculum* (American Association of Colleges, 1985). The most egalitarian proposals for educational policy appeared in a New World Foundation report called *Choosing Equality* (1985), authored by Ann Bastian, Marilyn Gittell, Colin Greer, Ken Haskins and Norm Fruchter. A sourcebook on these years of reform-from-above was compiled by Ronald and Beatrice Gross, *The Great School Debate* (1985). Chapter 4 of Ira Shor's *Culture Wars: School and Society in the Conservative Restoration, 1969-1984* (1986), offers a comprehensive analysis of what this great debate was all about.

[2] Richard Hoggart, *The Uses of Literacy* (London, 1957); Noelle Bisseret, *Education, Class Language and Ideology* (London, 1977); Shirley Brice Heath, *Ways With Words* (Cambridge, 1983). *See also* Richard Ohmann, "Reflections on Class and Language," *College English*, Volume 44, Number 1, January, 1982, pp. 1-17. Ohmann's *English in America* (Cambridge, 1976) is another key text on language and politics.

CHAPTER 1

How Can Teachers Become Liberating Educators?

Reinventing Ourselves: Challenging Tradition and Mass Culture

Ira   I want to begin with questions asked often by teachers and by students: How do I become a liberating educator? How do I transform myself?

Teachers and students have few opportunities to be in liberatory classrooms. Training programs are mostly traditional and schools discourage experimentation. So, the problem of models is a first question raised. Part of this problem involves companion questions: How does liberating education differ from traditional teaching? How does it relate to social change?

Paulo   Yes, I have also received these kinds of questions in North America, and in Europe, too.

Ira   Maybe it's a good idea for us to discuss our own learning and re-learning, to see how we came to do liberating pedagogy.

Paulo   Why don't you say some things first and then I can speak after.

Ira   I had a very traditional education. As a kid, I disliked school but loved learning, especially old maps, ancient cultures, astronomy.

So, I would read on my own, do the homework, and resent going to class. Boredom made me mischievous in school, and I became what they call a 'discipline problem.' Yet, I was extremely curious about things, even though school bored me and bored the other kids also. We were much smarter than school allowed us to be. We were being treated like morons and turned into robots and I rebelled against the stupidity.

The other students, my friends, were not happy either. They caused problems too, but I became an 11-year-old leader of student resistance. I started an unofficial school newspaper, which the principal promptly banned. This was an early lesson in our freedom of the press, very different from what the textbook said. I remember reading about freedom of the press in terms of what a colonial printer named John Peter Zenger did in 1735! The evil British jailed him way back then for printing unapproved papers, but now we were all free!

At the same time, I was wooed by the teachers, who told me I was smarter than the other kids, and who asked me to play by the rules so I could do well in the future. My mother had to come to school to discuss my behavior with my teacher, and a lot of pressure was put on me to shut up. My mother took a day off from work and complained that school was boring me, but my teacher embarrassed her by saying she'd just have to find the money to put me in private school if I needed such special classrooms. Ashamed of being working-class, my mother backed down and told me to obey the teachers. I caved in and kept quiet for a long time. I became a star student and a teacher's pet. The tables of power were nicely turned here. The teachers began to love me and my friends began to hate me. I had switched sides in the culture war of the school. I went on like this in a cocoon of being good and silent until the upheaval of the 1960s started, with the civil rights movement. I started marching and got swept up into the new protest culture. It was wonderful to fly again and protest with others.

Many people in the 60s began discussing a different kind of education. New ways of learning emerged, like the alternate school movement, free schools, radical teaching experiments, teach-ins, informal seminars attached to one movement or another. And I did some experimenting with college courses, then, as a graduate student teacher. I must confess that I learned a lot about politics, Vietnam, racism, sexism, and capitalism but very little about pedagogy, and very little about mass culture and consciousness. Later, in 1971, when I arrived at a working-class college in New York, the movements of the 60s were declining while the classroom remained open at my college for experiments. I began testing pedagogy in the middle of a new war to defend Open Admissions, the recent policy in the City University of New York to admit non-elite students without prejudice regarding their poor records in high school. At that historic opening of the University to working class students, I had no idea how to teach in the mainstream.

The problem of pedagogy forced itself on me in this new situation, unscholastic students en masse in higher education, a powerful clash of cultures, mass versus elite. In the past, only a scholastic fraction of worker-students like me had been admitted to the academy. Now, millions were in. What kind of teaching could make critical learning happen? The situation looked ideally structured to fail, underfunded, large classes, poor facilities, and already the authorities were moving to close the opening of the academy to students from the bottom, to end the period of cultural democracy.

I'm embarrassed to say it, but I confess I started out in community college as a traditional teacher. I lectured on writing. I began teaching grammar. I was concerned with correct usage.

Paulo   (Laughing)Yes! This was also my beginning! Many years ago. The big difference is that first I was a teacher of Portuguese syntax. And I loved to do that! Of course, at that time, I was very far from the necessary understanding of social class dimensions in language. But, I started like you.

Ira   I *liked* grammar when I was a kid. It was a puzzle. I learned the structures and experimented with sentences. But grammar and writing were not just creative puzzles to me. I used them as ladders to climb out of the working class. Intellectual study was my road to upward mobility. I was the fraction of working-class school kids tracked on to a Ph.D., so I had a big social stake in the rules of correct usage. They were my tickets of admission to medical school, my goal then. I knew I'd have to read and write like the elite to become a doctor.

When I began teaching working class students, I wanted to transfer my own knowledge to the students. You see the problem? I naively imposed my own experience on them. I didn't know what it meant to critically reinvent knowledge with them from their place in society. I had a different social relationship to the rules of grammar than they had, because they were barely allowed into a budget community college, while I was there after time at two elite universities. They were anything but scholastic stars and teacher's pets. So, how could they have the same stake in the rules as I did? How could correct usage insert itself into their lives in the way I took to it? I didn't understand how to situate education in their experience. I didn't understand their language or their expectations. Yet, I knew exactly how to teach them!

It took me several years to discover the real interferences to critical learning, including my ignorance and arrogance, as well their own immersion in a disabling mass culture. But, at the start, in my inexperience, I thought because I swallowed the rules of grammar, so should they. Of course, Paulo, I had marvelous rationales for what I was doing! I thought I was a 'creative grammarian.' I would teach grammar in *such* an exciting way that everybody would *love* grammar! (Laughing) It was such a mistake!

Paulo   Yes! It is almost impossible. In some moments, you have to fight *against* grammar, in order to be free to write. I also thought like you did, when I was 19 years old. But now, for example, I remember how ugly I wrote at that time. Nevertheless, I was following the so-called 'literate' patterns of the language.

Ira   I did the same thing. I wrote poetry, too, that was exactly like the pre-Romantic poetry of the British 18th century. I wrote these sickly poems by copying the correct forms in school, completely uninformed about freedom in modern poetry. I would just copy whatever I saw printed on paper. My creative writing teacher in college was astonished at my precision in mimicking Gray or Collins. He was sure I had copied their pre-Romantic verse and handed it in as my own! He also looked down on me with contempt, as a sadly unsophisticated person from the wrong class. And I began teaching this way, from the printed forms of writing.

Paulo   It's very interesting because there are some very good writers in Brazil who saved me. By reading them in my early 20s I was saved. Jose Lins do Rego and Graciliano Ramos are two of these writers; Jorge Amado; Gilberto Freyre, the great sociologist and anthropologist who writes so well was another important influence on me. But these writers were *not* preoccupied in following grammar! What they searched for in their writings was an aesthetic moment. I read them a lot. And in this way they also recreated me as a young teacher of grammar, because of the aesthetic creativity of their language. I remember today how I changed the teaching of syntax, when I was around 20.

The question then was not simply to deny the rules. When I was young, I learned that beauty and creativity could not live with a slavish devotion to correct usage. This understanding taught me that creativity needed freedom. So, I changed my pedagogy as a young teacher towards creative education. This was also a foundation for my knowing later on how creativity in pedagogy related to creativity in politics. An authoritarian pedagogy or political regime prevents the freedom needed for creativity, and creativity is needed for learning.

But, before I speak about my own transformation, I am curious to hear from you more about the change in you from traditional to liberating education.

Traveling Without Maps: A Trip Towards Liberating Education

Ira   When I began as a young professor just out of graduate school, I hadn't studied alternative education systematically. I simply wandered unequipped into the boiling predicament of Open Admissions. Once in that tough terrain, I did what I knew best and planned traditional courses courses hour by hour. I had a scenario for what Monday or Wednesday should be. I studied hard how to present the rules of grammar and correct usage and rhetoric. The results were uninspiring, so I had to ask what was going wrong—small results from so much effort. I met weekly with a group of other young teachers in our new remedial writing program to discuss our classes. Together, as a staff, we helped each other, taught each other, re-educated ourselves on-the-job, year after year. Teachers who want to transform their practice can greatly benefit from group support like that. A staff development seminar is a first need of teachers, a place for peers to engage in mutual re-formation.

While I was trying to re-form myself as a teacher, at least there was little student hostility to me. I often wondered why the students were so tolerant, even though I was stumbling along and laying out a menu of grammar and rhetoric, most of which they heard before. I think my enthusiasm showed them I meant well, even though I did not know what I was doing. They very generously tolerated my confusion! (Paulo laughs) I was grateful to them for letting me learn at their expense. I was happy to be in the room with them, so I didn't broadcast any contempt for them, as non-elite college students, and no contempt for myself, as a Ph.D. teaching in a marginal, mass college. I wanted to be exactly where I was, in a mainstream classroom, teaching working students I grew up among. The upheavals of the 60s made me want social change, and I chose to be in a mainstream college. At least I had the good sense not to lecture the students on politics. I was to the left of them, but I didn't lecture them on capitalism, war, and so on. I intuitively knew this required discussion, and that we'd study writing by writing on the themes that mattered to them.

In the micropolitics of the classroom, my attitude was that we were doing something very important. This made a difference. Even though I was confused *pedagogically* about methods, I had some *political* clarity, about power and class vis-a-vis Open Admissions students, the first in their families to attend college, who hated school up to now thanks to their disempowering educations, who were surrounded by a disabling mass culture. I began to study their language and their reality with them, to discover what was preventing critical study.

You can imagine my confusion in the early months. I went through the 60s, and still I came to class teaching grammar! All this is amazing and embarrassing now, but, as they say, that was another country, or is it water under the mill. Whatever the metaphor, I'm glad it's behind me!

It felt back then as if a bankrupt New York and its bursting City University were collapsing around our ears, just when many of us were inventing an Open Admissions frontier. Each classroom and bitter faculty meeting seemed ready to explode outward into the collapse. Protesting students forced the University to put in Open Admissions five years ahead of schedule and to allow non-elite students access to the better four-year colleges. When I arrived in 1971, the crisis disrupted business as usual, opening up unsupervised space for experiments, a wonderful moment partially and temporarily vacated by the authorities. Tradition was on the defensive, so we had some freedom to experiment. By 1976, the authorities regained the offensive, and the experimental period ended with a conservative restoration.

But, in the open years, I learned a lot, especially from other experimenting teachers, and from student language. People from dominated groups speak several idioms, depending on their situation. When authorities are around, they use a defensive language full of artificial ploys and constructions to 'get by.' These forms of discourse are the linguistic shapes of the larger power struggle in society. I heard these different idioms and felt the class was going well when they spoke in nondefensive voices. They did this often enough for me to learn about their culture, their consciousness. They are very clever in hiding from the teacher, to say what the teacher wants to hear, to confuse the teacher with defensive statements and copycat answering from the teacher's own words. This defensive language prevents teachers from finding out what the students really know and can do.

Predictably, when the students spoke to me or to others about their reality, their animation became more intense. This was the intrinsic motivation you spoke about, Paulo, in our first session (see the "Introduction"). Motivation was in their relation to the subject matter and in the social relations of the classroom. The growth of their literacy could not be subtracted from critical contact with themes from their world or from the egalitarian milieu of our work together. I slowly understood what I was doing. The reality-themes we looked at were saturated with critical inquiry so that we wound up inside and outside everyday life at the same time, studying the ordinary with extaordinary scrutiny.

In our discussions, I would hear some words and phrases I didn't understand. Sometimes, I'd say sentences the students did not understand. So, I would stop the conversation to ask for an explanation of their language or to explain my statements. This helped create a linguistic meeting ground. I was attempting to reconstruct my language and also to overcome the separation between us. I spoke an intellectual idiom I learned at the university. They spoke the language of mass culture. Both our idioms were products of a society divided by race, sex and class. My language was not the 'ideal' or the goal of student development because I had left graduate school unable to communicate with worker-students. So you can see the project for liberatory discourse, inventing democratic communications, what I think of as verbal exchanges which contradict hierarchy, transforming the power separation between teacher and students. There is an idiom of reconciliation I searched for which represented the changes in our socialized speech. The problem I set for myself was finding a desocializing discourse for the classroom.

What mattered, I think, was my refusal to install the language of the professor as the only valuable idiom in the classroom. My language counted, but so did theirs. My language changed, and so did theirs. This democracy of expression established a mutual atmosphere which encouraged the students to talk openly, not fearing ridicule or punishment for being 'stupid.' I wish I could repeat to you their surprise at my interest in their words, their culture. Very rarely had a professor taken them so seriously, but the truth is that they had never taken themselves so seriously either.

They had a lot to say, too. They had family problems, and work problems, and school problems, and commuting problems, and so on. It was not my job to convince them they were unhappy. What a silly thing that would be, like being a negative crusader. Besides, to call them unhappy would be a gross oversimplification. They were happy and unhappy, optimistic and cynical, angry and resigned.

They were many things all at once. I created conditions in class where people could speak the themes of their lives. Those who responded to this invitation revealed the problem-areas of most interest to them. I questioned them about their statements, posed critical problems, and tried to educate myself into what such utterances meant, as windows into mass consciousness and as roads outward to transformation. The students' lives and language were social texts which neither they nor I understood, but which presented to me patterns, motifs, themes, characters, imagery, as clues to meaning. So, all in all, maybe I understood that the liberatory process could be a window and a road to the students, to see their own conditions and to envision a different destiny. The face and voice of the teacher can confirm their domination or can reflect enabling possibilities. If students see and hear a teacher's contempt or boredom or impatience, they learn again that they are people who inspire disgust and weariness. If they perceive the teacher's enthusiasm in their own moments of living, they can find subjective interest in critical learning.

These understandings came to me long after experiencing them in the classroom. I experimented first and reflected after. Later on, Paulo, I read your books and got a philosophical framework for what I was doing.

Student Responses: Resistance and Support

Paulo   And Ira, to the extent you challenged the traditional way of relating to the students, the way of approaching the object to be known by the students, what kind of reaction did the students demonstrate to these changes?

Ira   There's been a range of reactions. Some students wanted to know why a liberatory class had been kept from them so long. They might have said in everyday language, Where have you been all my life? All your life you carry around unmet needs that you don't exactly understand. When you reach a moment that meets that need, you say, Where have you been all my life? Finally, you can be revealed for the person you are but none of life's situations have yet permitted this feeling. That was one reaction that I noticed.

Then, there was also anger and anxiety. Students might want to ask out loud, What the hell do you want? Why don't you just fill the hour with teacher-talk and let me copy down the answers silently, staring at you with glassy eyes, making believe I am listening to your words flying through the air while in fact I am dreaming about beer or dope or sex or Florida or the big football game or the party this weekend. Students are long-habituated to passive schooling, which made some feel I had no right to make critical demands on them. As I understand it, the liberatory classroom is challenging, not permissive. There are demands that you think about issues, write and read about them, discuss them seriously. The school system has convinced many students that school is not serious about them, so they stopped being serious there. A bloc of students can't overcome their learned disgust with intellectual work in school.

Then, there were also some students who saw the possibilities of an empowering class but were still unable to speak about it in discussion. I would read their papers but could not ease those writers into class debates. I had to respect the distance they wanted. Another kind of reaction from students was not much participation and not much resistance, but they would come back for another semester or two, to be around an atmosphere that appealed to them. They might say to me, It was real! I think this meant that the course gave them contact with their own subjectivity and with my subjectivity, instead of blocking our contact with each other and with reality. I didn't present a distant, teacherly manner and didn't expect them to be disabled characters in a traditional school script. Both of us were free to be natural.

Still others were actively hostile, challenging me in ways to stop the critical thrust of the class. They were committed to tradition and saw the class as a threat to their established values. They were often a large enough bloc in class to force me to become traditional for that course. If I found the liberatory appeal rejected by students in a large bloc, I was dragged backward into transfer-teaching. I can't impose liberatory pedagogy against anybody's will to receive it. It was disappointing but easy enough to do old-fashioned transfer-teaching, even if it doesn't work. The accepting group of students reacted differently by sometimes bringing friends, lovers and relatives to class with them.

What helped me at the worst moments was understanding the limits of my own powers. It was often true that my class was a one-of-a-kind experience in the students' lives. On the other hand, a course is only a three to four month episode in a larger curriculum, and education is only one piece of larger lives in an even larger society. Mass culture socializes people to police themselves against their own freedom. So, it made sense for some classes to reject the liberatory invitation I offered. What we do in the classroom is not an isolated moment separate from the 'real' world. It is entirely connected to the real world, and is the real world, which is both the power and the limits on any critical course. Because the world is in the classroom, whatever transformation we provoke has a conditioning effect outside our small space, but the outside has a conditioning effect on the space also, interfering with our ability to build a critical culture separate from the dominant mass culture.

Maybe I should say also that the resources for transformation are unevenly distributed. If I come in front of a new class, I can't presume that this class will repeat the development or transition of the last class. Neither can I assume that they will repeat the prior class's resistance to transformation. I have to rediscover the distance that this new group can travel. It may resist transition all the way, even if I am teaching the same course that produced noticeable transformation just the term before. I can take very little for granted from class to class.

This unpredictablity of student reaction was bad news and good news at the same time. The bad news was the need to expect anything, no uniform development or conditions to work in. This was my education into 'situated pedagogy' or situating the learning process in the actual conditions of each group. On the other hand, because student consciousness so determined the outcome of any class, I could stop blaming myself for classes that didn't go anywhere. If a class did not work out, it did not invalidate the process of dialogue. If a course did not transcend the transfer-of-knowledge pedagogy, it did not make me feel like *I* was a failure. I just concluded that the situation was not open to transformation. The human beings in the process could not begin transformation at this time, in this place, through this means.

I think this is a very important point for teachers, because if you try a transition to liberatory education, you may need constant successes to convince you that you made the right decision.

Paulo   (Laughing) Very good! The traditional ideology is so strong that we need *successes*, in order for the young teacher above all to feel that he or she is right.

Ira   Successes may not come in the first year. What do you do then? You need someone to reasure you that they may appear in the second or third year, and even then, when you are so much better at transformative teaching, it still will not be a uniform experience. It leaves me thinking that 'change' is inevitable in human experience, but liberatory transformation is a potential sometimes available. When possible, it is not necessarily realized by the means used in another setting. This is why liberatory learning cannot be standardized. It has to be situated, experimental, creative—action that creates the conditions for transformation by testing the means of transformation that can work here.

So, Paulo, this is how I think about my transition to liberating education. Why don't you speak now about your development. What made you decide when you were a teenager that you wanted to be a teacher?

Paulo   I have to say first of all that being a teacher became a reality for me *after* I started teaching. It became a vocation for me only after I began to do it. I began teaching very young, of course, in order to get some money, an income, but when I started doing it I created in me my vocation for being a teacher. I was teaching Portuguese grammar but I began to love the beauty of language. And I have never lost that vocation for teaching. I can't say that when I was six or seven I had a thought in my mind to become a teacher. Of course this can happen. But for me, in my first experience teaching someone who knew less than me, I felt that teaching was good. I was maybe 18 years old, teaching privately, tutoring high school students or young people working in stores. They wanted to learn grammar.

By teaching, I discovered that I was able to teach and that I loved it. More and more I began to dream of being a teacher. I learned how to teach the more I loved teaching and studied it.

Ira   When did you begin transforming yourself in a liberating direction?

Paulo   It's very interesting to remember that now. I recall that while I was teaching Portuguese in secondary schools in a very dynamic way, some students came to me and told me that the classes made them feel more free. They used to say to me, Paulo, now I know that I can learn! It meant undoubtedly a kind of liberation from something. At an individual level, some students were suffering self-restraint because of an external restriction coming from other teachers, who told them they were not capable of learning. To the extent I could prove to them that they could learn, when I challenged them, they felt more free. I perceived this kind of progress in students, but at that time I was still very far from seeing the politics in this situation.

Students told me about their feelings of freedom in classes of 30 or 35 as well as individually in their homes when I tutored them privately. I got very dynamic feelings from them. My teaching was a mixture then of traditional and critical ways of instruction. I explained the rules of correct usage in class but above all I challenged them to write small papers, which I read and then used one at a time as the text for a whole hour's class, using their own writings as examples of grammar and syntax, analyzing what they were writing about. I taught them grammar based on what they were already writing, not from a textbook. And I also used readings from very good Brazilian authors.

Ira   What kinds of questions did you ask them to write about?

Paulo   I asked what they did on the weekend, for example. I did not ask them to write about abstract things or concepts. I always found that kind of exercise wrong. I kept the questions concrete, sometimes about a few pages of a text we were reading, sometimes about moments from their experience. And our class hours would be discussions on the themes and also the writing, but a critical discussion on what they said and wrote, not a textbook lesson.

From the beginning, I was convinced that I would have to have dialogue with the students. If you ask me if I had some systematic notion of what dialogue meant, I would have to answer no. I had no epistemology worked out to help me design my teaching. I had intuition. I guessed that talking with them should be the beginning. That is, not to just give classes to them, explaining things to them, but instead to challenge them critically about what I was saying. Finally, after leaving high school teaching, I started teaching adult workers in Recife, in the northeast of Brazil, my home area. There, I reinforced all these ideas. That was my second moment of formation, among workers and peasants in Recife. And I made mistakes. I was traditional but I was capable of going beyond.

My work then in Recife was for a private institution in local neighborhoods and in rural areas, and also at the university. I worked a lot trying to establish the relationship of schools to the lives of the workers and peasants. The more I discussed with them the problems of schools, and kids, the more I became convinced that I should study their expectations. All the things I am trying to theorize now did not come up suddenly or accidentally. They came from a series of experiences.

I could underline three or four moments of my development. The first was when I was just a student, my childhood partly in Recife and then in Jaboatao. My family left Recife in order to survive the economic crisis of the Depression of the 1930s. A great moment in my life was the experience of hunger. I needed to eat more. Because my family lost its economic status, I was not only hungry but I also had very good friends both from the middle class and the working-class. Being friends with kids from the working class, I learned the differences of classes by seeing how their language, their clothing, their whole lives expressed the totality of class separations in society.

This moment was very good in my life. Every time I remember it I learn something from it. By falling into poverty, I learned from experience what social class meant.

A second moment important to me was in adolescence. I wanted very much to study but I could not because our economic conditions did not permit it. I would try to read or to listen in class and I could not understand any of it because I was so hungry. It was not stupidity on my part. It was not lack of interest. My social conditions did not permit me to get educated. Experience taught me again about social class and learning. Then, because of my problems, the eldest in my family began to work and help our condition, and I began to eat more. At that time, I was in the second or third year of high school, experiencing difficulties. To the extent I began to eat better, I began to understand better what I was reading. That was precisely the moment I began to study grammar a lot, because I loved the problems of language. I studied philosophy of language on my own, preparing myself at 18 or 19 to understand structuralism and linguistics. Then, I began teaching Portuguese grammar with the love of language and philosophy, and with the intuition that I must understand the expectations of the students, and should engage them in dialogue. At some point between 19 and 23 years of age, I was discovering teaching as my love. Also important at this moment in my affective life was when I met Elza, who was my student, and then we got married. I was her private tutor. I prepared her for an exam to qualify for school principal. There was a syntax part in the exam.

At that moment, I was invited to work for a private industrial institute in Recife which allowed me to meet adult workers. Before that, in my childhood, I had friends who were working-class kids. Now, as a young adult, getting to know adult workers was for me a rediscovery of what I knew before. It was a second chance to reknow what I learned about working life. In this new setting, I began to learn different lessons, another moment in my transformation. It was precisely my relationship with workers and peasants then that took me into more radical understandings of education.

Of course, they did not intend to teach me what I learned by working with them! But, I learned there from my relationship with them that I should be humble concerning their wisdom. They taught me by their silence that it was absolutely indispensable for me to put together my knowledge from intellectual study with their own wisdom. They taught me without saying that I should never dichotomize these two sets of knowledge, the less rigorous one from the much more rigorous one. They taught me without saying that their language was not inferior to mine. Their syntax was as beautiful as mine when

I examined its structure and listened to it. They never could say what critical analysts know about language and social class, of course, but they introduced me to the beauty of their language and wisdom, through their witness, their testimony, not through lectures about themselves. How many times some of them called my attention to their concrete exploitation as workers.

The people can teach us many things, but the way the dominated teach is different from the way the dominant teach. The workers teach silently by their example, their situation. They are not acting as teachers to us. Because of that, we as their teachers must also be absolutely open to being their students, to learning by experience with them, in a relationship that is by itself informally educational.

Ira   That's how I learned a lot, informally, by listening and by studying with students who didn't know they were my teachers. Did you learn then as a young man that reality was socially constructed and could be reconstructed, that we are made into who we are?

Paulo   Yes! Of course! That was one kind of knowledge I got in a very concrete way from them, not through the university but by teaching workers. If you study social science at the university according to a certain approach, you learn that reality is one thing, a research or statistical model. But, the other thing is to learn by feeling reality as something concrete. To learn that concrete feeling, there is nobody better than workers as teachers. They are experiencing the things we need to study.

Changing Through Experience: Teachers Learn With and From Students

Ira   Learning from reality is important, but more than just 'going to reality,' you accepted worker-students as your teachers. That adds political depth to 'experiential' learning, which is a common idea in progressive education. The teacher learns from the students and the academic professor is informally educated by workers. This agenda is different from the traditional curriculum, and more democratic than simple student-centered teaching.

If I followed, your informal education among workers pointed you away from a purely scholastic career in linguistics or epistemology. What was the next moment in your transition?

Paulo   In the university and also in the periphery of the city, I continued my work among adult workers, peasants, accepting them as my teachers as well as students. This was a long 15 year period for me in Recife, searching silently, organizing mentally some of the principal aspects I have written down in my books. It took 15 years in that period in order for me to say: Look! There is something different for teaching people how to read and write! These years are an apparent gap in my life when I was extremely active researching a pedagogy that was not a genius invention but rather something from common experience that showed a different way of education, with good results in its beginning.

Then, in 1963, I was invited by the Ministry of Education to organize an adult literacy program, which started a new public moment where I became known in Brazil. But, that moment was very short, less than a year, because of the coup d'etat, and I came out of Brazil. My next moment of radicalization or transformation, my recognition that an educator is a politician also, came soon after the coup, in exile in Chile. The exile is the last period of my development in pedagogy and in politics, for my understanding of the politics of education.

The exile made possible my rethinking of the reality in Brazil. On the other hand, my confrontation with the politics and history of other places, in Chile, Latin America, the States, Africa, the Caribbean, Geneva, exposed me to many things that led me to relearn what I knew. It is impossible for a person to be exposed to so many different cultures and countries, in a life of exile, without learning new things and relearning old ones. The distance from my past in Brazil and my present in different contexts kept provoking my thought.

Ira   What kinds of lessons did you draw in exile, especially about the coup and education?

Paulo   A lesson about the global limits of education was a lesson above all that I received from reflecting on the coup of 1964. Of course, the Brazil coup, and the ones after in Latin America, challenged me to see clearly the limits of education. I don't say that before 1964 I was absolutely convinced that education could be the tool for transforming society. But, I was not clear on this question. I have criticized some of my naiveté on the global limits of teaching, in an essay I wrote in 1974.[1] But, the coup d'etat raised this question very clearly, and it taught me the limits. Of course, it does not mean that we should constantly have coups to learn good things!

Yes, it is true that after 1964 I grew more aware of education's limits in the political transformation of society. But nevertheless, through education, we can first understand power in society. We can throw light on the power relations made opaque by the dominant class. We can also prepare and participate in programs to change society.

I would say that before the coup I gave to education some powers that were really beyond it, but the moment then was very optimistic. With some exceptions in left groups, there was almost a certainty that we would move forward to power. There was a great generalized hope that I was part of. In this atmosphere, it was not difficult to teach students. The moment was extraordinary. The young were absolutely motivated historically to participate in the transformation. I remember that one time we needed 600 students to work as teachers in adult literacy for an area in Rio de Janeiro. We announced it in the newspapers and we had 6,000 candidates show up! It was terrible! We had to make the interviews in a stadium to select the 600, at the end of 1963. It was a time of fantastic popular mobilization, and education was part of it, one of the elements, until the coup.

Ira   In the late 60s in the States, and in parts of Europe, education was also a radicalizing part of society. I'm wondering if the 60s showed the power of education to radicalize society or the limits of education in transforming society, or both at the same time. In terms of the coup in '64, if you read education the same way the military read your work in adult literacy, you might say that education is an unacceptable threat to oligarchy, inequality, authoritarian rule. The military and its upper-class backers concluded that education could not be ignored. It was part of the mass mobilization and had to be restricted. This suggests that education's role in social transformation was very significant at that moment.

Paulo   That's very interesting. Maybe now I should say that precisely because education should be the lever for social transformation, it cannot be!

Ira   You mean that it will not be allowed to be what it should be? The elite forces in society will not permit education to transform the political structure?

Paulo   Yes! (Laughing) If education could only have a conversation with biology, for example, and say, I have to understand how limited I am obliged to be because of the political limits I am not allowed to go beyond, then the living game of social limits would be easier to see! I began to understand the nature of limits on education when I experienced the shock of the coup d'etat. After the coup, I was really born again with a new consciousness of politics, education and transformation. You can see this in my first book *Education for Critical*

Consciousness (1969). I don't make reference there to the political nature of education. This reveals some of my naiveté back then. But, I
was able to learn after that about history. All these things taught me
how we needed a political practice in society that would be a permanent process for freedom, which would include an education that
liberates.

Ira   How can these lessons help teachers and students in their
transformation?

Paulo   For transformation, we need first of all to understand the
social context of teaching, and then ask how this context distinguishes
liberating education from traditional methods. Let me begin again
with the important point I became clear on after the coup: education
per sé is not the lever of revolutionary transformation. The school
system was created by political forces whose center of power is at a
distance from the classroom. If education is *not* the lever of transformation, how can we understand liberating education? When you
arrive at this doubt, you must have a different moment in your reflection.

Liberatory education is fundamentally a situation where the teacher
and the students *both* have to be learners, *both* have to be cognitive
subjects, in spite of being different. This for me is the first test of
liberating education, for teachers and students both to be critical
agents in the act of knowing.

Another point is that education is a moment in which you seek to
convince yourself of something and you try to convince others of
something. For example, if I am not convinced of the need to change
racism, I cannot be an educator who convinces you. No matter what
a teacher's politics, each course points in a certain direction, towards
some convictions about society and knowledge. The selection of materials, the organization of study, the relations of discourse, are all
shaped around the teacher's convictions. It is very interesting because
of the contradiction we deal with in liberating education. In the liberating moment, we must try to convince the students and on the
other hand we must respect them, not impose ideas on them.

Through your search to convince the learners, your own testimony
about freedom, your certainty for the transformation of society, indirectly you must underline that the roots of the problem are far
beyond the classroom in society and in the world. Precisely because
of that, the context for transformation is not only the classroom but
extends outside of it. The students and teachers will be undertaking
a transformation that includes a context outside the classroom, if the
process is a liberating one.

What really happens inside a seminar if you are a professor engaged in liberatory education is that you give a testimony of respect for freedom, a testimony for democracy, the virtue of living with and respecting differences. Inside the context of the classroom, you give all these kinds of witness, the witness of your radicalism, but never of sectarianism. Yet, you know that the political struggle to change society is not solely inside school, even though school is one part in the struggle for change. Then, in the last analysis, liberatory education must be understood as a moment or process or practice where we challenge the people to mobilize or organize themselves to get power.

Ira   One question that comes up often is the connection between empowerment inside and outside the classroom. I agree that connecting classroom work to the transformation of society is basic for a teacher's transition to liberatory methods, but the classroom and the rest of society remain physically separate areas of practice. The language, the methods, the expectations, of transformation work best when situated in the real context we are in. Connecting classroom work to the outside society is key, but it is not the same as equating the classroom with nonacademic settings.

As a writing, mass media, and literature teacher, I say to myself I will discover the transition possible in any particular class, given the situation I and the students are in. I say something very North American about the results—transformations come in all sizes. I have a goal of social change, but I am working to provoke the transformations possible in each discrete class. Often, all I can accomplish in any single course is a moment of transition from passivity or naiveté to some animation and critical awareness. Sometimes I can't make a dent in the hold of mass culture on the students' expectations. If students do engage each other in critical dialogue, I see that as an act of empowerment because they chose to become human beings investigating their reality together. If they examine critically some texts or articles I bring in, then I take it as a sign that their resistance to critical culture is declining and their immersion in mass culture is weakening. If they seriously study racism or sexism or the arms race, I read this as a starting point of transformation which may develop in the long-run into their choices for social change. In thinking about what a classroom can accomplish, I see a gradation of transforming moments.

Paulo   Yes, there are different levels of transformation.

Ira   I look for gradual development in the classroom dialogue and notice the changing behaviors of students vis-à-vis the critical inquiry.

I look at the social interactions, to see if naive or fatalistic attitudes are changing. Do they discuss the college, commuting, work or family life with different recognitions? I try to think broadly about the channels through which any group can display transformation. If teachers don't think in terms of phases, levels, and gradations in a long process of change, they may fall into a paralyzing trap of saying that everything must be changed at once or it isn't worth trying to change anything at all. Looking only for big changes, teachers may lose touch with the transformative potential in any activity.

Liberating Methods Reveal Dominant Ideology

Paulo   Your consideration led me to some other kinds of reflections. For example, the liberating educator has to be very aware that transformation is not just a question of methods and techniques. If liberating education was just a question of methods, then the problem would be only to change some traditional methodologies by some modernized ones. But that is not the problem. The question is a different relationship to knowledge and to society.

The criticism that liberating education has to offer emphatically is not the criticism which ends at the subsystem of education. On the contrary, the criticism in the liberatory class goes beyond the subsystem of education and becomes a criticism of society. Undoubtedly, the New School Movement, the Progressive or Modern School Movement, brought many good contributions to the education process, but generally the criticism from the New School Movement stayed at the level of the school, and did not extend into the larger society.

For me, one characteristic of a serious position in liberating education is to stimulate criticism that goes beyond the walls of the school—that is, in the last analysis, by criticizing traditional schools, what we have to criticize is the capitalist system that shaped these schools. Education did not create the economic base in society. Nevertheless, in being shaped by the economy, education can become a force that influences economic life. In terms of the limits of liberating education, we must understand the very subsystem of education. That is, how is systematic education constituted or constructed in the overall picture of capitalist development? We need to understand the systematic nature of education to act effectively within the space of the schools.

We know that it's not education which shapes society, but on the contrary, it is society which shapes education according to the interests of those who have power. If this is true, we cannot expect education to be the lever for the transformation of those who have power and are in power. It would be tremendously naive to ask the ruling class in power to put into practice a kind of education which can work against it. If education was left alone to develop without political supervision, it would create no end of problems for those in power. But, the dominant authorities do not leave it alone. They supervise it.

We have had in the 70s, a variety of theories trying to understand education as part of the reproduction of society, which Henry Giroux has studied very well.[2] The fact is that the relationships between the subsystem of education and the global system of society are not mechanical relationships. They are historical relationships. They are dialectical and contradictory. It means then, that, from the point of view of the ruling class, of the people in power, the main task for systematic education is to reproduce the dominant ideology.

Dialectically, there is nevertheless another task to be accomplished. That is, the task of denouncing and working *against* the reproduction of the dominant ideology. Who has this second task of denouncing dominant ideology and its reproduction? The educator whose political dream is for liberation. The second task cannot be proposed by the dominant class, whose dream is for the reproduction of their power in society. Transformation has to be accomplished by those who dream about the reinvention of society, the recreation or reconstruction of society. Then, those whose political dream is to reinvent society have to fill up the space of the schools, the institutional space, in order to unveil the reality which is being hidden by the dominant ideology, the dominant curriculum.

Of course, this unveiling is one of the main tasks of liberating education. The reproducing task of the dominant ideology implies making reality opaque, to prevent the people from gaining critical awareness, from 'reading' critically their reality, from grasping the *raison d'etre* of the facts they discover. To make reality opaque means to lead people to say that A is B, and B is N, to say that reality is a fixed commodity only to be described instead of recognizing that each moment is made in history and can be changed in an historical process. An example of an obscuring myth is that unemployment in the U.S.is caused by 'illegal aliens' who take jobs away from native workers, instead of seeing high unemployment as a policy of the establishment to keep wages low. This is obscuring reality. This is the task of the dominant ideology. Our task, the liberating task, at the institutional level of the schools, is to illuminate reality. Of course, it is not a neutral task, just as the other one is not neutral either.

To make reality opaque is not neutral. To make reality lucid, illuminated, is also not neutral. In order for us to do that, we have to occupy the space of the schools with liberating politics. Nevertheless we cannot deny something very obvious. Those who make reality opaque through the dominant ideology, through spreading, multiplying, reproducing the dominant ideology, are swimming with the current! Those who demystify the reproducing task are swimming against the current! Swimming against the current means risking and assuming risks. Also, it means to expect constantly to be punished. I always say those who swim against the current are first being punished by the current and cannot expect to have a gift of weekends on tropical beaches!

And for me, finally, at least finally for this moment, in liberating education, the transforming teacher uses the education space without being naive. He or she knows that education is not the lever for the revolutionary transformation precisely because it should be! (Laughing) This contradiction is at the heart of the problem. In order for education to be the tool for transformation it would be necessary for the ruling class in power to commit suicide! It would have to give up its dominant power in society, including its creation and supervision of the schools and colleges. We never had in history such a case and I don't believe that in this century they will give the example.

Ira   The authorities mandate a curriculum which they think will sustain the present structure of society. But school is not fully under their control. Education is not effectively reproducing the dominant ideology. It breeds student resistance—everything from political movements to vandalism. Teachers witness a lot of disorder in the classroom. On the other hand, school is not exactly out of control either. It is an area of political contention dominated by the authorities, where opposition ideas and democratic culture can be organized by those who want to transform society, and where student alienation prevents the curriculum from working.

Paulo   Yes, that is an important addition. Before we leave this question, I want also to emphasize one important point you said before, about a frustration experienced by educators when they see that their teaching practice was not able to make the revolution they expected. In fact, they approached liberating education in an idealistic fashion. They expected from it what it cannot do, transform society by itself. In discovering finally its limits, they may start denying every effort, even important ones in the field of education, and fall into a negative criticism, sometimes almost a sick one, of those who continue to act as dialectical thinkers but not as liberatory educators. They continue to know intimately how society works, how power operates in society, but they are not able to use this understanding in the classroom. We need to know the limits and possibilities of teaching, reach to the limits, and extend ourselves beyond education to avoid this despair.

Our discussion so far has been about liberating education as a democratic education, an unveiling education, a challenging education, a critical act of knowing, of reading reality, of understanding how society works, just at the level of the school. But there is another place for the existence and the development of liberating education which is precisely in the intimacy of social movements. For example, the women's liberation movement, the environmental movement, the housewives' movement against the cost of living, all these grassroots movements will have emerged into a very strong political task by the end of this century. In the intimacy of these movements we have aspects of liberating education sometimes we don't perceive.

Other Places: Education in Movements and Communities

Ira   In these movements, there are educational activities also— seminars, teach-ins, publications. The authorities didn't set up op- position movements the way they constructed the school system. Movements have an autonomy lacking in formal classrooms, a dis- tance from official control that gives them more freedom to act for social change and for critical education.

Liberatory teachers often wonder where to do most of their work, in classrooms or in movements or in community-based organizations. What if the classroom is not the primary place for transformation? There are movements here relating to the arms race, intervention in Central America, apartheid, women's equality, racism, and more. There are many community groups sponsoring local education. Is the classroom then a secondary place for liberating education?

Paulo   Sometimes it is. Let us suppose that in some moments, my participation, our participation, in seminars at universities is a sec- ondary place for liberating education. But, what we cannot deny is that it is important. It is also a question of choice and of historical possibilities. It is a question even of taste! I personally prefer to work with the social, popular movements in the periphery of the cities, instead of working in schools. But my preference for working outside does not make me uncomfortable inside formal classrooms. I love them both and have always done both. Nevertheless, another edu- cator can tell me, But look, Paulo, I feel that my place is inside schools. I can say I prefer to work in the periphery, but others can say that it is not their place, that they feel lost on the outside. They don't feel competent to work there, but feel more competent discussing economics with students, for example, putting light on the capitalist way of production. This is also important.

For me, the best thing possible is to work in both places simultaneously, in the school and in the social movements outside the classroom. But, one thing you must avoid is to be ineffective in both places, to do both poorly because you try to do too much.

Ira   Do you think that the professional training and work demands of teachers will most likely lead them to choose the classroom first and social movements second? Does this need correction, given the importance of movements in transforming society? Are you interested now in bringing to teachers' attention the value of outside movements and community education? The training of teachers is like official training in any profession, your expertise does not include taking part in opposition politics.

Paulo   I think if it were possible for lots of teachers who work just inside school, following the schemes, the schedules, the reading lists, grading papers, to expose themselves to the greater dynamism, the greater mobility you find inside social movements, they could learn about another side of education not written in books. There is something very important outside formal education, which the people are creating. It would be for teachers an experience of opening windows. Nevertheless, I respect teachers when they say they prefer to stay here in the schools, but even there it is necessary to be critical inside the system.

Being Critical of the System While Teaching Inside It: Lecture versus Discussion Formats

Ira   Educators in formal classrooms have one place for making critical culture, for criticizing the system from inside. But, traditional teachers may claim that they are illuminating reality also. They give informed lectures about their subject. The expert teacher speaks and the students copy down what they hear. From the traditional point of view, who is best-informed and thus best-qualified to do illumination, than the teacher? So, for the traditional teacher, 'illumination' is familiar, too. The method we have in mind is not a lecture-transfer one, not a 'banking' method of education which you described elsewhere in *The Pedagogy of the Oppressed* (1970). Traditional teachers could reply that the bank of existing knowledge is rich and they have a right to draw from it, lecture from it, assign long reading lists from it, and make deposits in the students' minds.

Paulo   But, Ira, it is also important to say that by criticizing banking education we have to recognize that not all kinds of lecturing is banking education. You can still be very critical while lecturing. For me the question is how not to put the students to sleep because they listen to you as if you were singing to them!

The question is not banking lectures or no lectures, because traditional teachers will make reality opaque whether they lecture or lead discussions. A liberating teacher will illuminate reality even if he or she lectures. The question is the content and dynamism of the lecture, the approach to the object to be known. Does it critically reorient students to society? Does it animate their critical thinking or not?

How is it possible for you to provoke critical attention by speaking? How to develop a certain dynamism in the interior of your speech? How to have in your speech the instrument to unveil reality, to make it no longer opaque? If you can do that in one hour for students! Afterwards the class takes your very speech as an object to be thought about. Do you see? You take your speech as a kind of oral codification of a problem, now to be decodified by the students and you. This is tremendously critical.

Ira   I hear many questions from teachers about the lecture format versus the dialogue format, so it's a good time to speak about the lecture as a verbal codification of reality, rather than as an oral transfer-of-knowledge from the teacher to the students, a problem-posing illumination which criticizes itself and challenges students' thinking rather than a delivery system of pre-packaged information passed out verbally in the classroom.

Paulo   This is important! I tell you, why don't you go on commenting, because you said something very good now. I think you grasped it very well, better than I. Your expression was happier than mine on this question. Here the importance is that the speech be taken as a *challenge* to be unveiled, and *never* as a channel of transference of knowledge.

Ira   All of us who come through traditional schooling have heard many lectures where there is nothing more than an oral transfer-of-knowledge, a verbal channel for knowledge-transferring. Very rarely were we provoked by a creative reinvention of knowledge in front of us, in an exciting way where the language compelled us to rethink the way we see reality. This takes some practice for teachers.

It also takes a political choice to enter the opposition, to see the difference between the transfer of expert knowledge through the lecturing voice and the posing of a problem which challenges official knowledge, animating students into motion. Many teachers ask, Do I have to stop lecturing altogether? It matters for the teacher's speech to avoid being a sleepy song of information or a sedating presentation that endorses the status quo. Instead, the liberatory lecture is a critical, inspiring appeal to students, which grows out of a dialogue underway with them. The teacher who steps forward to make a presentation has to ask how his or her words are rooted in the discourse already shared in class, rather than being an academic performance in language and materials far from the student's consciousness.

One example of the dialogic lecture is in reversing the lecture-discussion format. Traditional schooling and conferences socialize us into expecting a speaker at the front to talk at length first, and then the students or the audience ask individual questions to the expert lecturer, in a one-to-one discourse. This is an hierarchical discourse which begins the learning process with the speaker's words dominant. Silent listeners are immersed in the words of the lone authority at the front. To desocialize us from this structure of elitism, I reverse the process when I lead a class or make a public presentation. I announce that I have a systematic talk or material to present, but first I ask the group to practice participatory pedagogy by answering a question or problem related to our study or theme. I invite the group to think over a question I pose, like "Is there a Literacy Crisis?" or "What is critical education?" or "What is 'news'?"(in a journalism class). The participants then report their initial thoughts to each other in small groups, after which I convene the whole body to hear each group's deliberation. This dialogic method systematically invites students or audiences to think critically, to co-develop the session with the 'expert' or 'teacher,' and to construct peer-relations instead of authority-dependent relations. Also, reversing the lecture-discussion format allows me to do in-process research into the group I am teaching for or speaking with, so that I can shape my language and analysis to fit the situation. I begin my systematic, situated presentation after a discussion where the group has already spoken words in its own voices, balancing my activity with its own.

I could describe this desocializing method in an actual course. In a Literature and Environment class, I didn't begin with a lecture on my understanding of ecology in society and in art. Instead, I asked the students to write down the questions that came to them when they thought about the problems of their environments. Next, in groups of three the students read their questions to each other and developed composite lists which each group then read to the class. As a recorder, I copied down the verbal reports and then read back the questions students raised. We had some discussion on the issues that stood out in the lists. Then, I asked each student to choose one environmental theme or question and write on it for 20-30 minutes in class. Once again, students read their essays to each other in groups of three, chose one to read to the whole class, and then let us hear what the person wrote. From this initial activity two themes emerged as predominant. One was familiar enough—cars. The second was a real surprise to me—kids cursing! This class had a bloc of students who agreed that the cursing of kids was a major issue in their environment. How could I have possibly known in advance that such a theme would move this group to critical inquiry? Believe me, whenever I thought of the environment, I found issues of acid rain, ozone depletion, industrial pollution, toxic waste sites, nuclear spills, lack of recycling, Utopian communes and Utopian novels, nutrition, etc. But, here, this group defined cursing as a "generative" theme, generated by them from their experience. So, I began with the class to study cars and cursing while asking them to read a small selection of books from the critical literature of the environment, which we also discussed in class.

I was adrift often in how to address the question of cursing, and much more at home in talking about cars or garbage or recycling. But when I figured out for myself an explanation, I left the discussion and made a dialogic lecture on my analysis of kids cursing. I discussed it in terms of "symbolic violence"[3] by the disempowered in a culture of macho violence where sex is visible and forbidden at the same time, where sex and body functions cause inhibitions and anxiety, where kids lack power and proper nurturing in school and in neighborhoods, where a corporate-controlled economy overinvests in the military and underinvests in children and social services, requiring an unnecessarily long work-week from working parents, draining the time and energy they need to nurture kids. I can't elaborate here how I presented these thoughts, but when I felt I had an illuminating lecture to offer, rooted in our on-going relations of dialogue, I left the group and spoke. My interest was to offer a global perspective on the economy to explain the generative theme of cursing, to give experience a political and conceptual dimension. The students listened intently to my presentation even though I knew it was a demanding exercise on them. Prior to my presentation, they offered their own analysis on the theme of kids cursing, blaming TV, radio, rock culture, movies, older kids, and bad parents as the forces that teach kids to curse. I wanted to tie together these single threads into a critical perspective on the system.

Through our study, they gained some critical detachment on their own daily life, what you call, Paulo, 'an epistemological relationship to reality.' They were previously immersed in reality uncritically. In my lecture, I asked them to consider unfamilar conceptual frameworks as the root causes of cursing by kids, powerlessness, alienation, social policy which injures family life and schooling, corporate policy which suits business needs but not parents and children. I not only asked them to analyze their previously unanalyzed experience and not only asked them to reflect on my interpetration of the theme, but I also suggested we discuss solutions to the problem. This was a moment when we practiced transcendent thought. Eventually, that class wrote several small booklets, on cars, kids cursing, garbage, and the potential impact of a 20-hour work week on daily life, a policy which neatly appeared in two of the Utopian novels I assigned as critical reading. This allowed us to absorb academic texts into our themes from everyday life.

At the heart of my lecture was my search for a presentation that could unveil a compelling reality to the students. I had to consider the theme and the mystifications condensing around this subject in the students' consciousness. These mystifications are constructed through the official curriculum, the media, and mass culture. In what language can dominant ideology be challenged here, in this subject, with these students? With this intimate knowledge of the subject matter, the context in which the subject matter exists in society, and the construction of knowledge in the students' minds around this material, and the confidence that the theme is generated from the students' own subjectivity, I then could make an oral presentation which provoked critical re-perception of daily life and of power in society. In the final weeks of the environment course, each student took over some class time for her or his own project presentations on a theme connected to their local situations. These presentations were stunning in their seriousness. Also, I brought in information about organized campaigns on the environment by local political groups, to connect the critical inquiry to social change outside the classroom.

This dialogical approach was not the same thing as an expert lecture passing on the official tradition in any field. I tried to challenge routine thinking as an invitation to students to begin their own challenge. But, one problem of the lecture we should talk about is that teachers receive it as the correct professional form of teaching. It is displayed to them in their training as the pedagogy for the professional, for the expert. Teachers see so few good discussion classes, that they shy away from testing their own skills as discussion leaders. They hear few compelling, critical lecturers. They also get little voice and drama training which gives them confidence in their own verbal creativity. On the other hand, students are conditioned to be passive when the teacher starts lecturing, so their inactivity is the trap waiting for us in the lecture mode. Even more, as you said before, Paulo, when you turn to a liberatory discussion format or when you decide to give lectures challenging the existing ideology, you are swimming against the current, revealing what the culture keeps hidden, and you have to expect some 'heat.' This risk of punishment restrains many teachers. You're on safer ground if you join the club and just lecture from the official knowledge.

Even if teachers have political space to deviate, to express some radicalism, we must believe that we too will be educated in the process, and not arrange the pedagogy so that transformation goes one way. Student subjectivity has to be mobilized. In the Literature and Environment course, I found myself studying issues not on my agenda. This threw me into uncertainty for a while, so the voice I offered in discussion and in my lecture was a searching one, creating itself in-process. The animated, inventing voice is crucial for the lecture mode. The trap of the lecture is more than the sleepy sonority of the teacher's voice. There is also the invitation to deliver knowledge, even radical knowledge, in neatly-bundled fully-formed packages, so that students exchange a diet of official words for a new diet of unofficial rhetoric.

This tendency of the talking teacher to silence students is greater in the lecture format. Even radical teachers can sound like talking textbooks. The students are simply less articulate, and less informed, so they'll shut up rather than intervene, ask the 'wrong' question, and risk humiliation. I also think that because the lecture-format is so dominant already from traditional schooling, it's easy enough to fall back on it and exclude other formats. Sometimes I like to talk about *parallel pedagogies*, where the teacher simultaneously employs a variety of classroom formats. If the dynamic, problem-posing lecture coexists with student presentations, group work in class, individual work, writing sessions, field work outside class, and so on, the form of the course itself will reduce the threat of teacher-talk in a transfer-of-knowledge lecture.

Teacher-Talk versus Dialogue, Domination versus Illumination

Paulo   I agree. That was a good example from your class. Let me go back to one point you made in your speech, about liberating 'illumination' versus the traditional teachers' claims that they too are 'illuminating.' I think that when we speak about 'illumination' we are in some ways using a metaphor. Of course, the dominant people may be angry because they could say, Why is *your* attempt to understand reality synonymous with 'illuminating' reality, while *our* understanding of reality is 'obscurity?' I would say that it is for me a very good metaphor. Because, for me, the domination by an elite, the exploitation of people by a minority, requires the ruling groups precisely to deny that they are doing it to someone else. They are required to hide it from the people who are dominated. Myths and explanations must be invented to hide domination and present it as something else.

I think of grammar and correct usage here. When did a certain form of grammar become 'correct'? Who named the language of the elite as 'correct,' as the standard? They did, of course. But, why not call it 'upper-class dominating English' instead of 'Standard English.' That authentic naming would reveal, instead of obscure, the politics of power and language in society. The struggle against that kind of obscuring, to liberate people who are exploited, demands light on reality. Then the metaphor is good, I think. But, finally, what does it really mean?

I think that once again it comes to education as an act of knowing. Look, I don't want to reduce the process of illumination into just an intellectualist task. No, it is not. It is really a process of knowing reality, how reality is made. The more you understand the mechanisms of economic oppression and exploitation, the more you understand what working for wages really is, the more you illuminate, the more you put light on some obscurity necessary for domination. The question is then, how to develop a kind of critical reading or critical understanding of society, even in the face of resistance by students and by the dominant class.

In doing this 'illumination,' what we are calling the transformation of the teacher and students, or their conversion, I think it is not just an intellectual game. We don't convert ourselves just because of some speeches we hear. It is a very complex phenomenon. In many ways, there have to be some levels of practice to make the transformation, moments of experience that make the conversion. Those levels of experience can take different forms, like teaching or being in a dialogic literature class, like working with trade unions, or marching in a protest. These experiences, more than hearing speeches or thinking about transformation, push forward your political development. In some moments of the teacher's and student's experiences, he or she begins to perceive more than before that education has something to do with politics. How to do this at moments of student resistance and restrictions by the authorities requires the teacher to be an artist as well as a politician.[4]

This is a great discovery, education is politics! After that, when a teacher discovers that he or she is a politician, too, the teacher has to ask, What kind of politics am I doing in the classroom? That is, In favor of whom am I being a teacher? By asking in favor of whom am I educating, the teacher must also ask against whom am I educating. Of course, the teacher who asks in favor of whom I am educating and against whom, must also be teaching in favor of something and against something. This 'something' is just the political project, the political profile of society, the political 'dream.' After that moment, the educator has to make his or her choice, to go farther into opposition politics and pedagogy.

The teacher works in favor of something and against something. Because of that, she or he will have another great question, How to be consistent in my teaching practice with my political choice? The educator may say, Now I have discovered the reality of society and my choice is for a liberating education. I know that teaching is not the lever for changing or transforming society, but I know that social transformation is made by lots of small and great and big and humble tasks! I have one of these tasks. I am an agent with humility for the global task of transformation. Okay, I discover that, I proclaim that, I verbalize my choice. The question now is how to put my practice next to my speech. That is, how to be consistent in the classroom. For instance, I cannot proclaim my liberating dream and in the next day, in behalf of *rigor*, be authoritarian in my relationship with the students.

Ira   Or give them the experience that learning is boring or to discuss ideas is to fall asleep in the classroom or to be passive in front of a talking teacher.

Paulo   Yes. Because of that, I also cannot be liberal, or even something more than liberal, liberalist! I cannot be spontaneist, a word we use now in Brazil. That is, I cannot leave the students by themselves because I am trying to be a liberating educator. Laissez-faire! I cannot fall into laissez-faire. On the other hand, I cannot be authoritarian. I have to be radically democratic and responsible and directive. *Not* directive of the *students*, but directive of the *process*, in which the students are with me. As director of the process, the liberating teacher is not doing something *to* the students but *with* the students.

I think, Ira, generally these changes happen in the history of many of us teachers. It does not mean that everyone must have the same experience. But, sometimes, it is a long process in which we learn a lot. Still, the more the educator becomes aware of these things, the more he or she learns from practice, and then he or she discovers that it is possible to bring into the classroom, into the context of the seminar, moments of the social practice in which he or she is. In the last analysis, education belongs to the social practice of society.

Ira   How would you bring social practice into the classroom? How did you learn to name 'capitalism' as the root of domination?

Paulo   First of all, I learned about capitalism concretely. I saw society divided into such different classes that it was shocking to me. In the same city, I saw millionaires living a very good life while millions of people were hungry, eating nothing. My first reaction was that many people accept God as the author of this inequality, as a testing of their ability to love Him and each other under such hard conditions. But, I began 'reading' reality for an historical explanation of these conditions and later on I studied scientifically—Marx, capitalism, economics.

Ira   Do teachers have to consider economics and social class as part of their own transformation?

Paulo   I think so, yes. Nevertheless, many aspects of this training in economics should be in the hands of teacher unions. In Brazil, we have very politicized teacher organizations. Teachers through their own organizations should take into their own hands not just the issue of their salaries, but also the right to have better conditions for their educational work. Secondly, teachers need to gain the right to continue their formation, their growth. Teachers whose dream is the transformation of society have to get control of a permanent process of forming themselves, and not wait for professional training from the establishment. The more an educator becomes aware of these things, the more he or she learns from practice, and then he or she discovers that it is possible to bring into the classroom, into the context of the seminar, moments of social practice.

Once you make a choice for transformation, you can bring into the seminar pieces of reality. You can bring in speeches of the President. You can bring in newspaper articles. You can bring in comments from the World Bank reports. You bring it in and you examine it! You can do that *even* if you are a teacher of biology, without sacrificing the *contents* of the program—which is a ghost that frightens many teachers—sacrificing the contents of the discipline. If you are a professor of mathematics or physics, and you cannot discover *some* item in the World Bank reports that has to do with your discipline, then I don't believe in your capablility, because there are ways to do that. Suppose you bring in World Bank reports into a biology class. If the Bank requires austerity for loans to Third World countries—higher prices, lower wages, and cuts in social programs—the biology class can calculate the effects on the family diet. How many fewer calories will people eat? What cheaper food will people turn to? Will this worse diet increase infant disease and death? All these things have to do with the 'illumination' of reality—to challenge the students to understand that knowing is not just *eating* knowledge and that eating is also a question of politics!

Knowing Is Not Eating Facts: Dialogue and Subject Matter

Ira   Nowhere is eating knowledge more prominent than in courses with giant reading lists. Teachers and students regularly ask how to apply the dialogical approach to subject-matter and technical-expertise courses. They suggest that writing courses, literacy programs, and communications departments are favored situations for doing liberatory education because there are smaller bodies-of-knowledge to teach. Communications courses, they suspect, lend themselves more naturally to a discussion method. The body-of-knowledge courses in science, engineering, nursing and social science leave those teachers wondering how to be dialogical when they have so much material to cover.

There is some justice to this question on how to use a dialogue-process in an imposing body-of-knowledge course. On the whole, though, I think the case is overstated. Because all of us have had so little chance to witness liberating models, it's easier to blame the subject-matter itself rather than to reinvent learning in dialogic discussion and lectures. Secondly, writing, commmunications, and literature courses can have bodies-of-knowledge as imposing as any other discipline. These courses have traditionally been taught in passive ways that alienate and silence students, through the sleepy voice of a teacher, and through materials remote from student interests. I can teach my English courses as drills in basic grammar, syntax, and rhetoric. I can teach literature courses that recite official canons. I can teach media courses as a textbook recital of delivery systems. My choice is to experiment with dialogic formats that absorb social issues and student themes. I know this choice is being made by teachers in other departments such as math and social studies.[5] Still, the most work done on liberating pedagogy here in the States has been in literacy, following your example in Brazil.

But, there is a tiredness, a 'burn-out,' in the traditional feeding of knowledge to students. Teachers who have too many students and too many courses, who have taught the same subjects for too many years, who teach in shabby schools or colleges, or who submit to one testing regime after another, often lack the will to believe in what they are doing. The official curriculum does not inspire teachers or students, so it is vulnerable to alternatives.

Speaking about the current 'burn-out' in education takes me back to your discussion of 'illumination.' I'd like to think of illumination as a teacher's reward. Liberating education can offer rewards hard to get from other approaches now. It calls upon teachers and students to see our work in a global context, giving it a Utopian spirit missing elsewhere. What many teachers want to know is how much extra work is involved, what new things do I have to learn? Traditional methods, the transfer-of-knowledge approaches, are burdensome precisely because they can't work! They produce a tremendous student resistance we have to trek through in class. The dialogical method is work also, but it holds out a potential of creativity and breakthrough which gives it unusual rewards, mutual illumination.

Paulo Yes. By talking about 'illumination,' it is very important for the liberating educators to know they are not properly the 'illuminators.' We must avoid thinking that *we* are *the* illuminators. I think that liberating education implies illumination of reality, but the illuminators are the agents together in this process, the educators and the educatees together. Of course, it may be, in this process, the educator has been in the world many years before the educatees, and so for many reasons the educator is *not* the same as the students. He or she is different, having more instruments of analysis to operate in the process of illuminating reality.

Being engaged in a permanent process of illuminating reality with students, fighting against the opacity and obscuring of reality, has something to do with avoiding a fall into cynicism. This is a risk which we have as educators, to the extent we work, work, work!, and often see no results. Many times, we can lose hope. In such moments, there is no solution and we may become mentally bureaucratized, lose creativity, fall into excuses, become mechanistic. This is the bureaucratization of the mind, a kind of fatalism.

Ira The world is finished and we just divide up what is known and hand it out? There is nothing more to create?

Paulo Yes, and it is interesting that generally the teachers who thought of themselves as missionaries end up by becoming bureaucrats! Because of that and many other reasons, I am convinced that liberating educators are *not* missionaries, are *not* technicians, are *not* mere teachers. They have to become more and more militant! They must become militants in the *political* meaning of this word—I don't know if in English it has the same meaning. Something *more* than 'activist.' A militant is a *critical* activist.

Ira   The militant, the critical activist, in teaching or elsewhere, examines even her or his own practice, not accepting ourselves as finished, reinventing ourselves as we reinvent society?

Paulo   Yes, yes, exactly! This is militancy.

Ira   We redevelop ourselves with the students. The illuminating process renews the educator to keep doing it. If he or she only brings illumination to the classroom, the teacher can easily get burned out. Militancy means permanent re-creation.

Paulo   It prevents you from losing hope. No, I can't say that it *alone* prevents losing hope. It is *part* of the process that prevents someone from becoming bureaucratic, mechanical. Of course, we can also have a distorted way of being militant. When I speak about militancy now, I am speaking about the militancy you explained very well before, a kind of *permanent effort* to grow, to create, even without sleeping! Because we don't have to sleep (Laughing). You know, we have to be aware constantly of what's going on, fighting to overcome limits.

Ira   Teachers might say, though, that they read the professional journals and new books, and keep up in their field, thus always redeveloping themselves. They go to conferences and teacher seminars to hear new ideas. But the notion of militancy is different. The liberating process is not a professional growth only. It is self- and social transformation, a moment when learning and changing society are joined.

   The teacher, then, is not an end-point of development for students to reach. The students are not a flotilla of boats trying to reach the teacher who is finished and waiting on the shore. The teacher is also one of the boats.

Paulo   Yes, but of course with great responsibilities for the teacher in these boats! Not as the owner of the boats. You see? Strongly present in the boats, leading the transformation.

Notes

[1] See Paulo Freire, *The Politics of Education* (Bergin and Garvey, South Hadley, Mass., 1985), Chapter 13, "An Invitation to Conscientization and Deschooling," pp. 167–173.

[2] See Henry Giroux, *Theory and Resistance in Education: A Pedagogy for the Opposition* (Bergin and Garvey, South Hadley, Mass., 1983).

[3] For a discussion of the concept of "symbolic violence" applied to official curriculum in schooling, see Pierre Bourdieu and J.C. Passeron, *Reproduction in Education, Society and Culture* (Sage, Beverly Hills, Calif., 1977).

[4] See Chapter 4 for a discussion of the teacher as an artist.

[5] See, for example: Marilyn Frankenstein, "Critical Mathematics Education: An Application of Paulo Freire's Epistemology," *Journal of Education*, Volume 165, Number 4, 1983, pp. 315-339; Henry Giroux, "Writing and Critical Thinking in the Social Studies," *Curriculum Inquiry*, Volume 8, Number 4, 1978, pp. 291-310. Also, Nina Wallerstein brought her liberatory skills to the University of New Mexico Medical School's community medicine department. See her "Literacy and Minority Language Groups: Community Literacy as Method and Goal," National Adult Literacy Conference, National Institute of Education, Washington, D.C., January, 1984. Wallerstein's *Language and Culture in Conflict: Problem-Posing in the ESL Classroom* (Addison and Wesley, Reading, Massachusetts, 1983), is a fine example of liberatory thematics used in second-language teaching.

CHAPTER 2

What Are The Fears And Risks Of Transformation?

Fear and Risk: The Results of Dreaming Inside History

Ira   We've discussed the transformation of students and teachers but I think we need to examine the special fears teachers have about transforming themselves. I've heard teachers talk directly and indirectly about their fears. They worry about being fired if they practice emancipating education instead of the transfer-of-knowledge pedagogy. They speak about the risks to their careers if they express opposition ideology, if they engage in opposition politics in their institutions. They also fear the awkwardness of relearning their profession in front of their students. Teachers want to feel expert, so the need to recreate ourselves on the job is intimidating to many. Dialogic classes are creative and unpredictable, invented in-progress, making some teachers worry that they will make mistakes in class and lose control or respect.

Teachers who fear transformation can also be attracted to liberating pedagogy. The regular curriculum often fails them, boring them and the students. They can feel stifled by the routine syllabus or by the familiar limits of their academic discipline. They want to breathe deeply as educators instead of taking gulps of air in a closet of official knowledge.

Teacher burn-out, student resistance, and conservative cuts in school budgets have made many teachers wonder why they are in education. It's never been a place to get rich or famous. The pay and prestige of the profession have fallen in the last fifteen years, in the United States. It has some amenities like long vacations and the morale of working for human development. Many teachers came into the profession inspired by the human good they could do, even as a public service, looking for their students to experience the joy of learning. But now more than ever, teachers are getting fewer rewards and more distress. They find it harder to celebrate their love of knowledge and their devotion to human growth. This is a moment of crisis in the teaching profession which opens some teachers to liberating dreams.

Those open to transformation feel a Utopian appeal but many feel fear also. They are attracted out of a conviction that education *should* liberate. They turn away because they understand the risks of opposition politics. They fear standing out as radicals, as people who rock the boat. The 70s and 80s have been lonely conservative years in which to take a stand against the authorities. The decline of mass movements since the 60s meant you no longer joined large crowds challenging the system. Your challenge now makes you individually more visible, and thus more vulnerable. If you're in the opposition instead of safely inside the establishment consensus (the official curriculum), you risk being fired, or not getting a promotion, or not getting a pay raise, or not getting the courses you want to teach or the schedule you want or the leave you apply for, or even in some cases you become the target of ultra-conservative groups.

When I speak with teachers, fear is like a damp presence hovering in the room. I suspect that more people feel this fear than speak openly about it. It's embarrassing to admit publicly that what stands in the way is not only the difficulty of experimenting with students, but also the professional or political risks accompanying opposition. There is also, Paulo, something I referred to earlier, a fear of the students' rejection of liberating pedagogy. A conservative restoration from Nixon to Reagan in the U.S. has made students less willing to take risks. Resurgent authorities have imposed on students such things as careerism, new testing and curricular requirements, ethics of self-interest, and dismal regimes in back-to-basics. Students worry about getting jobs. They are anxious and impatient. They want to know how any course helps them gain skills and credentials for the tough job market. They face under-employment and declining entry-level wages, while shabby schools and colleges pursue them with tests, tests, and more tests! Such a repressive, business-oriented milieu makes students resist experimental pedagogy.

We should investigate this cloud of fear above the teacher's head when she or he holds class. Fear of punishment may be only the beginning of other kinds of fear that inhibit teacher transformation. Are these fears unreasonable? Are they sensible? Are people *so* socialized into fearing punishment that *we censor ourselves* in advance of becoming an effective oppostion, or even before attempting opposition? How can dialogical pedagogy deal with the teacher's fear of student rejection, student resistance?

Paulo   First of all, I think that when we speak about fear, we must be absolutely clear that we are speaking about something very concrete. That is, 'fear' is *not* an abstraction. Secondly, I think we must know that we are speaking about something very normal. Another point I find right now when I am trying to touch the question is that when we think of fear in these situations it leads us to reflect about the need we have to be very, very clear concerning our choices, which in turn demands some kinds of concrete procedures or practices, which in turn are the actual experiences that provoke fear. To the extent that I become more and more clear concerning my choices, my dreams, which are substantively political and adjunctively pedagogical, to the extent to which I recognize that as an educator I am a politician, I also understand better the reasons for me to be afraid, because I begin to foresee the consequences of such teaching. Putting into practice a kind of education that critically challenges the consciousness of the students necessarily works *against* some myths which *deform* us.

Those deforming myths come out of the dominant ideology in society. By challenging the myths, we also challenge the dominant power. When we begin to feel ourselves involved in concrete fears, like losing our jobs, having to walk from college to college sending out curricula vitae without receiving positive answers, or the fear of little by little losing credibility in our profession, when we see all these things, we have to add some other clarifications to the original clarification of our political dreams. We must establish some limits for our fear.

First of all, we recognize that having fear is normal. Having fear is a manifestation of being alive. I don't have to hide my fears. But, what I cannot permit is that my fear is unjustified, immobilizing me. If I am clear about my political dream, then one of the conditions for me to continue to have this dream is not to immobilize myself in walking towards its realization. And fear can be immobilizing. At this moment, I am trying to be didactic, in the interpretetation of this problem. Now, I am recognizing the right to have fear. Nevertheless,

I must establish the limits, to 'cultivate' my fear. (Laughs) To cultivate means to accept it.

Ira   Instead of denying it?

Paulo   Yes. Look, of course, I don't need to make public speeches about my fear. But, I don't need to rationalize my fear and I must not deny it, to call it something else and to give the impression that I am not afraid. In the moment in which you begin to rationalize your fear, you begin to deny your dream.

Ira   Fear comes from the dream you have about the society you want to make and to unmake through teaching and other politics.

Paulo   Yes! Fear exists in you precisely because you have the dream. If your dream was to preserve the status quo, what should you fear then? Your fear might concern the forces in society which are fighting *against* the status quo. Do you see? Then, you don't have to deny your fear, because you would have the power of the elite behind you in protecting the status quo. If your dream is one of transformation, then you fear the reaction of the powers that are now in power.

If you rationalize your fear then you deny your dream. For me, it must be absolutely clear concerning these two points: Fear comes from your political dream and to deny the fear is to deny your dream.

Ira   Making a dream of transformation concrete puts you in experiences that involve risk, but if you do not get to those experiences then you prevent your dream from entering reality. But, Paulo, let's think also about the *heroism*, even heroic posturing, that often accompanies being a radical, someone who dreams of revolutionary transformation. There's a mystique of heroism, of personal sacrifice, that possesses many people who want radical change. They might feel obliged to act heroic and to show no fear. This burdens them with the need to deny what they feel and distorts the kind of work they do. They might feel that having fear makes them an inadequate person, an inadequate militant. Fear is a sign of inadequacy from this point of view, rather than a sign you are testing ways to make your political dream concrete, to make it real in society.

Your analysis is entirely different. You say that fear is a sign that you are doing your transformational work well. It means that you are making critical opposition, engaging the status quo in a contention for social change. Your dream is entering reality, contending in history, and provoking unavoidable reaction and risk.

What Fear Can Teach Us: Limits and Lessons

Paulo   The more you recognize your fear as a consequence of your attempt to practice your dream, the more you learn how to put into practice your dream! Do you see? Look, Ira, I never had interviews with the great revolutionaries of this century about their fears! I never asked Fidel Castro, for example, about his fears. I could not ask this question to Amilcar Cabral, another fantastic revolutionary. Or to Che Guevara, for example. But, *all* of them felt fear, to the extent that all of them were very faithful to their dreams.

But there is another point which I think is very important. This understanding of fear is not something which diminishes me but which makes me recognize that I am a human being. This recognition gains my attention in order to set limits when fear tells me *not* to do this or that. Is it clear? I have to establish the limits for my fear.

Ira   First you make some concessions to it, and then you understand the concessions you make, saying I can't do *this* because I am afraid, but I won't allow my fear to prevent me from doing *that*.

Paulo   This is what I am trying to say. What happens as a consequence is that in some moments instead of rationalizing fear, you understand it *critically*. Then, the recognition of the fear limiting your action allows you to arrive at a very critical position in which you begin to act according to the dialectical relationships between tactics and strategy. What do I mean?

If you consider that strategy means your dream, the tactics are just the mediations, the ways, the methods, the roads, the instruments to concretize the dream, to materialize the strategy. This relationship cannot be dichotomized. Tactics cannot be allowed to contradict strategy. Because of that, you cannot have authoritarian tactics to materialize democratic dreams. Another thing: the more you bring strategy and tactics into agreement, the more you recognize the space which limits your actions.

In some moments, for example, you discover that today historically it is not possible to do a certain kind of action because the repression should come easily on you. Then, it is as if your fear is more or less domesticated by your clarity. You just know that in that moment it is impossible to walk one kilometer. So, you walk 800 meters! And you wait for tomorrow to walk more, when another 200 meters can be walked. Of course, one of the serious questions is how to learn the *position* where the limit is. You don't find that in books! With whom do you learn how to establish limits? You learn by practicing it. You learn by experiencing. You learn by being punished! (Laughs)

Ira   The same idea applies to educational politics. Teachers learn the limits for doing liberatory education by doing it. It's the same for any act of political transformation. By attempting transformation, we learn how to do it and also the limits within which we act. When we learn limits, *real* limits in our classrooms or in other arenas of society, we also gain some concrete knowledge on how much or even how little can be accomplished right now. Then this concrete feedback on our attempts protects us from wild fantasies of fear that could immobilize us, or which could drive us into ultra-militance if we fail to recognize limits or if we feel we have to deny our fear and act heroic. If we read our reality well, we don't imagine repression, don't project our future punishment for daring opposition, but rather test the actual circumstances of our politics and design our interventions within those limits. This calls on the teacher to take a very experimental attitude in her or his classes. But the experimental attitude is common to all transformational politics. You might say that politics inside or outside the classroom requires on-going research. You research your field of action to see the results and limits of your interventions. Then, you discover how far you can go or if you've gone beyond the limits. For example, these limits could mean, in the classroom, the transformational potential of the students. One way to go beyond the limits is to violate student openness to accepting the liberatory option offered by the teacher. You raise 'correct ' issues of racism or sexism or nuclear war or class inequality, and get no response from the students, who are hearing you speak in tongues, as far as they're concerned. If you go beyond student desire or ability, or if you work outside their language or themes, you see the results, their resistance. Your approach was not systematically rooted in the real potentials for change.

Another way to violate the real limits in a school or college is to organize a militant action which is abstractly 'correct' but practically disastrous. This happened at my college in 1973 when a racist geneticist came to lecture, at the President's invitation. Our small group of activist teachers and students wanted to disrupt the event. I argued that the student majority would not support such an action and that the liberal adminstration would go after the militants instead of uniting with us to keep the conservative majority of the faculty at bay. I marvelously failed to convince anybody of my point of view and the group militantly disrupted the lecture. The aftermath was a break between the left and the liberal administration including the firing of some radical teachers. In addition, because the left shouted down the speaker, the issue became 'free speech' on campus, instead of racism in school and society. This was one step forward and three steps back, thanks to a wrong assessment of the limits. The limits back then suggested we could engage the racist in a big public debate, win the contest, and increase awareness about the nature of racism.

There are authorities policing the teacher. If the teacher tries to squeeze through a political opening too small for the project she or he has started, the teacher will feel the pressure of official response, some form of reaction or repression, which is a sign that the limits have been stepped over at this moment, in this situation, using these kinds of methods. In the incident I cited above, I could see the administration mobilizing for this event in ways that threatened the position of the left. Repression calls upon us to do a tactical retreat and figure out a new way to work. If you are fired, you are erased as a factor in that place and have to begin somewhere else. Getting fired often makes people more cautious politicians wherever they wind up next. In many cases, it silences the teacher, especially those with families to support. We've had so many examples of radical teachers being fired at all levels of education in the U.S. The mere threat of losing your job is enough to silence many teachers. Teachers who speak up, organize, or deviate from the official curriculum are made an example of, and the example of their disappearance is not lost on the faculty who remain.

I remember also, Paulo, when I was just out of graduate school, starting as a professor, when the 60s upheavals were winding down. It was 1972 and my college was hit by political attacks against Open Admissions. The traditionalists wanted a return to the old elite curriculum and the previous decorum. The civil authorities and the private sector wanted to restrain the mass movements of the 60s, one of which was a struggle for open access to higher education. They wanted to reverse the politics of equality and also to cut the costs of education and other social services to working people. So, waves of attacks on Open Admissions and on free tuition started in New York in the spring of 1972, my first year as a professor.

I recall that we were in the large college auditorium for a crisis meeting, and I was sitting there with another professor, a friend ten years older than me. During the hot faculty debate on what to do with threatened budget cuts, I raised my hand to speak. As my hand went up, my professor friend grabbed my arm and pulled it down quickly. I looked at him in surprise and saw real concern, even a cynical wisdom in his face. He said to me, "If you want to keep your job, shut up and publish!" He was a a liberal and he had a wonderful

New York sense of humor. But, the lesson he shared with me at that moment of crisis was to shut up. I felt sorry for him. I felt sorry that he feared talking.

I did feel fear also. I wanted to keep my job—I needed the money and I liked the work. It had taken me two years to find that job, even though I was the top student in my graduate department at the University of Wisconsin. No senior professor went to bat for me there because my politics offended the old boy network. I heard that one of them put a poison pen letter in my job file to discourage other colleges from hiring me. So, after nine years in college and a Ph.D. in my pocket, you can imagine how I felt racing all over the country looking for work. This was one price of dissent here in the States. I felt fear once again because my whole doctoral committee was fired for political reasons. I finished my thesis just before my major professor's contract expired. Still, sitting in my budget-college auditorium in 1972, it was my habit to put my hand up, and speak at crisis meetings. That year, in my English Department, I faced being fired by conservatives, and was observed in my class five times in five months. It was a hard time that almost gave me an ulcer, but I managed to keep my job and do politics, feeling fear. Each year was a research for me in new political conditions.

Paulo   You are right—politics is a research also.

Ira   But not a very genteel research, not safely locked away in the archives. I can understand the fear of doing this kind of research, this testing of political practice. The moment you begin opposition you reveal yourself, you expose yourself for the 'dream' you want and against the 'dream' held by the authorities and their supporters.

Acting In Spite of Fear

Paulo   This is the question. But, you know the limits of the establishment to the extent you work or act in your location. That is, without acting you never can know what the limits are for you.

Ira   My professor friend in 1972 was stopping short of the limits we had to act. But, he had a family to support and he had already lost one job.

Paulo   The problem is to act without being paralyzed by your fear. In the case of teachers, for example, it's very good when we take risks in different spaces, not just in the schools. Now, I said 'risks' because this is one of the concrete parts of the action. If you don't command your fear, you no longer risk. And if you don't risk, you don't create anything. Without risking, for me, there is no possiblity to exist.

Let us suppose we work in a faculty of education in some university. We are afraid because we are trying to do something different. What is terrible is that what we can do in some faculties is nothing that could seriously endanger the establishment. But, the establishment is *so* demanding concerning its preservation that it does not allow anything, even something naive, which can say NO! to it. Then, facing the sensitivity of the establishment, *we* are afraid. But, as I said before, we are clarifying our choice. We are knowing more or less what we would like to do. I think that one of the first things to do is to begin to know the space in which we are. This means to know the different departments of the faculty, the dean of the faculty and his or her approach, his or her comprehension of the world, his or her ideological position, his or her choice. We need to know the teachers in the different departments. It is a kind of research. I call it making an 'ideological map' of the institution.

By doing this, sooner or later, we begin to know who we can count on at certain moments. Acting alone is the *best* way to commit suicide. It's impossible to confront the lion romantically! You have to know who you can count on and who you have to fight. To the extent you more or less know that, you can begin to be *with* and not to be *alone*. The sensation of not being alone diminishes fear.

Let me say here, now, why I insist constantly on the politicity of education. There was a time in my life as an educator when I did not speak about politics and education. It was my most naive moment. There was another time when I began to speak about the political aspects of education. That was a *less* naive moment, when I wrote *Pedagogy of the Oppressed* (1970). In the second moment, nevertheless, I was still thinking that education was *not* politics but only had an *aspect* of politics. In the *third* moment, today, for me there is *not* a political aspect. For me, now I say that education *is* politics. Today, I say education has the quality of being politics, which shapes the learning process. Education is politics and politics has *educability*. Because education is politics, it makes sense for the liberating teacher to feel some fear when he or she is teaching.

Then, when I am convinced of this, and being convinced that education is politics does *not* abolish fear, I treat my fear not as a ghost that commands me. *I* am the subject of my fear. This command over fear did not happen soon. It took time in my life. When rumors of a coup came up in early 1964, many people in Brazil preferred not to believe them. Instead of 'cultivating' their fears, they chose to say a coup was impossible. My feelings then were different. I felt the coup was possible, even though I leaned towards thinking that maybe it wouldn't happen. Before the coup I had less fear of a military move because of the optimism of the people at that time. After the coup, everyone's fears and mine in general increased. Getting control of fear is not the same thing for everyone. It depends on the intensity of the practice. It depends on the results of your practice. For example, my experience in jail was very good for me. No? (Laughs) Every time I say that I insist on adding that I am *not* a masochist! But I learned a lot in jail.

Some months after the coup in 1964 I spent 75 days in jail. I had different experiences there, concerning the kinds of cells, the kinds of human relationships with the people in prison and with the people who *put* us in prison, many things. My experience in exile taught me a great deal also.

Ira   Such punishments for teachers are still extreme here in the U.S. It's easy to lose your job for radical teaching or for opposing school policy or for organizing students, but it is far less likely that you would be put in jail, unless you broke some laws. It is almost impossible to be forced into exile. At this moment, those are punishments that teachers in the U.S. do not have to face for being in the opposition.

My doctoral committee in Madison was fired during the Vietnam era because they were outspoken against the war and also took militant stands against racism, sexism and authoritarian education. But they were not put in jail. They lost their jobs, their incomes, had their careers broken, and their families' lives disrupted. You might say they were forced into a kind of internal exile, because they had to leave town, give up their homes, pack up their families and move far away. Could you say something more of your experiences in jail or in exile, concerning fear?

Paulo   I had several difficult moments of cultivating my fear after I was arrested at my home in the coup.

One afternoon, I was in my cell with five or six colleagues, intellectuals, lawyers, doctors, liberal professionals. Lunch was just given to us by the jailers, but we had all thrown away more than we had eaten of the horrible food. Some of us were silent, some talked. Then, a policeman marched into the cell and demanded, "Who is Paulo Freire?" I answered "Present!" like a student in school. He then said, "I love prisoners like you with a good sense of obedience. Take your things and come with me." I asked, "Where to?" But he only answered, "You'll find out when you get there."

He put me in a jeep which sped off. While the jeep was moving, I felt fear enveloping me. I asked myself, "Where am I going now? What is my destination? Am I going somewhere I can return from? How can I let Elza know I am being moved?" For a prisoner, being moved is something to worry about. The jeep traveled 30-40 minutes during which I was invaded by fear of the unknown. At some moment in the ride, I realized that if I did not get control of my fear, it would destroy me.

To get some control, I established a relationship between my individual experience and the larger political moment I was in. This comparison of my situation with the problems of the country gave me some detachment. Also, I perceived that my class position as an educator might protect me, at least at that moment in the coup. Those 40 minutes in the jeep were my strongest moments of wrestling with my fear, even though I had felt fear earlier, when I was first arrested.

When the jeep finally stopped, the police handed me over to a lieutenant in an army barracks. Now I had a new fear to overcome after dealing with my first fear of the unknown in the jeep. At the barracks, they put me in a box, a kind of small closet perhaps two feet by three feet, with no windows. I spent a day and a night in that box. When I first recognized the barracks and knew where I was, my fear of the unknown decreased, but I then had a second fear, whether or not I could survive biologically in such a box, and how long would they keep me in it. I was not sure I could deal with such a space. My body would have to invent surviving in a box where the walls were rippled so that I could not rest against them without pain.

After finally accepting that I was in such a box, I had to confront the size of the space to avoid its damaging effects, how to sit or stand or kneel, and so on. While I was deep in thought about this, a sergeant suddenly came to the box and spoke to me when he knew we were alone. He said through an iron grate in the door, "Professor, I know who you are and I also know you have no experience in being in such a space. Don't stand up or sit down too long. You must walk in the box. Every hour or so, call for me or someone else on duty and say you need to go to the toilet, even if you don't have to, just to get out, and don't hurry back in." This advice helped me a lot to deal with my fear in the box.

My story took place during the coup. But, in terms of dealing with fear, I can also speak of a fantastic testimony about this question a few years ago from a black worker in Brazil, when I was visiting a Christian base community, a Catholic grassroots community. There was a public meeting of about 1000 people where I was received in the community. This was in 1980, when I had just arrived back in

Brazil after my exile since 1964. This community was in a local neighborhood in Sao Paulo. The meeting was especially for us to have a conversation together after sixteen years of separation, when I was far from Brazil.

At one moment, this man, a tall, strong, beautiful man, began to talk. He said, "Some years ago, I learned how to read and to write with the proposals of this man here," and he put his hand out like this, pointing to me. He then said, "But to the extent that I began to read, to write the words, simultaneous with understanding better how Brazilian society worked, I became strongly motivated to do the same with other workers who also could not read. And then I became a teacher of literacy. I began to teach some other people, to do with them what the other teachers did with me. Of course, I began to discuss with the others the problems of Brazil, the coup d'etat in Brazil, the violence against the workers. One day the police came, and arrested me. They took me to the prefect's office, the police station, to put me in jail."

He said then, "When I was going to the police office, to be put in jail, to speak with the prefect, I began to think of my seven children. And the more I thought of the seven children, the more I was afraid. When the police car stopped at the station, they took me out and I was introduced to the chief in the district office. He stared at me and said, 'Look, I have some information about you. They say you are a good man, not a bad man. Your behavior is good. But, they say you were influenced by the ideas of a *bad Brazilian*, the so-called Paulo Freire, and now you are teaching people according to the ideas of this bad Brazilian. I brought you here to tell you this is your first time, your first warning, so I will let you go back, but please stop teaching people with the ideas of this bad Brazilian.'"

The black worker from the community looked around and then said, "At the moment when the chief made his speech to me I had the temptation to feel happy because I was being released. And I almost denied using Paulo Freire. And I came home feeling happy because I was free, crying out, I am free! I am free! I embraced my kids and I kissed my wife, and I spent three days without giving class. On the fourth day, I said to myself, No, it is impossible, I must continue to teach. At the same time, I said to myself, What am I going to do with my seven kids? I can't go on teaching because of the kids. Finally, I taught the classes. The next week I was called in again to the police station, by the same man. He said, 'You did not accept my suggestion, so you will stay here now. I don't know when I will let you go.'"

I can't forget the speech of this man, his testimony! I must always think of him as one of *my* best educators, one of *my* best teachers.

And then he said, that in jail, he began to think again of his seven kids, and about his wife. Finally, some people intervened and he was released. When he got out, he insisted again on teaching the classes.

This story is beautiful because we can see in it the question of fear associated with the dream, how he learned to control fear *without* rejecting it.

He said that the third time, when he began teaching the classes, he was called again to the police station. The chief said to him, "Look, it was just told me that you know fifty percent of the slum in which you live. And fifty percent of the people know you. Why don't you leave this area? Why don't you forget Paulo Freire? Why don't you go far away and live in another slum where you don't know anyone, start a new life?"

The answer he gave to the police chief was, "Oh, Mr. Prefect, yes I know fifty percent of the people of my slum. How can I leave the slum right now when I must get to know the *other* fifty percent?"

The worker stopped his story and stared at me in the great silence of this big meeting. I am sure he heard the silence gripping the attention of the people there. Finally, he said, "And about my seven kids, *what* happened to them?"

He answered his own question in such a *fantastic* way! Look, I am sweating from the memory of his speech! He said, "There was a moment in my fear in which I discovered that *precisely* because of the seven kids I could not be silent!" Do you see?

Ira   His dream was their hope for the future. His fear meant that their hope was alive, their future was coming to life.

Paulo   Yes! His dream, absolutely concrete, is his future and his hope. In no sense was there a future for his kids without his hope. Then, knowing this, he overcame his fear. No paralyzing fear. This, Ira, is what is not easy to explain, or to live with. After seeing the sweetness of this fantastic man, this Brazilian worker, this story of his fear, when I left the meeting that night in Sao Paulo, I also felt more or less changed. That is, finally, that man added to me some dimension of courage.

Ira   The Brazilian worker was knitted into a community that helped him know what he was fighting for, but he also faced more severe repression than teachers face in the First World, who may lose their jobs but won't be locked up for doing liberatory education.

When I think of getting knitted into a location and acting for a dream of transformation, I'm taken back to the 'ideological profile' you spoke about earlier, as a way of preparing myself for opposition. I know I didn't understand this in the 60s, when the upheavals were immature and not well-organized. Now, I see better the value of research and preparation, to make opposition count, and also as a way of reducing fear by reducing mistakes and unnecessary risks. If you do a careful institutional profile, a map of who is on what side politically, then you can find allies, scout your enemies in advance, get a feel for what terrain offers some political opening. This preparation not only reduces the chances of miscalculating the room for opposition, but it also starts knitting you into your location. I found that I also had to learn what the history of politics had been in my college before I arrived there as a new professor. It's very easy to discredit yourself if you stand up naively and propose something that had been just fought over before you arrived.

The black worker in your story had friends who could intervene for him. He worked in concert with others in his community so the police could not simply isolate him. He wasn't a romantic hero. If teacher-militants can become 'institutional citizens' knitted into the school or college, the authorities cannot so easily uproot us or characterize us as outsiders. Doing the institutional profile helps this knitting, I think. Another political method that helps is called 'deviance credits.' I think of this as taking on some of the harmless tasks of the institution so that you get recognized as a legitimate part of the scenery. There are many things formal schools or colleges do, from buying books for the library to planning how to decorate the buildings to judging student essay contests and appeals on grades. On the whole, society and its subsystems like education are authoritarian. But, not every piece is captured by authority or closed to democratic opposition. Finding cracks in the wall helps, like locating less obnoxious parts of the school or college to take part in for deviance credits. If you take part in a variety of small tasks, you begin slowly to root yourself in the life of the institution. The recognition you get for doing this is like an account of credits that allows you more room to deviate.

Confrontations are inevitable over pedagogy and policy, so there will be some risk and fear. You are bound to make interventions that offend the status quo. It matters to pick our battles carefully, but we also can store up weapons for the fight. If you accumulate deviance credits, the right to deviate, you gain more legitimacy for radical criticisms, for liberatory experiments, for opposition programs. You are not a total outsider and you are not a total insider. You have one leg in the life of the institution and one leg outside. Gaining this kind of credibility by doing some legitimate institutional tasks strengthens your chance to make opposition. You could say that it prolongs your life in the institution because you did something for the life of the institution as you found it when you arrived. This will simply make it harder for the authorities to fire you. After all, the point of making opposition is not to get fired fast!

Paulo   Yes (laughs).

Ira   The goal of opposition is not to get fired, but to make long opposition, so you can gradually research your efforts and feel out your territory, slow enough to cope with your fears, like the black worker in the story. If you can prolong your opposition, you'll take it farther. There's no way to avoid risk, fear, or offending the status quo, but maybe you can limit the response by the authorities, by keeping them off-balance, with something like deviance credits. I think the black worker in the story had deviance credits because of his association with the Church in Brazil, which is a powerful and legitimate insititution there, and here in the U.S., too. He not only had half the slum as his acquaintance but he was also inside one of the pillars of his society, which made it harder for the police to pull him out and eliminate him. The police had less running room because of his connections. Still, he, a liberatory educator, had to work through his fear and convictions, to use the possiblities of his environment.

The Fear of Student Resistance

Ira   Paulo, I'd like to go on here to talk about a different fear teachers speak about in the U.S. They fear *student* rejection of liberating pedagogy. Teachers who are transforming themselves to liberating methods often complain that students resist the invitation. The students often have traditional expectations.

Now, in the U.S., there are discipline problems. Students are reacting to resurgent authorities full of tests and new requirements. The economic crisis is also anxiety-producing. The job-market is poor, the cost of living high, the cost of college going up. So students want to know quickly what the market value of a course is. They resent taking required liberal arts courses that 'waste' their time by distracting them from their career majors in business, nursing, engineering, or computers, the new hot programs that pushed humanities into a depression in the 70s.

Students worry about their futures. How do they get a good job out of this education? Liberating educators face student cynicism on a grand scale. Teachers often find themselves possessing a dream for society that is light years distant from the universe of their students.

Some student militancy is reviving now, especially around apartheid in South Africa and the arms race and the war in Central America, but the premier problem has been a decade of careerism rather than liberating possibilities. How would you speak to this question?

Paulo   This fear of student rejection is a very concrete problem. First of all, it is *not* the students' thinking about jobs and money which makes society like it is now. On the contrary, it is society *becoming* a certain way which creates this preoccupation among students. There are some very concrete, historical conditions which create students' expectations about pedagogy. Secondly, I think that expecting a job after traditional education is *not* a problem for the official curriculum, not a problem for teachers who use the transfer-of-knowledge approach. Getting a job is a very concrete and realistic expectation which easily fits into the regular way of schooling. It is normal for traditional classrooms to respond to the students' preoccupation with getting a job. They agree with the status quo, including the job market the students must enter. Thirdly, I think that *both* the traditional and the liberating or democratic educator, in my view, have to answer the expectations of the students. Let me be more concrete.

Because I, the liberating educator, have some dreams perhaps completely different from the students, I don't have the right to accomplish my tasks in an irresponsible way. I cannot teach only to their demand that this course do nothing but help them get a job. Is that clear?

Ira   It's an important point. Explain it again.

Paulo   Both the traditional and the liberating educator do not have the right to deny the students' goals for technical training or for job credentials. Neither can they deny the technical aspects of education. There is a realistic need for technical expertise which education from a traditional or a liberatory perspective must speak to. Also, the students' need for technical training in order to qualify for jobs is a realistic demand on the educator.

Nevertheless, what is the *only* difference a liberating educator has on this question? The traditional educator and the democratic educator both have to be competent in their ability to educate students around skills needed for jobs. But the traditionalist does it with an ideology concerned with the preservation of the establishment. The liberating educator will try to be efficient in training, in forming the educatees scientifically and technically, but he or she will try to *unveil* the ideology enveloped in the *very* expectations of the students.

Ira   The traditional educator offers technical training in a way that strengthens the hold of dominant ideology on student consciousness. Training does not reveal the politics of doing such work. The liberatory teacher does not mystify jobs, careers or working, but poses critical questions while teaching them?

Paulo   Yes! No mystification.

Ira   Job skills must be criticized at the same time they are learned because the current conditions of society require students to enter a predatory job market.

Paulo   Yes, it is required! How is it possible *before* transforming society to deny students the knowledge they need to survive? For me, (laughing) it is an absurdity.

Ira   Then, our task as liberating educators with the necessity of training students for jobs is to raise critical questions about the very training we are giving. The students must earn a living, and no one can deny that need or have contempt for that expectation of theirs. At the same time, the pedagogical problem is how to intervene in the training so as to raise critical consciousness about the jobs and the training, too.

Paulo   I don't deny or question the need for training. But I absorb this aspect into my criticism of the whole system, in the class. Still, what is impossible is to be an *incompetent* educator because I am a revolutionary! (Laughing) Do you see? It would be a contradiction. The more seriously you are engaged in a search for transformation the more you have to be rigorous, the more you have to seek for knowledge, the more you have to challenge the students to be scientifically and technically prepared for the real society they are still living in. If the students use the course *just* to get jobs and be happy with that, you *cannot* kill them! (Laughing) You have to challenge them at the very same moment you are helping them to be prepared.

Ira   Won't students see this as a confusion? You are endorsing and criticizing the material at the same time.

Paulo   Ah, no, it is not a confusion. It is a contradiction. They must understand what contradiction means, that human action can move in several directions at once, that something can contain itself and its opposite also. For example, at the same time that architecture or nursing students get competent training, the liberating teacher has to raise questions about how people live in slums, and what are their medical and housing needs. It is not enough to prepare students to build for the rich or to treat the rich only. Neither is it enough to feel sorry for the poor. The politics of housing and medicine have to be integrated into the program.

Ira   Right now, vocational, career, and professional programs, like nursing, accounting, computers, engineering, business, marketing, teach job skills that funnel students uncritically into an unpredictable job market. The critical side of the curriculum resides almost exclusively in some liberal arts courses, in the college program. Sociologists, philosophers, anthropologists, historians, literature teachers, in some courses, not all, ask students to think critically, and only a small part of this reflection is actually devoted to critical scrutiny of work, careers, or domination in the job market. In my book *Critical Teaching and Everyday Life* (1980), I devoted some chapters to writing courses where 'work' was investigated as a theme. There is now a radical separation in the curriculum between the programs that do the most concrete training for jobs and the programs that do the most critical reflection. This separation is political, not accidental. It prevents future labor from escaping dominant ideology. It segregates critical thinking from training. Such job preparation reduces the capacity of workers to challenge the system.

   The problem for liberating educators is that they often wind up in the departments which do the *least* job training, with the least career orientation, like me in an English Department teaching writing, media and literature courses, with very few English majors at my college. My courses are filled with business, tech, nursing and computer majors, who are pumped full of career anxiety by their prime programs. So, from the start, students arriving in my classes or in other humanities courses know that the education offered there will be marginal to their career goals, to their getting the training required by the job-market. Still, I like to make a virtue of necessity, so I've found that the writing course has been able to raise some critical awareness even though it is not a career program. Perhaps that's because reading, writing and thinking have been defined as basic job skills, required for all careers, even though writing itself is a limited career choice for most students. The writing teacher can insert critical literacy closer to the job world precisely because writing classes can absorb social themes as their subject matter for literacy development. The techniques of writing need concrete subjects to create compositions, so the writing class is open to critical study of the most anti-critical theme of education, career training.

Paulo   Let me go on with your example of the writing course or the writing teacher. Think about two English teachers. One is a convinced reactionary who does not want anything concerning social change. He or she thinks all things that exist are good and should stay that way. He thinks that those who fail are to blame for their own failure. The other English teacher on the contrary knows that his colleague is wrong. From the point of view of the interests of the mass of the people, he or she knows the reactionary is wrong, but the liberatory educator also knows that the traditional writing teacher is absolutely right from the point of view of the dominant class, which has the greatest stake in keeping things as they are.

Then, the liberatory educator has a different approach concerning language, teaching, learning. She or he knows very well that language is an ideological problem. Language has to do with social classes, the identity and power of each class being expressed in its language. But the liberating teacher also knows that today the standard that rules language is a very elitist one. The powers that rule society at large also have a standard by which language is judged. If the liberatory teacher wants to teach competently, he or she must know well the elite criterion by which language is valued. This is a hard criterion of language for common people from lower economic backgrounds to achieve, something which the liberatory teacher accepts without blaming the students for their problems with correct usage. By understanding the elite and political aspects of standard usage, the liberatory teacher avoids blaming the students for the clash of their own language with the ruling forms. Knowing these things, the liberatory teacher works with students who must gain a good command of standard English and correct usage.

Ira   You are saying that standard English is a job skill, a social skill that students must possess? The liberating educator is obliged to teach correct usage?

Paulo   Yes, the liberatory teacher has to know this, or see the language problem in this way. The so-called 'standard' is a deeply *ideological* concept, but it is necessary to teach correct usage while also criticizing its political implications.

Now the question is, knowing all these things, does the liberating educator have the right not to teach standard usage? Does he or she have the right to say "I am a revolutionary so I don't teach the 'good' English?" No. In my point of view, she or he will have to make it possible for the students to command standard English but here is the big difference between him or her and the other reactionary teacher. While the traditionalist teaches the rules of the *famous English* (Laughs) he or she *increases* the students' domination by elitist ideology which is inserted into these rules. The liberatory teacher teaches standard usage in order for them to survive while discussing with them *all* the ideological ingredients of this unhappy task. Do you see? This is how I think teachers can reflect on their fear of student rejection and also on their fear of standard usage.

Ira   We study standard usage and technical skills because of political realities facing students and teachers both, the fact that society is not yet an egalitarian one where elite standards no longer dominate. What we need to invent are liberatory methods which develop student command of correct usage and of job skills while encouraging them to respect their own idioms and to criticize the very nature of the unequal job-market. This is a complicated dual task which has taken up my attention since I began teaching at my worker college, to develop language skills and criticism of domination at the same time.

Paulo   Yes. This is the position I take in Brazil when I talk to teachers. A year or two ago, I opened a Brazilian congress of teachers of Portuguese. In my speech, I talked precisely about how the standard form or correct usage can be absorbed into a democratic pedagogy. This problem is very great for teachers in Brazil because there is such a vast social class difference between the Portuguese I speak and the Portuguese the workers speak. They are two separate worlds of language. The syntax is completely different. The structure of thinking is also different. The problem of concordance between subject and verb, for example, is constantly different from one class to another in Brazil.

To my thinking, teachers in popular areas of Brazil need first to give testimony to common students that they respect the language of the people. Secondly, they would have to give testimony that the language of the people is as beautiful as ours. Thirdly, they would have to help them believe in their own speech, not to be ashamed of their own language, but to discover the beauty in their own words. Fourthly, teachers who work among ordinary people would have to demonstrate that the common form of language also has a grammar which is invisible at the moment to them. Their ordinary way of speaking also has rules and structure. Their language exists because it is spoken. If it is spoken, it has a structure. If it has a structure, then it has grammatical rules too. Behind this ordinary speech, there is an unwritten grammar and an unrecognized beauty, which of course the dominant class would not draw to the attention of the common people. To organize such knowledge and make it clear to the people would be to challenge the dominance of the elite forms and thus of the elite class itself.

Finally, teachers have to say to students, Look, in spite of being beautiful, this way you speak also includes the question of *power*. Because of the political problem of power, you need to learn how to command the dominant language, in order for you to survive in the struggle to transform society.

Someone may ask me, But, Paulo, if you teach correct usage, the poor or working-class student may just get ruling ideology through the elite usage. Yes! It is a danger. But dominant ideology is not being reproduced *exclusively* through language or through school. There are other ways of reproduction in society, and language is only one mechanism. For me, what we cannot deny to working-class students is the grasp of some principles of the grammar common to the dominant class. Not grasping the elite forms would only make it more difficult for them to survive in the struggle. The testimony that must be given to students as we teach the standard form is that they need to command it not exclusively in order to survive, but *above all* for fighting better against the dominant class.

Ira   This is political wisdom for liberatory teachers. Still, I must criticize the word 'survival,' because 'survival' is a conservative theme that put teachers and students on the defensive after the egalitarian 60s. The word 'survival' has poisoned the educational atmosphere in the States with more fear than is necessary. The student fear of survival has helped conservatives tilt the curriculum towards careerism and back-to-basics. By alarming students, teachers and parents about survival, conservatives in the recent period were helped in narrowing the experimental and democratic curricula from the 60s. From another angle, I'd say that the overblown talk about survival is also an unnecessary paternalism by teachers. Students are very resourceful in dealing with the predatory job market. They know that connections, aggressiveness, luck, moxie, and chutzpah play as big a role as paper credentials. Students need critical education, skills, degrees, and adult mentoring, but they don't benefit from an alarming picture of reality, where careerism and back-to-basics are falsely posed as the keys to a fearful kingdom. Fears of survival only strengthen conservatism by encouraging students and teachers to think of career programs as the solution, while critical learning and politics are only distractions. Jobtraining and vocationalism have always been the curricula of choice by business forces for the mass of students. Work-based programs also have a poor historical record of connecting schoolish training with future employment.

I said these things because the theme of survival has become too angelic in my culture. I always remind myself that the great masters of survival are the cockroaches of New York! I've read that they reproduce every few generations a new breed that resists the insecticides deadly to their grandparents. Cockroaches can beam with pride at their children's survival powers. I've also read that cockroaches are likely to be the best survivors of a nuclear war. Not too long ago, the 60s was a time when masses of people thought about 'thriving,' not just 'surviving.' Cockroach 'survival' has served the authorities' need to restrain the mass movements of the 60s and to limit demands for power, equality and prosperity.

When the political pendulum swings back to social movements, fears teachers have about student rejection of liberatory education will change with the changing tides of history. These fears, I think, are the size of this conservative age. You're right, Paulo, about the need to make concessions to the limits of the moment, the need to insert critical learning into correct usage and career issues. But, conservative eras that set such limits are made and unmade in history. As conservatism ebbs and popular militancy returns, student resistance to transformative learning should decline. Will teachers then fall behind the experimental desires of the students?

CHAPTER 3

Is There Structure and Rigor in Liberating Education?

Structure Against Structure: Liberating Classrooms Transform Traditional Authority

Ira   We spoke before about the fears and risks of transformation. At this point, we should talk about structure, rigor, and authority in liberating pedagogy.

Teachers ask about structure in a dialogic and transformative classroom. They want to know what kinds of rigor operate there. From their training and from department requirements on the job, teachers have set before them a very normative program. In the lower grades, standard syllabi are often developed at the centers of authority, in official curriculum groups or state committees. College teachers inherit an official reading list which is the traditional shape of their subject matters. These standardized programs give teachers and students little autonomy to re-invent existing knowledge.

State and school authorities seek a standard curriculum that is even teacher-proof. Just imagine that, legislating the individual teacher out of knowledge-making. These mechanical curricula often tell the teacher how many pages should be read in a week, how many words a student should produce on an essay, how many tests should be given at what intervals, how many lab experiments and how many years of history should be covered in a term, and so on. Such pedagogy presents itself as a professional model of teaching, very architected, with learning easily quantified and measured, easily tested, conveniently monitored by supervisors. The managerial counter-revolution in education has installed a curriculum shaped for administrators and accountants. The school bureaucracy absorbs a huge chunk of school monies and thinks that schools could be run perfectly if only teachers and students didn't get in the way.

There is a 'great chain of being' here. Business interests predominate in society and control the election of public officials through mass media, lobbies, campaign contributions, and the two-party system. Business-oriented officials then construct and administrate a nominally 'public' education system. This 'public' schooling mandates a curriculum which socializes each new generation into the values of private enterprise. Education is thus a complicated and indirect agency through which corporate interests are promoted in the public sector. To get pro-elite outcomes from such a subsystem, state and local administrators impose mechanical curricula to control what teachers and students do in each classroom. This hierarchy finds the transfer-of-knowledge approach the most suitable pedagogy for sustaining elite authority. The transfer-method is thus no accident or mistake. It is not a question of informing the authorities on 'more effective teaching.' The inequality and hierarchy in our corporate society simply produce the curriculum compatible with control from above. That chain of authority ends in the passive, transfer pedagogy dominating schools and colleges around the country. It also ends in teacher burn-out, student resistance, and the continual eruption of liberatory reforms from below.[1]

Teachers are at the bottom of this great chain of elite power, one link up from students. If we ask teachers to consider transformation to liberatory methods, they often wonder if there is a structure to the new way of working which can compete with the standard syllabus. In attempting an illumination of reality and an empowerment of students, they wonder if they'll be systematic and competent. Is the liberating approach a helter-skelter, do-your-thing episode without direction? Is it chaotic and permissive? We need to speak about the rigor and structure we see in dialogical classrooms.

Paulo   I think this is a very, very good question. And I'm also asked about that, not exclusively in the United States, but also in Europe, Brazil, and other places in Latin America. There are some very interesting aspects to be touched exactly in the way you put the question.

For example, I have the impression, but perhaps right now I am *not* being rigorous! (laughs) , because I am saying 'I have the impression,' when some young teachers and young students ask a question like this, emphasizing improperly the rigor in the traditional curriculum, of choosing the contents of the programs, emphasizing the authoritarian dimensions of this traditional approach, giving to this mechanistic way of thinking and of doing curriculum the name of 'rigor,' for me it is *not* 'rigor.' The standard, transfer curriculum is a mechanistic, authoritarian way of thinking about organizing a program which implies above all a tremendous lack of confidence in the creativity of the students and in the ability of the teachers! Because in the last analysis, when certain centers of power establish what should be done in the classroom, their authoritarian manner denies the exercise of creativity among the teachers and the students. The center is above all commanding, manipulating, from some distance, the activities of the educators and the students.

Let's go back, Ira, to the beginning of my reflection. When students or young teachers ask the question you put on the table, my impression is that by thinking of something different, which the students or young teachers are naming 'dialogical education' or 'liberating education,' they are so used to following orders that they don't know how to be responsible for their own formation. They have not learned how to organize their own reading of reality and of books, understanding critically what they read. Because they are dependent on authority to structure their development, automatically they think that liberating or dialogical education is *not* rigorous, precisely because it asks them to participate in their own formation. I don't know whether I am being clear in my explanation.

Ira   Students and teachers inventing liberatory education and reforming themselves may feel so unfamiliar with being responsible for their studies, that they think the dialogical approach lacks rigor. Participatory learning begins from a history of their non-participation. The elite transfer-pedagogy laid everything out in advance and just asked us to follow along step by step, preventing democratic learning and the intellectual habits needed for transformation. In this transitional moment, it is easy to mistake chaos from below as the antidote to control from above. Those of us who ask about liberating structure may also intuit the effort that participation requires and can feel tired by the energy it takes to 'illuminate' reality, to overcome the limits of traditional education. People can know *a priori* the rigor of transformation, which may make them long for a mechanical, undemanding route to liberating education. We have been allowed to know only *one* definition of rigor, the authoritarian, traditional one, which mechanically structures education, and discourages us from the responsibility of recreating ourselves in society.

Paulo   Yes, yes! To the extent what has been *said* to be rigorous means *precisely the distance* from being responsible. At the moment in which you say, Look, but now, I invite you to be responsible!, immediately they think in opposition that your hypothesis is not rigorous. Do you see? It is very interesting. I said before, I have the impression, but now, I am almost quite sure about that! (Laughing) And what can we do in such a situation? I am sure, Ira, that we have to fight with love, *with passion,* in order to demonstrate that what we are proposing is *absolutely* rigorous. We have, in doing so, to demonstrate that rigor is not synonymous with authoritarianism, that 'rigor' does not mean 'rigidity.' Rigor *lives* with freedom, *needs* freedom. I cannot understand how it is possible to be rigorous without being creative. For me it is very difficult to be creative without having freedom. Without being free, I can *only* repeat what is being told me.

I think that we have to understand with patience that the question of rigor in liberating education is not asked to provoke us in the bad sense of the word. This question is really a curiosity of the student or young teacher, but if we are not able to demonstrate that the dialogical approach is very serious, very demanding, very rigorous, and implies a permanent search for rigor, if you are not able to demonstrate that through doing it, not through speech, I think that we fail in our proposition.

Ira   Yes, we have to show in practice that liberatory or dialogical education works rigorously. In my book *Critical Teaching,* I wrote five chapters about actual courses I tested from this approach, to situate the ideas in real classrooms. When I speak with teachers or students at a conference, I remind myself to do critical and participatory learning with them, instead of only talking about it or talking at them. But here, I also wanted to say something more about the single definition of rigor we have now, coming to students and teachers from the official curriculum.

Teachers and students are socialized into a mechanical way of education, year after year, and its form becomes synonymous with professional rigor. This mechanical program silences and alienates the students, with less than one percent of class time devoted to open, critical discussion and less than three percent of the hour showing any emotional tone, according to Goodlad's recent study.[2] There is little experience in doing education any way other than teacher-talk. Because central authorities mandate a standard syllabus and each discipline sets the appropriate language and subjects of its own academic territory, the official proposition is that learning in any course or classroom can be quantitatively measured. With testing and measurement, the authorities decide if the money invested is well-spent or not, cost-effective or not, as they put it. Then, they know if the school hour is well used or not and if the professional educator is earning his or her money. A certain amount of information transfered to a certain number of students in a certain time period equals rigor, school money well-spent, and teaching wages well-earned. You can see again the business culture behind traditional 'rigor.'

We have by now *internalized* the traditional forms, the old architecture of transfering knowledge, the authoritarian habits of teacherly discourse in the classroom. So, I think, Paulo, the problem is not only to criticize the center of authority which many students and teachers feel oppressed by, but then to define the creative rigor of dialogue so that we know how to begin with confidence in the new method. In doing this, we have to accept that the *distant* authorities who mandate curriculum are by now inside us also, and will have to be expelled from our thinking.

Another obstacle to our confidence in transforming education is lingering doubt from the last great period of experimentation. The experimental 60s often raised a permissive, unstructured classroom as a new 'liberating' education. This image of license instead of deliberate freedom allowed elitists and conservatives to claim that creativity, experimentation, breaking with tradition, meant an absence of seriousness and rigor. Such an historical background almost requires us to discuss how liberating education is not a permissive, undirected pedagogy.

I'm thinking also about the limits for us as we talk here. The limits are that we can't develop *in anyone else's* classroom the kind of specific curriculum that will be suitable for those students and teachers. This would violate the creativity of the pedagogy we have in mind. If I understand it correctly, liberating culture is situated in the real conditions of the people who are making and remaking their society, so their day-to-day curriculum cannot be invented by someone else from a distance, delivered or imposed on them. On the other hand, we can report on our own process of learning, our own teaching, and reflect on what they suggest. So, Paulo, why don't you speak more about the creative rigor of dialogue-education?

Creative Rigor: Democratic and Directed

Paulo   I would like to say some things to you about that. Fifteen days ago, I had a very interesting weekend at the Universidad Autónoma de Mexico, in Mexico City. Three days of work with 25 professors at a very high level of seriousness and competency. We talked together each day for four hours, and in some moments we discussed your question of rigor and dialogue. A Mexican professor who thought like us (most of them were in the same perspective) said something very interesting. He said that a dialogical experience which is not based in seriousness, in competency, is *much worse* than a 'banking' experience where the teacher merely transfers knowledge. I am *absolutely* in agreement with him. From the point of view of the students, a dialogical teacher who is incompetent and not serious provokes worse consequences than a serious and well-informed 'banking' educator.

Ira   What are the consequences?

Paulo   Ah! For example, the first one and the worst one is the testimony of irresponsibility, of intellectual irresponsibility.

Ira   That learning is impulsive and disorganized?

Paulo   Yes, that knowing is something that happens...

Ira   Out of the blue...

Paulo   And it is not! Knowing demands discipline! Knowing is something which demands many things from you, which makes you tired in spite of being happy. It is not something which just happens. Knowing, I repeat, is not a weekend on a tropical beach!

An irresponsible educator, talking about his or her practice as if it were a dialogical one, works against a kind of revolutionary education. And a second consequence as bad as this one, is that irresponsible behavior, *self-named dialogical*, convinces the authoritarian educators that *they themselves must be authoritarian.*

Ira   You think that undirected 'liberating' classrooms present an image of aimless, flaky education which allows the authorities to claim that a strong central power is needed? Irresponsibility and disorder justify authoritarianism or help make it legitimate?

Paulo   It justifies their traditional methods. I think, then, Ira, that those like us who believe in liberating education, not because we were *told* that it is good, but rather because of our *political* choice, have really to be strongly demanding. That is, we cannot give the students the impression that crossing the courses we participate in is something easy. Because if we do that, we work against these ideas. Because, look, many things are against them! Tradition. Authoritarianism all over the world. Even many *left* colleagues, who are also authoritarian, *tremendously authoritarian!* Who cannot accept dialogical methods.

Many in a left position are convinced *religiously* that they received a mandate from God, in spite of not believing in God! To *save* the students, to *save* the people. They think they have *the truth* in their hands and their task is to walk all over the world as Peregrines of the Revolution, not discussing 'truth,' simply putting it inside as many heads as possible.

Ira   Like injections of revolutionary wisdom.

Paulo   Yes, injections! We *must* say that this is reactionary and *not* a revolutionary attitude.

Ira   Let's talk more about the revolutionary attitude, how it works in favor of creative rigor. Suppose we want to reject the authoritarian way of transfering knowledge to students. We also want to avoid being left-wing crusaders who mimic the transfer-teacher by injecting "Revolutionary Truth" into students' minds. We have a creative pedagogy which seeks to reinvent knowledge situated in the themes, needs and language of the students, as an act of illuminating power in society. How can we describe the rigor of this process in even more intimate detail? You know what I'm getting at. There is in official schooling a range of tangible, seductive products, such as the final exam, the term paper, the multiple-choice test, entry skill-exams and exit competency-exams, it goes on and on, a closet full of cultural tools.

If you can't program a course in advance and can't test results mechanically at the end, how do we demonstrate the rigor of the liberatory course? How do we demonstrate to ourselves, to interested teachers, to our critics, and even to our enemies that rigor exists here?

Paulo   Yes, but look, to demonstrate to our enemies is very difficult because they are absolutely inserted into their comprehension of rigor. For example, one of the connotations of rigor for them is never to try to interpret reality.

Ira   Yes, like we discussed before, especially among some physical scientists and social scientists.

Paulo   As a teacher, even though you humbly do not *proclaim* that you are a scientist, you have to give witness, testimony, to the students that they have nothing to do with interpreting or, even worse, changing reality. Reality is not there to be interpreted or changed but to be described, observed, according to the traditional way of teaching.

And it's very funny, because for traditionalists, scientists, who claim rigor but deny interpretation, the concept of observing implies an observer who has to put a glass in front of his or her face and put some gloves on their hands in order not to touch, not to make contact with reality, not to...not to...

Ira   Contaminate yourself with the real conditions of living.

Paulo   Yes, not to contaminate reality and not to be contaminated by reality.

Ira   They propose no critical exchange between the knowing subject and the object to be known. They also propose mystifications as false general explanations, like monopoly capitalism is 'free enterprise,' that anybody can go as far as you want if you only work hard enough, and if you fail it's your own fault, that we enjoy freedom of the press instead of a highly monopolized, censored mass media.[3] Whether we are taught to merely describe limited parts of society or to see through distorted overviews, we are kept from contacting reality.

Paulo   Reality, they say in their weak rigor, is a *positum* waiting for your observation and not for your action, as if it were possible for you to continue *to be* if you *just* observed. We are *becoming* something more because we are learning, are knowing, because *more* than observing, we *change*. This is for me one of the connotations of creative rigor in dialogue-education, one of the most important ones. If you don't change as you know the object of study, you are not rigorous.

Traditionalists are defenders of the status quo, opposed to democratic changes from below, so I am not so interested in demonstrating to them that *I* am rigorous. But, what I have to demonstrate to the students is that I have another way of being rigorous, precisely the one in which you do more than observe; you try *to interpret reality.* Then, the more I approach critically the object of my observation, the more I am able to perceive that the object of my observation *is not yet because it is becoming.* Then, more and more I begin to note in my observation that the object is not in-itself but it is being related dialectically with others which constitute a totality. The more my observation goes beyond a mere description or opinion of the object, and I get to a stage in which I begin to know the *raison d'etre* which explains the object, the more I am rigorous.

I also recognize in my approach to reality that the very fact of being rigorous is being done in time, in history. First of all, it is not just an individual attitude. It is also a social activity. I am knowing something in reality, with others, in communication with others.

I think that in terms of curriculum, you can do these rigorous studies through reading. Serious reading is part of the rigor of the dialogical class. Of course, the students *have* to read. You *need* to read, to read the classics in your field. The students have to read Marx, for example, independent of their rejection or acceptance of the Marxist rigor. What for me is impossible is to deny the existence of Marx, as well as to deny the existence of the Positivists, of the Structuralists, of the Functionalists. You see, then, I don't accept a kind of *scientific racism*, where some classics are not allowed to be read, not considered part of the fundamental literature.

Ira   So, Paulo, you think that students need to study the classics of any discipline, but *not* as objects of worship?

Paulo   Studying *really*, reading seriously, critically. For example, some years ago a graduate student said to me that a teacher in a course he was taking gave for one semester a bibliography with *300 books!* And the student said to me, "I am crazy. I don't know what to do besides reading. I have no time. I am creating a serious problem with my wife and my kids." Look, I cannot understand how this is possible! I confess also, I don't know whether this very professor who gave 300 books had really read all of the books. And if he really read them, I am not quite sure if he understood all these books. For me, it is necessary to underline this point to the students: When I criticize this professor and the reading list, I do not mean the opposite that I see no need for reading books. Then, our position is very difficult because I think it is absolutely necessary to make clear to students that we need to read seriously at least some books.

Another question when we think of this (and I don't know if you have in the States the same phenomenon we have now in Brazil) is that the new generation of Brazilians are arriving at the universities without knowing how to do the kind of reading which the universities demand. I said 'the kind of reading the universities demand' because they really know to make *other* kinds of readings. But not the kind demanded at the universities. Of course, most of them also don't know how to write in the way demanded by the universities. This is a problem. Some professors say, "I have nothing to do with this because my task here is to teach Hegel. If they are not able to understand Hegel, this is *their* problem, *not* mine."

I don't see things like they do. First, because I don't believe that the students come to me at the university without knowing that they are responsible for a certain kind of reading and writing. They are responsible for knowing that but there are reasons why this is not yet inside the level of responsibility of the youth, which explains this situation. If I am an educator looking for a possible social change in my country, I cannot say to the students, "I have *nothing* to do with that! And I put down a *zero* for you!" No. If I can help them, maybe they can understand better the need to transform Brazilian society. Some professors, even *left* ones, demonstrate their rigor by *annihilating* the students, dropping them from the program. My rigor is too much influenced by my political choice, with which I try to be consistent.

Then, my rigor and my political position lead me to help the students by teaching them how to read. How can I do that? I do that *simultaneously* with reading Hegel! That is, instead of telling the students, you have to read the first chapter of this book by Hegel or this book by Gramsci, I read one chapter with them in the whole time of the seminar. I read with them, without telling them I am teaching them how to read, what it means to read critically, what demands you make on yourself to read, that it's impossible to go to the next page without understanding the page you are on, that if you don't understand some words you have to go to a dictionary. If a normal dictionary does not help you, you have to go to a philosophical dictionary, a sociological dictionary, an etymological dictionary! Reading a book is a kind of permanent research. I do that with the students.

Two years ago I suggested to a group of graduate students to read *six pages* of a printed transcript containing a statement made by a peasant in Brazil. This transcript was from a tape done by an anthropologist, a great friend of mine, who taped this conversation he had with a peasant. This transcript of the conversation became the preface for a book he organized. The six pages by the peasant are one of the best texts which I found in Brazil after my return there in 1980, after sixteen years of exile. The peasant criticizes education in Brazil, as it is being done now.

I suggested to the students that they read this text, and that at our next meeting we read it in class, but first they should read it at home. The next week, I took my copy and at nine o'clock we started reading. We had three hours with a coffee break, but the coffee break did not exist, because the students did not want to stop reading! In order to give my demonstration of serious reading, my testimony of critical illumination, I started reading, but when I came to the first period, I stopped and said to the students, "Right now for me it is impossible to go on if I don't stop in order to think about what I read. I want to understand better what I read here, so let me go back to the beginning of the sentence." I went back to the first word and read little by little. When I stopped again, I said, "Right now I think I understood better, and I will try to tell you how I interpret what is behind this speech by the peasant." And then, I began to speak about what I was reading, and I read two or three more pieces of the speech, doing the same thing. When I stopped, I said, "Who would like to continue?" One of them began to read.

We did that for *four* sessions with *three hours* each session to read *six pages.* Twelve hours. When we finished, in the last day, one of the students, a sociology professor in the faculty of medicine, doing a graduate degree in education, came to me smiling and said, "Paulo, I have something to tell you. When you suggested one month ago to read this text, I bought it and Sunday evening, the day before the first session, I read it in twenty minutes, and I said to myself smiling, 'I want just to know what Paulo will do with this tomorrow. Because we have three hours in seminar and what will he do with this text which I finished in twenty minutes!' After spending twelve hours reading this text of six pages, my conclusion is that I did not know how to read before." Do you see?

What is my opinion on this? (Maybe I am not rigorous now because I begin with only my opinion!) My thesis is that for me it was better for that group of graduate students to have spent twelve hours reading with me six pages. The sociologist showed me how her notebook was full of notes she made during the discussions. My impression is that after that exercise it should be more easy for students *to read alone.* To understand what it means to read. To go on by themselves. I think that from time to time if you can read with students for one chapter like this, challenging them, and after that suggesting other chapters to read alone and discuss with you, it is better than to impose the reading of 300 books, which rests on a certain faith in a very, very problematic epistemology, which is, If you insist on something, you end up getting it. But 'knowing' is not that, not just getting what you insist will be the end result of an exercise. This is a problem and not a certainty.

But do you see, Ira, how difficult is our land, our territory?

Ira   Yes. On the one hand, we want the 'illuminating' course to be serious and on the other hand it has *to develop* the habits of intellectual seriousness in a cultural field that discourages students from being critical. Even worse, the students are habituated to the wrong model of 'rigor,' one of mechanical study and memorization. We have to develop critical rigor in a pedagogy that asks students *to assume their own direction.* This amounts to directing self-direction. Then, also, the liberating class seeks to absorb themes and materials from *social contexts* which direct critical attention to reality. We also try *to give value to texts which traditionally are not taken seriously,* like the political critique of Brazilian education by a peasant, whose words are studied along with the classics of education written by professors. I think also that your anecdote showed *the professor learning along with the students,* not knowing in advance what would result, but inventing knowledge during the class, with the students. This is a complex moment of study. The habit of study is itself developed while studying. The material of study is transformed. The relationship between the professor and the students is re-created. A critical relationship of the seminar to society is established. All these thrusts converged at a single moment in the intense study of the peasant speech. That makes the territory full of structure and purpose, a rigorous exercise, but the final result of such an educational moment cannot be predicted in the way a professor may test memorization of a 300-book reading list. The final test is how students change by knowing the material, change in relation to study and to their participation in society. This is the re-creative rigor of liberating education.

Your scrutiny of a small text invited students to become critical readers of texts *and* of reality *and* of nontraditional subjects at the same time. This sounds like a way to make education into social research during the class hour itself. Education is not gulping down books, here, but is transformational of the relationships between students, teacher, school and society.

There is a strong elite tradition which always looks backward to a Golden Age to increase the number of books students must read and the number of essays they must write. In the great ghost of the past, the honored reading lists were all 300-books long! Those who worship the past think standards are declining and their answer is authoritarian, to get tough on students and teachers, to use reading and writing as punishments and discipline-devices. This conservative ideology is being criticized now in the United States from several progressive quarters.[4] Perception is growing that the oversaturated, authoritarian curriculum is itself a major obstacle to learning.

The point is not to assign fewer books so that students will have time to memorize *more* of what they read. Learning is not a memory olympics! The idea is to make critical reflection on society the fundamental activity. The idea is to avoid flying over the words in an heroic effort to reach the end of the reading list, flying over society also in such a way as to avoid knowing how learning relates to reality. Simply shortening the syllabus is not the same thing as investing the pedagogy with a critical purpose.

What I hear a lot from teachers is that they are always rushing 'to cover the material,' 'to cover the syllabus,' 'to get through the basics or the fundamentals.' They are oppressed by this race to the end of the term. They are under pressure to use certain textbooks or to cover certain mandated topics in a prescribed order, in too many classes with too many students. There will be mandated exams at the end and the next course in the curriculum will expect the previous course to have covered certain material. Teachers who deviate from this procedure worry about looking bad if their students do poorly on standard tests or in the follow-up courses. Their reputations could decline. They could be fired. Your example of scrutinizing a small amount of non-traditional material lifts the curricular albatross hanging on the teacher's neck.

Rigor is Depth and Change: Understanding versus Memorizing

Ira   Another question also came to me as you spoke about the peasant speech your class studied. I want to focus some attention on another aspect teachers ask about. You mentioned the notebook of the student who wrote for twenty pages on the small peasant text. This is one concrete product from the process. It is a tangible result which can show the impact of the program on the student. Teachers want to know about the results, the products of liberating classes. What else would you want to demonstrate which shows end products? What else can show that the process was productive, constructive, and rigorous? Teachers ask for witness to the process.

Paulo   Yes, yes, this is important. I have had in my experience in Brazil at the end of the semester papers at *such* a level of criticism and creativity that I sometimes ask the authors to give me copies of what they wrote. I have some of these papers in the education center we created in Sao Paulo, with the authors' names, so that other students can read them. Sometimes they write very interesting critical analyses of their own experiences, in these papers.

But, I want to add that if you have to measure the efficiency of a course by measuring knowledge in centimeters, you will come up with total failure from this kind of liberating method! For me, what is *impossible* is to measure knowledge with rulers as if we made twenty feet of knowledge today in class! (Laughing) I repeat, the question is to know whether the students in this semester, even though not having read 200 books, but having read *some* good books, some central and fundamental books, went beyond the stages of mere opinions about the facts and got much more critical understanding. This is for me 'rigorous rigor.' This means to overcome opinionating by grasping the *raison d'etre* of the facts.

Ira   Many teachers will agree with you. They want the students to go deeper than surface facts and mere opinion. The *size* of the official syllabus sabotages this goal of theirs, but the *content* of what is read interferes with student seriousness also, because textbooks and professional articles are written in an artificial language and in a political idiom which stops students from knowing the power conflicts of any age, any discipline, any issue. It will be good news to teachers if they have a smaller required syllabus but they will have to discover what materials or texts can provoke dynamic student reflection.

Another thing, teachers may have to 'let go' like you did in that class, by learning the material in front of the students, with the students. This by itself signals a creative moment, that knowledge is happening right there. The teacher validates creative learning by learning creatively in-process.

I can tell you what it feels like to drown in a syllabus or a textbook. You know one thing I do on the subways of New York? I talk with high school or college students who are carrying textbooks or who are reading books. I ask them what they think of the texts. They complain about the size and even the weight of the tomes. The college students complain about the costs, at my own college also. The textbook business in the U.S. is a billion-dollar-a-year industry. Each textbook is two pounds of wisdom and thirty dollars of knowledge! But, few students report the joy of learning from these whitewashed versions of history, science and society.[5] Textbooks used to be an inch wide, then two inches, and now more. The body-of-knowledge is growing fast and eventually textbooks will be gigantic bodies of print carried on stretchers through the subways of New York! (Paulo laughs) And it will take *two* students to carry the book to school, one on each end. They will begin reading the text in high school and end at retirement.

If we propose a radical reduction in the transfer-of-information in class or in textbooks, in favor of prolonged scrutiny of materials drawn as *problematic texts* on social life, we can hope to get farther than the dismal results of the regular curriculum. But I want to draw out one consequence, one spillover result from the saturation of students with dull information. All this educational activity in the official syllabus has not spoken *their* language, not developed their critical desire, not related to themes intimately rooted in their lives. The students in my courses do not speak the English of the textbooks, or of the professors. Their themes, their daily issues, are about sex, family life, money, work, food, sports, growing up, music, drugs, safety in the streets, cars, and more. They already know that the school, the *very* place where learning is supposed to go on, has little to say about the things that matter most to them. What the school does say isn't in the language they speak! You can imagine how easy it is for students to become anti-intellectual under these conditions.

Here in the U.S., mainstream students assume that just about any material brought to class by the teacher will be irrelevant to their interests. They ask themselves if they will be able to put up with it, and don't expect to be inspired enough to digest it word by word. Offering *less to read* will not be enough by itself to change this perception. Right now, just about anything students want to do from eating a hamburger to roller-skating is more appealing than education. The less that is chosen and how the less is presented are fateful decisions. Not least of all is the student perception that a teacher who assigns less, expects less from them.

Paulo   Yes, I understand what you are saying. And it's very interesting. I remember when I was teaching at the University of Geneva, at the end of the seminar, at the evaluation we tried to do together, one of the students made a very interesting criticism to me which has to do exactly with what you said now.

By attempting the methodology in practice with them, as an object itself for reflection in our mutual evaluation of the seminar, the student said to me, "Paulo, today after our experience this semester I have something to tell you which is a criticism. But for me it is a necessary criticism and I hope I can help you." I said, "Okay," and he went on to say, "Look, Paulo, you committed just one mistake but it is a serious mistake in working with us. When you arrived here in the beginning of the semester, you thought we were ready to assume the responsiblity of shaping ourselves with you, but you had no right to think like this. You assumed something that was not tested."

He told me, "And what did you do? *You committed suicide* as the teacher. Instead of that, you should have exposed yourself to our assassination! (Ira laughs) We would have to kill you as the only professor in the seminar for you to be re-born as a student who is also a professor. Instead of that, you committed suicide in our presence and it created in us a feeling of being orphans." (Paulo laughs)

I smiled and said, "Yes, I agree with you completely. I did not have the right to commit this mistake."

And I think that this is precisely what you are saying now. In some situations, in some circumstances, the democratic goal of liberating education can lead to irresponsibility if the students perceive it as expecting less from them. The responsible educator has to be at least *six* people as the teacher, leading as the professor and learning as the student, making an open atmosphere in a number of ways, but never, I repeat, never an atmosphere of *laissez-faire, laissez-allez*, never, but a democratic atmosphere yes. Then, by doing that, the students begin to learn a different way. They really learn how to participate. But what is impossible is to teach participation *without* participation! It is impossible just to speak about participation without experiencing it. We cannot learn how to swim in this room. We have to go to the water. Democracy is the same. You learn democracy by making democracy, but with limits.

Freedom and Limits in a Liberating Classroom

Ira   This is an important departure point between traditional and liberating education. The official curriculum constantly lectures us about democracy without allowing students the freedom to practice it. Your story about Geneva is a lesson in how the practice of democracy needs to be situated in the developmental limits of the students. Directiveness and freedom have to be located anew for each class.

As I understand it, in a liberating classroom, the teacher seeks to gradually withdraw as the director of the learning, as the directive force. As the students keep exercising more critical initiative, the teacher encourages their self-organization, their participation in setting the agenda of the curriculum. It would be impossible to expect traditional authorities to plan their own resignation from power in any institution, including school. The self-organizing goal of the liberating class is a delicate one, as your Geneva seminar showed. You can let go of authority too soon, just as you can let go too late. Making that calculation is precarious, which more than many other moments involves the teacher as a politician, scientist and artist, synthesizing from many indications and exercises an understanding of when and how to pass on authority to the students.

In contrast, the traditional teacher is always in charge from beginning to end. His or her authority is fixed at an unchanging distance from the students. This authority must be fixed so that the programmed curriculum all the way from Lesson A to Lesson Z can be implemented on schedule, by virtue of the teacher's initiative. The fixed authority of the teacher here interferes with the students' own critical emergence. The teacher is empowered to be active, while students are made reactive.

Paulo   But, look, Ira, for me the question is not for the teacher to have less and less authority. The issue is that the democratic teacher never, never transforms authority into authoritarianism. He or she can never stop being an authority or having authority. Without authority it is very difficult for the liberties of the students to be shaped. Freedom needs authority to become free. (Laughs) It is a paradox but it is true. The question nevertheless is for authority to know that it has its foundation in the freedom of the others, and if the authority denies this freedom and cuts off this relationship, this *founding* relationship, with freedom, I think that it is no longer authority but has become *authoritarianism*. As well, if the freedom side of the dialectic does not meet authority because authority renounces itself, denies itself, the tendency is for freedom to stop being freedom in order to become license. In both cases, we cannot speak about democracy, we cannot speak about discipline, we cannot speak about creation, democratic re-creation of society, no. We have license from below and we have imposition from above.

Because of that, I am convinced that the educator, no matter if she or he works at the level of preschool or primary school or the university, has to assume the necessary authority which he or she must have, without going beyond it, in order to destroy it, by becoming authoritarian. And this is not easy to do. We have different ways of being authoritarian, no?, including a very false and very hypocritical way in which you make a manipulative appeal. Something is A and you try to say it is B. We can be authoritarian in sweet, manipulating and even sentimental ways, cajoling students with walks through flowery roads, and already you know what points you picked for the students to know. But, you don't want them to know your plans, your map.

Ira   You're right in making this distinction between authority and authoritarianism. I use authority and need authority to begin and direct my classrooms. I am open to sharing it and to having the students emerge as co-directors of the curriculum. The more the students have confidence in me as an authority who directs a productive course, who can maintain discipline, who has a good command of knowledge and how to gain more knowledge, the more the students will trust my interventions. I agree that liberating educators have to use authority within the limits of democracy. How to do this in practice is harder to demonstrate. Each classroom, each group of students, each situation will require individual teachers to adjust the equation of authority and freedom. While you can't know in advance exactly what this equation should be for any class, you do gain experience in practicing authority with freedom, and you can see easily from the behavior of the class if your method is working or not. What I wanted to point to also is the mobility of the teacher in a liberating process. I learn and change as the class proceeds. I've written elsewhere about the variety of formats the liberating class might take.[6] When I spoke of the traditional authority being 'fixed' at a permanent distance from the students, I wanted to suggest that the liberating educator can adjust his or her role in the classroom to the needs of the study. This willingness to be a mobile authority is one aspect I see in the transformation of the teacher. The teacher may lecture, may lead a discussion, may organize small study groups inside the classroom, may supervise field research outside, may show films, may compensate for points of view missing in class, or may act as a librarian to help study groups find materials, or may give over long class hours to student presentations, etc. The willingness to move with the class involves a willingness to be flexible in the form of authority the teacher exercises. This flexibility is a signal to the students about the openness of the course.

You make me think that the teacher's authority must always be there, but it changes as the students and the study evolve, as they emerge as critical subjects in the act of knowing. The teacher also is recreated if the process is working.

Together, But Not Equal: Teacher-Student Differences

Paulo   Yes, this is the ability to be creative. That is, to understand the development of the practice of being a teacher. It is not something immobilized. Your way of working this semester is not necessarily the same in the next one.

I don't know whether you are also asked by students and teachers about this question of authority in a dialogical classroom, whether the teacher is or is not equal to the students. It is very interesting, this question. The experience of *being under* leads the students to think that if you are a dialogical teacher you definitely deny the difference between you and them. All at once, all of us are equal! But, it is not possible. We have to be clear with them. No. The dialogical relationship does not have the power to create such an impossible equality. The educator continues to be different from the students, but, and now for me this is the central question, the difference between them, if the teacher is democratic, if his or her political dream is a *liberating* one, is that he or she cannot permit the necessary difference between the teacher and the students to become 'antagonistic.' The difference continues to exist! *I* am different from the students! But I cannot allow this to be antagonistic if I am democratic. If they become antagonistic, it is because I became authoritarian.

Ira   You were not open to change.

Paulo   Yes, I became rigid, closed to democracy. And it's very interesting. The students in a certain moment test you. They are so conditioned by authoritarian professors that when you come and say we in this class are different, we have the right to think and to ask questions and to criticize, not only the right but the duty, it's possible that one of the students (and it's beautiful!) makes the first test! Then he or she can provoke you by doing something which should be punished by an authoritarian professor. He or she does that in order to know whether what you said is real. If you punish that student, you really were not honest. Your speech did not have any value. But, if you do not say *anything* to the student, your speech *also* did not have value. Do you see how difficult it is?

Ira   Yes, students are very clever in the power struggle of the classroom.

Paulo   The student needs to know that in some moments freedom must be punished, when it goes beyond the limits of democratic authority. And the punishment has to be made by the authority. For example, Elza and I never failed to punish our kids every time it was necessary. We never beat them. It was not needed. They are absolutely virgin of this. But, we punished, we talked seriously with them. Yet, we never said 'no' unless we gave reasons why we were saying 'no.'

I've had other situations like this in my life. Two years ago in Brazil in a graduate course, a woman did something like this test I spoke of above, testing my testimony of freedom, on the first day. In the last analysis, I am sure she was expecting me to put her out of the room, in order to demonstrate that I was really not open. In my speech I could not do that, but I could not just smile either. When she stopped speaking, making an incredible *a priori* criticism of me I spoke seriously to her with the authority of the teacher but I did not expel her from the seminar, and by the end of the term she got a good grade. She was a capable woman. We did not become friends because I think she also did not want it.

This is the kind of situation you have if your choice is a liberating one to use democracy, freedom and authority together. You cannot accept the invitation to authoritarianism which the dominant ideol-

ogy makes to you *through* the test of a student, who challenges you
with the very freedom we believe in! (Laughs)

Ira   The student is the ironic messenger, inviting the liberatory
teacher to fall back into rigid relations.

When I'm facing student tests of democracy or my authority in the
classroom, I try to remember all the ways students learned to manipulate the teacher. In the day-to-day culture war of the official
curriculum, students practice keeping the teacher and the institution
at bay. Sometimes the challenges to me come from a number of
students, one after another or at the same time. I try to remind myself
to behave in ways which reverse student expectations and thus interfere with their routine behaviors. Still, all my reasoning and ingenuity and good intentions are not always enough, and I have to
regularly ask students to leave the course. I can't let them wreck my
work or the learning possible with the other students, so I tell them
to drop the course if they don't change or else give them work to do
outside the classroom. The other students are often relieved that I
asserted my authority to expel such a disruptive person from the
room. I do this because it has to be done. I do believe that our
economic system creates some human damage that cannot be repaired
with our present resources, including the resource of liberating education. I think it's important to say that many teachers in U.S. public
schools and in some colleges often face antagonism, alienation and
resistance, which *no* pedagogy at this moment can reverse. The problem requires something more than a teaching philosophy or a classroom method.

In my experience, I find that student antagonism is harder to man-
age in large classes. The number of tests coming at the teacher from
the students multiplies. Smaller classes will make it easier on the
liberating educator to negotiate student alienation. It's easy enough
to say, in terms of school reform, that a bad process with 40 students
will be a bad process with 20. Transfer-education or 'banking' education is not better just because you do it to with only half as many
students. The nature of the process is the first problem; the social
relations and contents of the curriculum matter first. Still, the size of
the class is an important issue also, because overworked teachers and
students in an overcrowded room will be less patient with an experimental process.

So, I think, Paulo, that the issue you raised about non-antagonistic
differences is important. The teacher is different from and not equal
to the students, even as we practice democratic relations in the classroom. This is another way of describing the leadership role that the

liberatory teacher has to play. The dialogic teacher is more intellectually developed, more practiced in critical scrutiny, and more committed to a political dream of social change, than are the students. We have to acknowledge these differences betweeen the teacher and the students. In fact, those differences make the liberatory project possible. A person teaching for transformation in schools or colleges works in situations set against freedom, where the curriculum obscures reality. A teacher in a community organization works in the middle of a mass culture which equally obscures reality. If the teacher is to challenge domination, he or she has to bring a political dream to places where this dream is only a possiblity. The teacher is different not only by virtue of her or his training but also because the teacher leads a transformation that will not happen in class by itself.

Notes

[1] For recent discussions of student resistance to the official curriculum, see Paul Willis, *Learning to Labor: How Working Class Kids Get Working Class Jobs* (New York, 1981); Henry Giroux, *Theory and Resistance in Education* (South Hadley, Mass., 1983); Theodore Sizer, *Horace's Compromise* (New York, 1984); and Arthur Powell, David Cohen, and Eleanor Farrar, *The Shopping Mall High School* (New York, 1985). For analyses of education as a public convergence of state and corporate policy, see Joel Spring, *Education and the Rise of the Corporate State* (Boston, 1972); Samuel Bowles and Herbert Gintis, *Schooling in Capitalist America* (New York, 1976); Martin Carnoy and Henry M. Levin, *Schooling and Work in the Democratic State* (Stanford, 1985).

[2] John Goodlad's eight-year study of public schools, *A Place Called School* (New York, 1983) drew on observations of a thousand classrooms to calculate that only 3% of the time in class had any emotional tone, while only 1% was devoted to open-ended critical discussion. For an earlier observation on the same failures, see Jerome Bruner, "Learning and Thinking," *Harvard Educational Review*, Vol. 29, No. 3, Summer, 1959, pp. 184-192.

[3] See Ben Bagdikian's *The Media Monopoly* (Boston, 1983) for one excellent survey and critique of monopoly ownership in the media, and the resulting pro-business censorship of the 'news.' Another good survey of political censorship in the media is Michael Parenti's *Inventing Reality: The Politics of the Mass Media* (New York, 1986). Parenti especially considers Cold War ideology in the U.S. media's biased presentation of the U.S.S.R. and the Third World.

[4] In the post-1983 reform crisis in U.S. education, there were some liberal demurrals to the larger conservative trend. These liberal statements identified the official curriculum itself as an obstacle to learning. This point of view can be found in the Goodlad and Sizer reports cited in footnotes 1 and 2 above, as well as in Ernest Boyer's Carnegie study, *High School* (New York, 1983). Two other commission reports in this period also pulled the pedagogical debate in a progressive direction, away from passive pedagogy: *Involvement in Learning* (National Institute of Education, 1984), and *Integrity in the College*

Curriculum (Association of American Colleges, 1985). Other key proposals for progressive pedagogy can be found in Charles Silberman's *Crisis in the Classroom* (New York, 1970) and Herb Kohl's *The Open Classroom* (New York, 1969) and Kohl's *Basic Skills* (New York, 1982).

[5] For discussions of the ideologized material of mainsteam textbooks, see Frances Fitzgerald, *America Revised* (New York, 1979); William Griffin and John Marciano, *Teaching the Vietnam War* (Montclair, 1979), and Jean Anyon, "Ideology and United States History Textbooks," *Harvard Educational Review*, Vol. 49, No. 3, Summer, 1979, pp. 361-386.

[6] See Ira Shor, *Critical Teaching and Everyday Life* (Chicago, 1987), Chapter 3, "Theory of Critical Teaching: Extraordinarily Re-Experiencing the Ordinary."

CHAPTER 4

What Is The 'Dialogical Method' Of Teaching?

Liberatory Discourse: Dialogue Transforms Communication

Ira   You've said, Paulo, that the teacher is an artist and a politician. However, the *politics* of dialogic pedagogy are clearer than its aesthetics. It is simpler to explain this method as *for* freedom and *against* domination, as cultural action inside or outside a classroom where the status quo is challenged, where the myths of the official curriculum and mass culture are illuminated. We need now to discuss how the dialogic teacher works so that he or she is an artist in doing these unveilings.

Why don't we examine first the heart of the process, "dialogue," and work through that idea to the aesthetics of the method. Teachers ask often about "dialogical education." They know some things about dialogue. Teachers have been students in courses using a socratic recitation following a lecture or a reading assignment, where the instructor asks questions to test students on the material covered. In addition, many teachers use nontraditional discussion-circles in class, to break down the formality. Still others engage students in conversation, and would consider that dialogue.

For the most part, though, teachers didactically lecture. In college, professors traditionally lecture to large numbers of students, who sit in big rooms either busily taking notes, or sleeping, or daydreaming, or doing homework from another course while sitting in this one, or talking to each other. A low-paid graduate student leads a recitation class afterwards, to review what the professor said or what the textbooks say. This is 'cost-effective' education, minimum personal contact between professors and students. Professor-contact is reserved for graduate students, or undergraduate majors, or honors classes, or for students at the most costly universities, where money is invested in small classes for the elite. In the lower grades, richer school districts and private schools also offer their students smaller classes, to give students more personal attention.

You can see the problem here for dialogue. The *right* to have a small discussion begins as a class privilege. The more elite the student, the more likely that he or she will have a personalized, discussion contact with the professor or the teacher. For the rest, there are large college classes mixed with recitation sections staffed by poorly-paid instructors, or large classes in underfunded public schools. If public resources were transferred from the military to education to fund smaller classes, that would make dialogue easier to have in school. Teachers and students would then have to confront our own inexperience in small-group, democratic communications. We are most familiar with 'monologue' or teacher-talk, in the transfer-of-knowledge approach. Even in discussion groups, student voices are often restricted by a dull or imposing teacherly voice that inhibits critical challenges to the syllabus.

The privilege of small classes and the predominance of transfer-teaching are the realities surrounding us. How does the dialogical method present a different model of learning and knowledge? How does dialogical teaching transform communication?

Paulo   I think, Ira, that first of all we should understand liberating dialogue not as a technique, a *mere* technique, which we can use to help us get some results. We also cannot, must not, understand dialogue as a kind of tactic we use to make students our friends. This would make dialogue a technique for manipulation instead of illumination.

On the contrary, dialogue must be understood as something taking part in the very historical nature of human beings. It is part of our historical progress in becoming human beings. That is, dialogue is a kind of necessary posture to the extent that humans have become more and more critically communicative beings. Dialogue is a moment where humans meet to reflect on their reality as they make and remake it. Something else: To the extent that we are communicative beings who communicate to each other as we become more able to transform our reality, we are able *to know that we know*, which is something *more* than just knowing. In a certain manner, for example, birds *know* the trees. They even communicate to each other. They use a kind of oral and symbolic language, but they do not use written language. And they do not know that they know. At least scientifically up to now, we are not sure whether they know that they know. On the other hand, *we* know that we know, and we human beings know also that *we don't know*. Through dialogue, reflecting together on what we know and don't know, we can then act critically to transform reality.

In communicating among ourselves, in the process of knowing the reality which we transform, we communicate and know *socially* even though the process of communicating, knowing, changing, has an individual dimension. But, the individual aspect is not enough to explain the process. Knowing is a social event with nevertheless an individual dimension. What is dialogue in this moment of communication, knowing and social transformation? Dialogue *seals* the relationship between the cognitive subjects, the subjects who know, and who try to know.

Ira   From another angle, I'd add that speaking either confirms or disconfirms the social relations of the people who engage in such communication. That is, communicating is not mere verbalism, not a mere ping pong of words and gestures. It affirms or challenges the relationship between the people communicating, the object they are relating around, and the society they are in. Liberatory dialogue is a democratic communication which disconfirms domination and illuminates while affirming the freedom of the participants to re-make their culture. Traditional discourse confirms the dominant mass culture and the inherited, official shape of knowledge.

Paulo   Yes, dialogue is a challenge to existing domination. Also, with such a way of understanding dialogue, the object to be known is *not* an exclusive possession of *one* of the subjects doing the knowing, one of the people in the dialogue. In our case of education, knowledge of the object to be known is not the sole possession of the teacher, who gives knowledge to the students in a gracious gesture. Instead of this cordial gift of information to students, the object to be known mediates the two cognitive subjects. In other words, the object to be known is put on the table *between* the two subjects of knowing. They meet around it and through it for mutual inquiry.

Of course, the educator has had a certain "gnosiological"[1] or intellectual experience in picking this object for study before the students meet it in the classroom, and in painting it or presenting it for discussion. This prior contact of the educator with the object to be known does *not* mean nevertheless that the teacher has exhausted all the efforts and dimensions in knowing the object.

Ira   The teacher selecting objects of study knows them *better* than the students as the course begins but the teacher *re-learns* the objects through studying them with the students?

Paulo   This is *exactly* the question! I could extend what you say in some conceptual language by saying, for example, that the educator *remakes* her or his 'cognoscibility' through the 'cognoscibility' of the educatees. That is, the ability of the educator to know the object is remade every time through the students' own ability for knowing, for developing critical comprehension in themselves.

What is dialogue in this way of knowing? Precisely this connection, this epistemological relation. The object to be known in one place links the two cognitive subjects, leading them to reflect together on the object. Dialogue is the sealing together of the teacher and the students in the joint act of knowing and re-knowing the object of study. Then, instead of transferring the knowledge *statically*, as a *fixed* possession of the teacher, dialogue demands a dynamic approximation towards the object.

Ira   The teacher can say in advance, I know the material, I know the science of oceanography, or this novel by Zola, or this lathe in front of us, or even the hamburgers we eat in the cafeteria, but in the dialogical process, I relearn the material when I study it again with the students.

Paulo   Yes! That is the point of dialogue-education. But look, let us take this point again, dear Ira. Why do some educators consider this perspective on the act of knowing *bizarre*? Something bizarre which came from the Third World? How is it possible to think like this? Dialogical education is an epistemological position, not a bizarre invention or a strange practice from an exotic part of the world!

What I do accept, for example, is that many people from the First World and the Third World say to me, "Look, Paulo, okay, it's beautiful, but nevertheless I don't accept such a position. Because, for me the role of the educator is to *teach* the educatee." I say, Okay this is your position, authoritarian. Okay, this is your understanding of epistemology, but this is not mine. This kind of debate about the differences I accept. But, what I cannot accept is saying that dialogue is a bizarre way of learning coming out of the Third World, as if I were making propaganda with curious tools. No. This is a debate on epistemology, not on demonic arts from a picturesque location.

Precisely because there is an epistemology here, my position is not to deny the directive and necessary role of the educator. But, I am *not* the kind of educator who *owns* the objects I study with the students. I am extremely interested in the objects for study. They stimulate my curiosity and I bring this enthusiasm to the students. Then, both of us can illuminate the object together.

Ira   You can imagine how disturbing this epistemology is to a traditional educator. I'm not surprised they want to call it bizarre. Think of the difference between describing a course as an expert syllabus, a long reading list, a series of lectures from a professor, a succession of question periods, and a final exam to test the knowledge, compared to a course where the professor enters knowing a great deal but leaves the course 'relearned' because of the dialogue-inquiry, the rediscovery of the material *with* the students.

The lecture method sets up the teacher as an authority who transfers fixed knowledge to students. Knowledge is already formed and must be verbally delivered to the students. Students in the traditional mode are expected to absorb preset formulations spoken by the teacher.

In contrast, the openness of the dialogical educator to his or her own relearning gives dialogue a democratic character. The domination of the official curriculum rests on many things, but surely fixed, expert knowledge is one pillar. If the dialogical teacher announces that he or she relearns the material in the class, then the learning process itself challenges the unchanging position of the teacher. That is, liberatory learning is a social activity which by itself remakes authority. In this case, authority is the form of existing knowledge as well as the governing behavior of the teacher. Do you see my point? These challenges demystify the teacher's power, open it up to change. They impose humility on the existing order. They invite the students to exercise their own powers of reconstruction.

Paulo   Yes, but nevertheless it does *not* mean that the educator first denies that he or she knows! It would be a lie, an hypocrisy. He or she has on the contrary to demonstrate his or her competency to the students. Secondly, it does not mean that every time, in every course, in every term, the educator changes his or her knowledge about this or that object. No.

For example, by discussing dialogue every day with students, I am not changing every day my understanding of dialogue. We arrive at the level of some certainty, some scientific certainty of some objects, which we can count on. What dialogue-educators know, neverthe-less, is that science has historicity. This means that all new knowledge comes up when other knowledge becomes old, and no longer answers the needs of the new moment, no longer answers the new questions being asked. Because of that, all new knowledge when it appears waits for its own overcoming by the next new knowledge which is inevitable. Sometimes I say that if scientists were as humble as knowl-edge is, we would be in a different world.

But, there are other aspects of dialogical situations which I think are important to add. The circumstances of a seminar where dialogue is the relationship between cognitive subjects and a knowable object is not a situation in which we can do anything we want to do. That is, it has limits and contradictions which condition what we can do. Dialogue does not exist in a political vacuum. It is not a 'free space' where you may do what you want. Dialogue takes place inside some kind of program and context. These conditioning factors create ten-sion in achieving goals that we set for dialogic education. To achieve the goals of transformation, dialogue implies responsibility, direc-tiveness, determination, discipline, objectives.

Nevertheless, a dialogical situation implies the *absence* of authori-tarianism. Dialogue means a permanent tension in the relation be-tween authority and liberty. But, in this tension, authority continues to be because it has authority vis-a-vis permitting student freedoms which emerge, which grow and mature precisely because authority and freedom learn self-discipline.

Something more: A dialogical setting does not mean that everyone involved in it *has* to speak! Dialogue does not have a goal or a re-quirement that all people in the class *must* say something even if they have nothing to say!

Ira   I see what you are pointing to. For them to feel pressured to speak even when they have nothing to add creates a false democracy, a fake moment of discussion. In a way, this is an imposition on the students, by a teacher who has made dialogue into a dogma, a tech-nique instead of into a genuine open exchange.

Paulo   Yes! In dialogue, one has the right to be silent! Neverthe-less, one does not have the right to misuse his or her participation in the development of the common exercise.

Ira   You mean your right to stay silent does not mean you have a right to sabotage the process?

Paulo   That's a good way to put it. If for example, someone tries to sabotage the process precisely because the class is dialogical and gives them an opportunity to intervene, he or she must be punished. Not physically, of course, but prevented from abusing the openness of the class or from interfering with the other students and the teacher.

Participatory Learning: Dialogue and 'Situated Pedagogy'

Ira   There is a necessary discipline in the dialogic class, which is not permissive. We spoke earlier about this. Here, we should talk more about what produces student participation in dialogue. Of course, we want students to accept the dialogic class, not stay silent or sabotage it. But, silence is their right and sabotage has to be prevented. Still, in my experience, allowing the students the right to stay silent can sink a dialogic class if a majority exercises this right. A dialogic class needs a critical mass of participants to push the process forward and to carry along those students who will not speak but who will listen.

This may be a good time to discuss 'situated pedagogy,' as one route to student participation. Teachers may follow the difference between lecture-socratic methods where knowledge is fixed at the beginning and liberatory dialogics where knowledge brought to the course is challenged and rediscovered...

Paulo   I must repeat something here, in order to be absolutely clear. At the moment the teacher begins the dialogue, he or she knows a great deal, first in terms of knowledge and second in terms of the horizon that she or he wants to get to. The starting point is what the teacher knows about the object and where the teacher wants to go with it.

Ira   Yes, the teacher starts with knowledge, a learning process and goals. This is her or his competency, and also the place where his or her politics are revealed. On the one hand, the teacher knows a lot about the object to be studied and the teacher has more familiarity with conceptual scrutiny. On the other hand, the teacher has a destination, or an horizon as you said. This is the learning process that moves the whole project forward. I understand that you want to emphasize the directive responsibility and the competency of the teacher who begins a dialogical class.

The question I want to raise now is how competency, knowledge, and horizon, and training in scientific method get situated in the dialogical process. The teacher's accumulated strengths can inhibit instead of promote the students' critical emergence. The idea of situated pedagogy is useful here, for investing the teacher's competencies in a participatory process, so maybe I can say a few things about it.

My understanding is that dialogic inquiry is situated in the culture, language, politics, and themes of the students. Teachers have some familiarity with experiential objects or materials for study. They bring in magazines from mass culture, or show popular films and TV shows. They ask students to write about events from their daily lives. But, in situated pedagogy we discover with students the themes most problematic to their perception. We situate the critical pedagogy in subjective problem-themes not yet analyzed by students. This gains intrinsic motivation from subject matter of key concern to students while also giving them a moment of detachment on their previously unreflected experience. In dialogic pedagogy, this turn towards subjective experience must also include a global, critical dimension. That is, we don't only look at the familiar, but we try to understand it socially and historically. The global context for the concrete, the general setting for the particular, are what give students a critical view on reality, what I refer to as "extraordinarily reexperiencing the ordinary." In this way, situating pedagogy in student culture does not merely exploit or endorse the given but seeks to transcend it. That is, the themes familiar to students are not thrown in as a manipulative technique, simply to confirm the status quo or to motivate students. There is this dual danger of confirmation and manipulation because material familiar to students can by itself stimulate more attention. But, then, does a critical challenge to the material and to the students' reaction follow? Do the material and questions open an investigating dialogue through which we reexamine the subject, until it is no longer the routine matter which absorbed uncritical attention before? We gain a distance from the given by abstracting it from its familiar surroundings and studying it in unfamiliar critical ways, until our perceptions of it and society are challenged.

I see a tension here between familiar objects and unfamiliar critical scrutiny. I see another tension between the routine curriculum of school which makes reality opaque and the critical classroom which tries to break through the official opacity. There is a third tension between the students' prior experiences of authoritarian education and the new liberatory class which proposes dialogue and self-discipline. Even more, there is a tension between the liberatory teacher's reflection on the themes and the students' own analyses. These are what I think of as the developmental forces in a dialogic class. They set the pedagogy in opposition to the disempowering logic of school and social experience. They also establish a relationship between the students' critical thought and the students' experience, as well as between the teacher's critical thinking and that of the students. Traditionally, familiar materials are studied in opaque or abstract ways, or else academic material is presented unrelated to reality. Either way, the curriculum is not situated inside student thought and language. Transformative tensions emerge if the study is situated inside the subjectivity of the students in such a way to detach students from that very subjectivity into more advanced reflections.

Choosing problem-themes from student culture is one pedagogical option. Studying academic or formal subjects in a situated manner is a second option, that is, inserting biology or history or nursing or economics into their social contexts. I don't think of situated study as only using familiar materials, or as using them because they are 'hip' and students can 'turn on' to them. There is something more oppositional here. Maybe it involves what you wrote about in other places, 'limit-acts' and 'limit-situations.' Situated study presents subjective themes in their larger social context, to challenge the givens of our lives and the surrounding system dominating daily life. These limits or givens are reperceived eventually as confining membranes around us, historical borders, politically constructed Great Walls, which we contact to discover vulnerable points for breaking through. Simply recognizing that we are surrounded by political membranes is an advance. Then, finding means to go beyond its limits is a social action goal of the dialogue.

There's another way I think of situated pedagogy, not only in terms of the object of study. I often think of it as located in the authentic levels of development presented by the students as the course begins. This means I'm researching my students' cognitive and political levels at the course's opening, to see what kinds of critical thinking, literacy and political ideas are operating. This informs me of the developmental situation in the class, the real starting point for making a liberatory invitation.

Paulo   I'd like to think out loud with you here about some of the things you mentioned for situated pedagogy. But, first, Ira, I think I have to begin to fly before I can land on the question! (Ira and Paulo laugh)

Many, many times I have thought about the following aspect: Our experience at the university tends to form us *at a distance* from reality. The concepts that we study in the university can work to amputate us from the concrete reality they are supposedly referring to. The very concepts we use in our intellectual training and in our work are abstracted from reality, far away from the concreteness of society. In the last analysis, we become excellent experts in a very interesting intellectual game, the game of the concepts! This is a 'ballet of concepts.

Then, our language risks losing contact with concreteness. The more we are like this, the farther we are from the masses of the people, whose language on the contrary is absolutely linked to concreteness. Because of this, we intellectuals first describe concepts while the people first describe reality, the concreteness. This is my first moment of flying on the question of 'situated pedagogy' before landing.

When I insist on dialogical education starting from the students' comprehension of their daily life experiences, no matter if they are students of the university or kids in primary school or workers in a neighborhood or peasants in the countryside, my insistence on starting from *their* description of *their* daily life experiences is based in the possibility of starting from concreteness, from common sense, to reach a rigorous understanding of reality. I don't dichotomize these two dimensions of the world, daily life from rigor, common sense from philosophical sense, in the expression of Gramsci.[2] I don't understand critical or scientific knowledge which appears randomly, by magic or by accident, as if it did not need to meet the test of reality. Scientific rigor comes from an effort to overcome a naive understanding of the world. Science is super-posing critical thought on what we observe in reality, after the starting point of common sense.

Ira   The moment you begin to seek a scientific understanding of your naiveté, you are no longer naive.

Paulo   Yes! If I am no longer naive, it means that I am no longer *acritical*.

Ira   You've made the first transition to critical consciousness, seeking a systematic understanding of your impressions.

Starting With Reality to Overcome It

Paulo   Let's go back to the question of the starting point. First of all, I am convinced that epistemologically it is possible, by listening to students speak about their understanding of their world, to go with them towards the direction of a critical, scientific understanding of their world.

I should say something here about a great friend of mine from Brazil, a physics professor at the University of Marcio Campos, who talks to me constantly, especially when we make our car trip of 90 minutes together from Sao Paulo to the University. I told him many times how frustrated I am that I am not able to audit his course and be one of his students. The course is 'From Astrology to Astronomy,' a kind of history of scientific rigor. By comparing astrology to astronomy he tries to grasp what rigor in science has meant, especially by analyzing the historicity of science.

One day, he said to me, "Look, Paulo, constantly I ask the physics students in the beginning of the course to do a simple neighborhood research over a weekend. I ask them to go to an area of common people and talk with fishermen, workers, peasants, people in the streets, to speak with them about how they understand the world, what is their cosmological vision, what is *the sky* for them? What do stars mean to them? What distance do they think there is between us and the stars? What is the world from their eyes? I also ask the students to put their own understanding down, to make some comparisons." This in a physics course!

This physics professor studies science with his students by beginning with their research into popular thinking about reality. When students come back the next week to his class, they report on how people think about night and day, the moon, the seasons, the tides coming and going, and compare all these things to their own positions. The assumption is that the students' own positions will be *less* magical, and they are.

Then, he begins to think scientifically with them on this material. For me, there is no problem here with situating the course in these concrete materials. Critics of such an approach might begin to worry about the program. What can we do with such contents, they may ask. The regular curriculum is more important, they say, the regular way of teaching physics. I say to them that I am not against a curriculum or a program, but only against the authoritarian and elitist ways of organizing the studies. I am defending the critical participation of the students in *their* education. Do you see? They have the right to participate and I don't have the right to say that because they might reject participation, then I assume the position of totally giving them their formation. No! I must recognize that students cannot understand their own rights because they are so *ideologized* into rejecting their own freedom, their own critical development, thanks to the traditional curriculum. Then, I have to learn with them how to go beyond these limits, beyond their own learned rejection of their rights.

Ira   This physics course is a good example of challenging the students' learned passivity, which is one starting point of their study, while the opinions of working people on the moon and stars is another. The students' situated research moves them beyond the limits that restricted them before. They take on responsibilities which are unfamiliar to them, outside the traditional curriculum. They become active researchers *prior* to listening to a lecture on reality. They are also university students who make serious contact with common people, to consider mass culture as a research problem. More than that, the democratic aspect comes from them having to consider their own thought a research problem, which they analyze comparatively with material from the street interviews. The interviews ground their academic training in reality, rather than in conceptual abstractions invented on campus. This is a textured situation of teaching. It opposes the passive and silencing methods of transferring knowledge. Students share in the illumination of several realities. I like this example because it is a dialogical method for a course in *science*, something with a very imposing body of knowledge. The question on my mind now is, can we say that this physics course which begins from several realities it tries to overcome actually 'empowers' the students?

Empowerment Is A Social Act

Paulo   Yes, perhaps we can say that the physics course 'empowers' students, but it is interesting to me how people in the United States are so preoccupied in using this word and concept 'empowerment.' There is some reason in this, some meaning to it. My fear in using the expression 'empowerment' is that some people may think that such a practice simply empowers the students, and then everything is finished, our work is done, over! I wish I could better express the feeling deep inside me about this desire to use the word 'empowerment.'

Ira   Do you worry that 'empowerment' gives us too easy a way out? Does it lead us to think of the teacher as a kind of lamp-lighter? The teacher walks into a classroom, provokes some illumination, like turning on a light-switch, and then walks out, mission accomplished. On to the next class, where once again the teacher lights some lamps and calls it 'empowerment.'

Paulo   You understand my feeling. It may make the situation seem too easy when it is not. And another thing: Let us even accept that the kind of experience which my friend the physicist offered to his students, which he invented himself, not because he read my books or wants to follow Freire, which he believes in as a scientist who knows that he is *not* the owner of the knowledge he has, or *is* having, let us suppose that his pedagogy develops in students a certain level of independence. What I want to say is that this level of autonomy is not enough to transform them for making the necessary political and radical transformation of Brazilian society.

Ira Can I explore this reservation you have? In the U.S., one school of Progressive thought seeks to develop 'self-directed learners.' In this pedagogy, the teacher is a 'resource-person' and a 'mentor-on-demand' when the student asks for something. The teacher is expected to come up with bright ideas and to untangle knots when students work themselves into a corner. Students are expected to design their own learning contracts and to be responsible enough to follow them and to ask for help. In many instances in the U.S., educators will point to the self-directed learner as an empowered student, a person who does not have to be watched, supervised, or graded. Now, this ability to self-organize your studies is real autonomy from authority-dependence. It is one form of education for people who disagree with authoritarianism, who see the autonomy of the individual learner as the measure of democracy and empowerment.

Paulo But it is not my conception of democracy and empowerment! It is *very* good that you put this question on the table. For example, when I am against the authoritarian position, I am not trying to fall into what I spoke of earlier as a *laissez-faire* position. When I criticize manipulation, I do not want to fall into a false and nonexistent nondirectivity of education. For me, education is always directive, always. The question is to know towards what and with whom is it directive. This is the question. I don't believe in self-liberation. Liberation is a social act. Liberating education is a social process of illumination.

Ira There is no personal self-empowerment?

Paulo No, no, no. Even when you individually feel yourself *most* free, if this feeling is not a *social* feeling, if you are not able to use your *recent* freedom to help others to be free by transforming the totality of society, then you are exercising only an individualist attitude towards empowerment or freedom.

Let me go more into the question of empowerment. Let us take again the example of the students working with my friend the physicist. Even though they can feel and perceive themselves after the semester as first-rate students, more critical students, better scientists and better people, it is still *not* enough for the transformation of society, this *feeling* of being free.

But now, I want also to justify, to support, the dialogical class of the physicist and also the efforts I make in this field. While individual empowerment or the empowerment of some students, the feeling of being changed, is not enough concerning the transformation of the whole society, it is *absolutely necessary* for the process of social transformation. Is this clear? The critical development of these students is absolutely fundamental for the radical transformation of society. Their curiosity, their critical perception of reality, is fundamental for social transformation but is not enough by itself.

Ira   It is one ingredient that needs others to complete their promise. The students' dialogic learning needs a relationship to other elements taking part in the larger transformation of society. If I understand, you want to ask here again for whom and against whom do they use their new freedom in learning. How does it relate to other efforts to transform society?

Paulo   Those are the questions I have in mind.

Ira   I feel how important this problem is in a culture like mine. Education for social change was a popular idea in the 60s. But, historically, the notion of empowerment in U.S. society has been captured by individualism, by private notions of getting ahead.

With our deep roots in individualism, we have a Utopian devotion to 'making it on your own,' improving yourself, moving up in the world, pulling yourself up by your own bootstraps, striking it rich by an ingenious personal effort. This is a culture in love with self-made men. Here, a lot of rich land and no backward aristocracy made the economy very dynamic. Also, the exploitation of black slaves helped build up the country's wealth, and the liquidation of Native Americans opened up the huge interior to pioneers, thieves and adventurers. The very economic dynamism of this society has had an impact on pedagogy, putting a lot of force behind individual empowerment, self-help, self-improvement, self-reliance, in the lower grades and in adult education. This emphasis on 'self' is the educational equivalent of the capitalist infatuation with the lone entrepreneur, that romantic and fading factor in an economy now monopolized by giant corporations.

In the U.S., there have been openings for clever individuals, enterprising white men especially, and commercial connivers. Even more than the *limited* ability to move up compared to the *unlimited myth* of the American Dream, there was a restless economy that produced an always changing culture, a dramatic modernization in the way each new generation lived. Class, race and sex inequalities remained but each generation could see visible changes in the style of life. So, individualism was fueled by a furious pace of modernization and economic growth. Even more, individualism triumphed here in economics and pedagogy because social movements had limited success.

Individualism did not drop from the moon and land in the U.S.; history was the midwife. As a result of our historical experience, the ideas of social intelligence and political empowerment have less credibility than individual efforts. Even more than individualism being a strident pillar of capitalism, self-absorption also serves the system's need to divide and conquer common people, whom it attempts to organize into a commercial, conformist culture, contradicting the very individualism it proposes, but at least displacing class solidarity with mass identity.

Class and Empowerment

Paulo   This is a very good moment for us to come back to the question. Is it possible for us here in North America to use a dialogical method that came from the Third World? How do you use this kind of liberating pedagogy here? For example, I will make a statement going beyond what you said in understanding 'empowerment' as a social activity. You began to analyze how difficult it is for the average American or teacher to understand this social context, because of ideology which by itself is not an abstraction but has been generated in very concrete historical situations. Now, I will go beyond, not *too* much beyond, in trying to explain better my comprehension of empowerment as 'social class empowerment.' *Not* individual, *not* community, *not* merely social empowerment, but a concept of 'social class empowerment.'

This statement may risk being even *more* outside the comprehension of average Americans and teachers. They may say that they do not understand this man. They may claim that such a kind of empowerment has nothing to do with them. Why? Because it is *one* thing to make a class analysis in Latin America, and it is something altogether different to make the same kind of analysis in the States. In an enormously complex society like the North American one, it is hard to make a class analysis. It does not mean that U.S. society is without social classes. There are classes here, but not with the almost geographical frontier, the powerful reality we have of social classes in Latin America. I always say that in doing class analysis in the U.S., Marxist instruments of analysis were valid once but now need to be refined, in order to be useful to such a complex society like the American one.

Another thing we should say is that when my understanding of empowerment has to do with social class, I am not trying to reduce *everything* to class, as some narrow Marxists do. I don't want to do that. I recognize that this preoccupation I have with 'class' has to be recreated for the States. The question of social class empowerment involves how the working class through its own experiences, its own construction of culture, engages itself in getting political power. This makes 'empowerment' much more than an individual or psychological event. It points to a political process by the dominated classes who seek their own freedom from domination, a long historical process where education is one front.

Ira   Social class empowerment is a problem of analysis as well as a problem of pedagogy. About class-relations, I find clarity and confusion in students at the same time. Consciousness is *not* uniform from student to student or group to group. Consciousness is often inconsistent within the same student. In my classes, you can hear students speak about the class division of wealth and power in the U.S. At the same time, you can hear others deny that this inequality is a big deal. Whether they acknowledge or deny class divisions or racial prejudice or sexual inequality, few feel that history presents limits or tasks for transformation. Then, in the next breath, you can listen to their sense of oppression, maybe disgust or disappointment or even cynicism, that a country proclaiming democracy should be full of inequality, deception, and elitism. Not long after that, some students can passionately defend the American Dream while others will criticize it as a myth that isn't working. A teacher in my college can hear all these contradictory statements from students and must design a pedagogy that inserts itself into the tangle.

This repeats, I think, the potentials and limits of liberating education. If the course is an illuminating one, it is empowering insofar as it connects to other efforts in society for transformation. Also, any one course is only part of a long educational experience. I wonder again if teachers in my society feel the need for quick results in the classroom to support their confidence and morale. Perhaps U.S. teachers are unusually impatient because of our commercial and individualist culture, quick fixes, dynamic changes, fast cures, practical methods, manageable remedies. The problems of society will not be resolved soon or in a single classroom. But, there is a nobility to this impatience because it drives us forward towards answers, so it is not only a trap that can lead to fake solutions or to cynicism in the absence of easy answers.

Paulo   But there is another point to this question of individualism, environment, and pedagogy. I don't know if you will agree with me, Ira, as an American, if I take environment above all as an instrumentality, an historical force, which weaves our cultural circumstance. For example, the quantity of books we find in the American bibliography on 'how to get happy,' 'how to be happy making love,' 'how to get a good job,' 'how to make friends.' Sometimes I think it should be a very interesting issue for a dissertation, to make a research into the books coming out in one year in the States about self-improvement. The project could be to make an ideological analysis of the books. On the one hand, they intensely stimulate individualism. On the other hand, they are consistently prescriptive.

Ira   I agree. Also, various self-improvement programs become fads followed *en masse*. You are enveloped into a mass exercise for improvement via the appeal to individualism. Our discussion here has strongly characterized self-improvement as an interference to critical consciousness. Does this North American phenomenon of individual answers stand in the way of social empowerment?

Paulo   Exactly! Such a literature and cultural endeavor are the opposites of a critical effort for social transformation.

Ira   Just imagine the complications here in the U.S. for the notion of social class empowerment. This was a rich terrain inhabited by native peoples whose technology was no match for European gunpowder and diseased blankets. White settlers seized the land from the American Indians, exterminated them, and then millions of black slaves involuntarily developed our agriculture, while millions of poor white immigrants streamed into the new factories. Such a vast enterprise required great expectations, great capacity for cruelty and inflicting hardship, and the courage to endure hardship and cruelty. This historical experience rooted on private dreams of prosperity and freedom, not ideas of class like in European and Latin cultures.

    Individual dreams of freedom and prosperity in slaves and immigrants as well as in slaveholders and captains of industry molded this society. Getting free of slavery or the crushing poverty of early factory life meant dreaming big about your future or your children's future. Transformation was demanded by our historical experience. But, the privatization of this demand, the deflection of its social aspect, created among other things a vast market for self-help books, weak popular organizations unable to restrain the destructive power of monopolies, and a problem for dialogical education.

Paulo   It is absolutely necessary to say how this fantastic country and this tremendously contradictory reality is also full of surprises, full of richness. This may be easier for me to see or to speak about than you, because I am a Brazilian, an outsider who looks in, and you are an American. It is a mistake, a *big* mistake, to think that everything in the States is stabilized. No! This would be impossible! First of all, *no* reality is stable. For example, I tell you it is not easy to find another city so challenging, so full of creativity, as New York. What fascinates me in the States is the conviviality of the myth and the reality, the way they congenially live together. Evil and Good, Devil and Angel in one culture, in such close relationship, caught together in a tremendous vitality.

The first time I came to the States, I came because of Elza, my wife. When I was invited, I said to Elza, I will not go because what can I learn in such an imperialist country? Elza said to me, smiling, "How contradictory you are, and how naive. It is impossible to think that this country is just imperialist. It is impossible for it to be exclusively like this. You have many things to learn there." Immediately, she convinced me and I came. Since then, I never stop coming here. I come every year and I always learn something, even if I only learn how difficult it is to learn about this culture!

Ira   Even if you are born here and grow up here, it is also difficult to learn how this society works. It is a huge country with extreme divisions of regions, climates, races, religions, classes. The consistent culture of self-improvement, for example, has always coexisted with periodic social movements for transformation. In our history, self-help has been the predominant ideology, but we also had periods of great political upheaval where the social fabric had to be rewoven. We've had several waves of women's liberation, decades of action for racial equality, labor movements, eras of progressive school reform. This spoken book we are doing stands on the egalitarian shoulders of the 60s movements. That political era shaped me and many others in thinking about school and society. At some moments, the dream of freedom is a collective vision and also an idea whose time has come. Then, the individualist American Dream, the Utopia of self-improvement, becomes absorbed into a movement. In the 60s, when I was a student, it was common to act for individual and for social transformation at the same time. The conservative restoration of the 70s and 80s split this political marriage of personal and social change by promoting the notorious 'me-decade.'

The Teacher As Artist

Ira   In terms of empowerment and pedagogy, I want to raise here another issue, the question of the teacher as 'artist.' The role of art in transformative teaching interests me greatly, so I'd like to say some things about it before hearing your perspective.

Saying the teacher is an artist can easily lead to misunderstandings. Artists work in predictable materials like oils or marble or music. In what ways are teachers like sculptors, painters, conductors and composers? One way I see this aesthetic aspect of teaching is posing the classroom as a plastic material already shaped into one thing and capable of being reshaped into another. This is another way of saying that liberatory learning involves desocialization. Students and teachers in a classroom are not educational virgins. We are very socialized beings in our schools and colleges. We have long been practicing an elaborate school script of how each is supposed to behave (and misbehave) . This routine script is the traditional relationship between supervising authorities and alienated students. The liberating teacher has to study this routine scenario in the classroom, see how the socialized limits express themselves concretely, and then decide which themes are the best entry points for critical transformation. From these access points to the inside of the situation, the teacher then has to re-present the material he or she knows of student culture or of the object to be studied. This re-presentation of a student theme or of an academic context or of a moment from society is the problem or 'codification' posed to the class for inquiry. This is an artistic process, uncovering key themes and access points to consciousness, and then recomposing them into an unsettling critical investigation, orchestrating a prolonged study.

I've needed in the classroom a creative ingenuity to adjust the pedagogy for each new group of students. As each course begins, I have to start exercises which develop the students' critical literacy at the same time they develop my knowledge of the students. If I learn the key themes and words from their consciousness soon enough, I then have to problematize that material so that we both gain a systematic appreciation of the material. I'm referring here to situating critical literacy inside the themes and language of the students, but I think creative formats for studying academic bodies-of-knowledge also require the teacher to be an artist. For example, your friend the physics professor in Brazil was being creative when he asked students to research the consciousness of common people, as the way to begin a history of science course. Reformulating academic knowledge so that it absorbs the students' subjective position takes a lot of imagination on the teacher's part. Also, another creative dimension is including in this reformulation a critique of society.

The creative disruption of passive education is an aesthetic moment as well as a political one, because it asks the students to reperceive their prior understandings and to practice new perceptions as creative learners with the teacher. Maybe we can consider ourselves dramatists when we rewrite the routine classroom scripts and reinvent liberating ones. The syllabus is as much a script as it is a curriculum. The classroom is a stage for performance as much as it is a moment of education. The classroom is not only a stage and a performance, and not only a format for inquiry, but is also a place that has visual and auditory dimensions. We see and hear many things there. How can we adjust the sights and sounds of this moment to stimulate unfamiliar critical attention in students? In terms of verbal texture itself, I think of aestheticizing the classroom by varieties of utterances. Human voices speak in many modes: questions, statements, generalizations, specifics, images, comedy, pathos, sarcasm, mimicry, sentimentality, etc. How much of this texture appears in any course? When does comedy appear? Where is deep feeling?

Let me be concrete about this question of verbal texture. The routine script of the classroom has the teacher speaking *very* loudly about official subjects marginally interesting to students. The remote curriculum and the authoritarian relations of the classroom require the teacher to speak loudly and a lot, to command some attention in the face of student resistance. On the other hand, if teachers are used to speaking a great deal very loudly, students are used to saying very little very lowly.

Paulo   (Laughing) Yes, that is the way in the classroom.

Ira   I enter the classroom with a loud voice and have a lot to say, if I am the teacher. I speak my words clearly separated from each other, to make it easier to take notes, if I am the teacher. I speak from the front of the room, barricaded behind a desk, and verbally emphasize the key words in my sentences which I want students to memorize, in preparation for a short-answer exam coming up soon. Now, if I am a student, I enter the classroom and sit as far from the teacher as I can. I speak as little as possible in as low a voice as possible, slurring my words, because no one is really listening to me, or taking notes from what I have to say, or worrying about a test based on my words, and the whole discourse is aimed at the correct short-answer anyhow, so why go on?

If I know these things as a liberating teacher, I begin my creative reversal in the speaking moments. I modulate my voice to conversational rhythms rather than didactic, lecturing tones. I listen intently to every student utterance and ask other students to listen when one of their peers speaks. I don't begin my reply after the student ends her or his *first* sentence, but ask the student to say more about the question. If I'm asked what I think, I say I'd be glad to say what I think, but why don't a few more people speak first to what the student just said, whether you agree or not. If I don't have a reply to what a student said, or don't understand a series of student comments, and can't invent on the spot questions to reveal the issue, I go home and think about it and start a next class from what a student said before, to keep signaling to students the importance of their statements. These small interventions contradict the verbal domination which has driven students into resisting dialogue. If I am recreating the teacher as a speaker and listener here, I am also inviting students to recreate themselves as listeners and speakers in a new classroom script. I think the art here is verbal reinvention, vocal recreation through dialogue.

Student silence is created by the arts of domination. Students are not silent by nature. They have a great deal to say, but not in the script of the traditional classroom. Reinventing the visual and verbal aspects of the classroom are two ways of addressing the destructive arts of passive education. Discovering a key student theme and then orchestrating it as a motif, variations on the theme to explore its character, is also an artistic use of dialogue.

From another angle, I would add that humor is one more creative moment, as a mutual comedy between students and teachers and not only a comic performance by an amusing instructor. One of the funniest and most revealing moments for me is the power of students to mock and mimic their superiors. When I walk down the halls of my college, I eavesdrop on student conversations, to learn how they talk to each other. I hear them making fun of teachers, bosses, etc., in wonderfully creative mimicry. If I ask them in class to write *my* introductory speech *to them* when the course begins, they are able to produce good renditions of a teacherly voice. They also can read this didactic voice from their pages with colorful characterization. They know how to sound like professors.

Paulo (Laughing) Yes. They know how we talk.

Ira   Yet, we often say they don't know Standard English or correct usage, even when they can mimic a professor. They know something about this official language of the authorities. They don't use it or study it consistently because correct usage is not their organic language, not organic to their subordinate development in school and society. They will perform in standard usage for creative moments when they want. Here is an example of critical aesthetics that teachers as artists need to draw out.

Paulo   I agree absolutely with you about this question of the teacher as an artist. I would just add two elements to it.

One is that no matter if education is exercised informally at home or formally at a school, through informal relationships between parents and kids or formally in primary school between teachers and students, education has to do with a permanent process of formation. Even though it is not strictly the task of the educator to form or to shape the students, no matter what the level of education, I am in my perspective a helper of the students in their process of formation, of their growing up. This process is necessarily an artistic one. It is impossible to participate in the process of getting shaped, which is a kind of rebirth, without some aesthetic moments. In this aspect, education is naturally an aesthetic exercise. Even if we are not conscious of this as educators, we are still involved in a naturally aesthetic project. What can happen is that, being unaware of the aesthetic aspect of education, we become very bad artists, but artists of a kind nevertheless, to the extent we help the students enter a process of permanent formation.

Another point that makes education once more an artistic event is precisely when education is also an act of knowing. For me, knowing is something beautiful! To the extent that knowing is unveiling an object, the unveiling gives the object 'life,' calls it into 'life,' even gives it a new 'life.' This is an artistic task because our knowing has a life-giving quality, creating and animating objects as we study them.

All the things you said participate also in this aesthetic nature of knowing and forming. Gestures, intonations of voices, walking in the classroom, poses: We can do all these things without being conscious all the time of their aesthetic aspects, their impact on student formation through teaching. What I think is that the aesthetic nature of education does not mean that we explicitly and consciously do it all the time. I think that from the moment we come into the classroom, at the moment you say, Hello! How are you?, to the students, you necessarily start an aesthetic relationship. This is so because you are an educator who has a strategic and directive role to play in liberating pedagogy. Then, education is simultaneously a certain theory of knowledge going into practice, a political and aesthetic act. These three dimensions are always together, simultaneous moments of theory and practice, art and politics, the act of knowing at once creating and recreating objects while it forms the students who are knowing.

I think, then, if the educator becomes more and more clear about these characteristics of teaching, he or she can improve the effectiveness of the pedagogy. Clarity about the necessary political and artistic natures of education will make the teacher into a better politician and a better artist. We do art and politics when we help the formation of students, whether we know it or not. Knowing what we are in fact doing will help us do it better.

Notes

[1] See the "Foreword" for a discussion of "the gnosiological cycle" of knowledge, the two moments in making knowledge, producing new knowledge and knowing what we have produced.

[2] See Antonio Gramsci, *Prison Notebooks* (Baltimore, 1973). Gramsci wrote about the educational role of intellectuals whose work organically interacts with people in daily life: "it is not a question of introducing from scratch a scientific form of thought into everyone's individual life, but of renovating and making 'critical' an already existing activity." (p. 330) See also Gramsci's *The Modern Prince and Other Writings* (International Press, New York, 1970).

CHAPTER 5

Do First-World Students Need Liberating?

Defining A 'Culture of Silence'

Ira   In this chapter, Paulo, I'd like to discuss further how to situate a liberatory program in our culture here, in the North. Some teachers question if the dialogical method can or should be applied to classrooms in developed countries. They know your epistemology evolved in the Third World under political and economic conditions very different from those in the U.S., the U.K., Canada, and Europe. For now, I'd like to focus on the society I teach in, the United States. Do the differences between North America and Brazil invalidate the method for U.S. classrooms? Can dialogical education work here in the prosperous North, whose culture is so different from that in Latin America?

Besides wondering if liberatory learning works only in the Third World, U.S. teachers question if it is even needed. Dialogical education emphasizes the development of democracy in school and society. Is this a special preoccupation of Third World teachers who often live under military rule? In our society here, teachers and students do not live in a dictatorship. This is a constitutional democracy without military coups. Thus, the emphasis of dialogical education on freedom may be culture-bound to the authoritarian politics of the Third World.

Teachers here also see an affluent society, a very complex, electronic, consumer society. Many students want to make it in a culture they perceive generally as democratic. Teachers wonder if the notions of liberation, empowerment, and 'the culture of silence' fit this student reality. Is it reasonable to apply such pedagogy here, with its vocabulary of domination and oppression?

These questions are valid and important. Such doubts can interfere with a teacher's ability or desire to test liberating methods. Maybe I should begin speaking from my own experience as a North American teacher.

I do find a 'culture of silence' in my mainstream American classrooms. These college students, many fresh out of high school, many working adults coming to evening courses, are mostly white and often the first in their families to go to higher education. The younger students pour out of crowded high schools and are often unclear what they want from college, but the bad jobs available to them now are worse than being in school. The older students largely come to college to get job-market degrees in business, computers, technology, or nursing, impatient with the hurdles placed in their career paths. It's familiar for me to enter a classroom and find students so alienated that they refuse to speak in the course. My experience with student withdrawal is reported by other teachers, also.

The 'culture of silence' I'm describing has several dimensions, including an opposing student response of aggression, which make it similar to and different from the silence of workers, peasants and students you described in *Pedagogy of the Oppressed* (1970) . One element is the students' internalizing of passive roles scripted for them in the traditional classroom. The official pedagogy constructs them as passive/aggressive characters. After years in dull transfer-of-knowledge classes, in boring courses filled with sedating teacher-talk, many have become non-participants, waiting for the teacher to set the rules and start narrating what to memorize. These students are silent because they no longer expect education to include the joy of learning, moments of passion or inspiration or comedy, or even that education will speak to the real conditions of their lives. They expect the droning voice of the teacher to fill the very long class hour.

Such student withdrawal can be simply passive or can be a smoldering, angry silence. Some silent students dutifully copy down notes and follow the teacher's voice. Others sit silently and daydream, unplugged from the repulsive conditions of the classroom. Still others sit in anger, provoked by the imposition of tedium and orthodoxy on them. These silences are varieties of alienation produced by transfer-of-knowledge pedagogy in U.S. schools and colleges.

A second dimension of this culture of silence is its aggressive side, the visible aggression of students in response to it, an aggression produced by the imposition of passive learning. It's a reality inadequately named by the phrase 'culture of silence.' I think the phrase 'culture of silence' suggests passive tolerance of domination. The passive response to authoritarian pedagogy is true as *one* aspect of the classroom. Many students simply withdraw into a speechless cocoon in class. Others simply swallow what the official curriculum offers, without enthusiasm, without questioning the syllabus. But, in addition, there is an aggressive, negative resistance as well.

Aggression is inevitable because passivity is *not* a natural condition of childhood or adulthood. There is a 'symbolic violence' in school and society which imposes silence on students.[1] It is symbolic because it is in the very order of things, not an actual physical beating, but an environment of rules, curriculum, tests, punishments, requirements, correction, remediation, and standard English, which establish the authorities as the ones in charge. This environment is symbolically violent because it is based in manipulation and subordination. It openly declares itself 'democratic' while actually constructing and reproducing inequality. The curriculum is presented as normative, neutral and benevolent, even as it 'cools you out,' adjusting most students to subordinate positions in society.[2] Inequality is presented as natural, just, and earned, given the differing 'aptitudes' and 'achievements' of various groups. The advantages of the elite are hidden behind a myth of 'equal opportunity' while the idiom of the elite is named 'correct usage,' another myth of symbolic violence against colloquial speech, making the idioms of ordinary people into inferior, outlaw languages. This social construction of inequality through schooling joins a constellation of other agencies repeating the messages and myths, in the mass media, mass advertisements, and the job market. For individual students, it becomes hard to see alternatives to 'the way things are and have to be.' But, it is also difficult to swallow your defeats. In school, many students rebel against their structured descent into cheap labor, the low-wage, high-tech future waiting for them after the depressant effects of public education.[3] Faced by illegitimate supervisors and teachers, many alienated students choose an aggressive response.

A 'Culture of Sabotage'

Ira The official curriculum is also filled with praises of democracy which hide as well as contradict the culture of silence. Students get some messages which encourage their speaking out against arbitrary authority. In addition, rebellion is provoked by the very act of symbolic violence, which pushes people into an unnatural silence that propels some of them to push back. If the symbolic violence of the official curriculum was a complete success, there would be no discipline problems in school. If it worked well, Paulo, you and I might not be speaking this book now. The widespread disorder in school means that the process is resisted by many students. Passivity or aggression are thus developed in society through our institutional experiences. Students are the objects of this development before they are old enough to understand it well or to challenge it effectively. A segment of the students is thrown into passive acceptance; another will not play by the rules and not rebel either but will scheme how to 'get by'; a third group will sabotage the rules by overt aggression; a fourth group will buy into the system and actively support the status quo. The element of aggression surfaces a lot in U.S. classrooms and is troubling to the authorities. Maybe it is good to name this aggressive rejection of silence as 'the culture of sabotage.' Students who sabotage the symbolic violence of the curriculum are defending their autonomy, in often self-destructive and confused ways, to be sure. But, nevertheless, they are responding defensively to the regime being imposed on them.

Their aggressive behavior interferes with the transfer-of-knowledge. Very often, their confrontation is verbal sabotage. To be clear about the politics of dicourse here, I want to specify the didactic voice this student aggression is challenging. You've spoken before, Paulo, about the 'sleepy sonority' of the teacherly voice, the narrating voice of the 'banking' educator who sings the students to sleep while filling up the empty accounts of the students' minds with deposits of knowledge. That sing-song voice intends a transfer of the official curriculum from the teacher and the textbook to the students. It tries to habituate students to taking orders and to denying their own critical thinking.

That didactic voice is also self-sabotaging. It is an invitation to casual listening and to resistance. By itself, it encourages nonattention. The traditional curriculum asks teachers to fill up the class hour with material that is not critically captivating or worthy of an hour's attention. So, what is the result? The teacher lapses into a sonorous voice which bores itself as well as the students, and in a way encourages the students to drift off. It even assists them in the role of casual listeners. I mentioned earlier how some lecturing voices are wonderful examples of this. The teacher will verbally emphasize those few words in a sentence or paragraph which count. By hitting certain nouns, verbs or adjectives with a pop of extra volume, the teacher sends signals to the students about the few key words to remember or copy down, which will appear later as the short-answers in a multiple-choice exam. Students know they can ignore the lecture and listen only for periodic emphases, often on the nominative case of spoken sentences, where names, places and dates are mentioned. This repulsive or just plain silly exercise in class convinces many students to withdraw into silence. It provokes others into anger, so they act to sabotage the process. The 'culture of sabotage' meets the symbolic violence of schooling with its own symbolic violence. The degree of student resistance or aggression now has become a crisis for the establishment, even though the student movements of the 60s are gone.

That crisis produces a stalemate in countless classrooms. Uncooperative students and unyielding authorities have fought each other to a stand-off, what I call a student 'performance strike.' Many students refuse to perform under the current conditions of school and society. They know how to sabotage the curriculum but they aren't able to change education in favor of their constructive freedom. Their skills are ingeniously negative. They don't know how to make organized demands for change. Instead, they get better and better at aggression and sabotage, or they fall into deeper silences, or more drugs and alcohol. The aggressive ones in some schools yell in class, make jokes, throw things, come late, leave early, walk around the classroom during the hour, listen to rock music on walkman stereos, eat in class, don't do homework, hire others to write their papers, etc. It's hard to teach with this level of resistance. Disorder demoralizes the teacher as well as the other students. This alienation cannot be solved by more passive pedagogy or by tougher authority. It requires a counter-alienation pedagogy, one creative, critical, and on the side of student subjectivity.

The conditions we teach under here deteriorate year by year. Is the situation similar in Brazil?

Paulo I think first that, all the conditions you mentioned, like 'culture of silence' and 'culture of sabotage' are really expressions of something larger. Once again we have to think in ways that avoid confusing one thing as the reason d'être for the other. It's important to know why students do what they do. Secondly, at least in a general way, I think that the aggressive attitude of American students in the classroom is not easily seen in Brazil. As far as I can tell, from six years back in Brazil after sixteen years in exile, we have students who in a very ideologized way wait for the speech of the teacher. In a very interesting contradiction, on the one hand they expect the speech of the teacher, while on the other hand they are very alive, fighting against the lack of freedom.

Ira   How do they fight against the lack of freedom?

Paulo   It is completely different from the kind of disruption you describe here now. They fight inside their organizations against the lack of freedom, above all in the global context of their larger society, against the government, for example. They fight in an organized way against such things as the private university's raising the tuition. If they belong to a state university, they demand the government give more money to the colleges. It is different, a political and organized opposition.

But, I don't know, Ira, if I am being very naive or not concerning this question of sabotage because I never confronted such a situation in any of the schools or universities I have visited in the U.S. The different colleges I've worked in here have been privileged places. I never had to confront in any of these privileged situations the kind of aggressive circumstances you talked about. But, the situation I have with students here is not the normal one. I suppose that the students who come to the seminars I offer here are paying a lot for attending. Of course, they pay a lot for their other courses also. They come to the seminars because they want to come, not out of compulsory attendance. The seminars are not a required part of the regular curriculum. Finally, I am a Brazilian and a foreign teacher so my situation is very different than what you and other American teachers experience in the classroom.

I think that if I was a regular teacher here and had to confront the kind of rebellion you describe, I would try to discuss with the students why they are doing this sabotage. Now, I would not assume an attitude of fear towards them. No, no, we would have to grasp the very rebellion as something absolutely concrete and to ask ourselves in the class about the reasons. For example, I might say to the students, "Okay, you are provoking not only me but also the group. This is a fact. I want to invite all of us right now to make a kind of parenthesis in our session today. Let's put a parenthesis around the object we were supposed to analyze today. Instead of the material we planned to cover, I would like to take the very rebellion now as an object of our curiosity. What really do we want in doing this? And why are we doing this?"

I'd like to ask your opinion on this. How do you confront this situation when faced by it? I think that at the moment in which we invite serious attention on the rebellion, but not out of fear, we challenge it to know it better.

The students will have to choose between two answers. The first answer is simply to increase the rebellion. The second is to be so surprised that he or she loses the impulse to rebel. If this approach fails, what else can the teacher do? Expel the students? Maybe physically the teacher is afraid to do this. To enter into the atmosphere of rebellion to try to stifle the disruption may ask more from a teacher than the teacher can physically do. This is what I ask you now, from your personal experience, and that of other teachers here in the States.

Ira   One way to address the disruption is to put aside the material for the day because the students have already put it aside for you. Then, challenge the students to discuss their own challenge. If you can make this work, you'll come out with an interesting class and stronger teacher-student communication. At these moments, when one of my classes is resisting the work strongly, I sometimes do what you proposed. I 'stop the music,' as we say here, and ask what is going on, and begin a dialogue on why we cannot go on with the work. I recall these detours as partial successes. But also, the level of sabotage I face in my mainstream college has rarely been high enough to make impossible some critical appeal to the students. I have had, though, a few classes that resisted all critical appeals. Some groups cannot be appealed to.

When I have a disruptive student I monitor him or her to see how far she or he will go. I look in the direction of the disruptive student and make eye and verbal contact to let her or him know I have noticed and want the disruption to stop. If the look doesn't work, I then say something to the student. If the student doesn't stop, I say something more and louder. If it goes on, I may have to stop class and ask the student to leave. I try not to interrupt class for too long, or to make a confrontation which exhausts me and the other students. If the disruption is severe, I ask the student to see me after class where I have a very open talk, show my dismay and make clear the precise rules for behavior. I tell the student to drop the course if her or his response to my words is equivocal. If the student responds positively, I invite him or her back. Sometimes I insist on the student taking a class off or a week off and doing outside work while she or he thinks of how to behave in class. Regularly, I have had a number of students who I do not let back in the course. In some classes, there are small groups of disruptive students that I either expel or ask to work alone outside of class. It's easier for me than for high school or junior high school teachers because I have fewer classes and fewer students and far fewer aggressive students to contend with. I also am dealing with adults who do not have to be in school by law. The 'culture of sabotage' I described earlier does not appear uniformly in all schools; some have it worse than others; some have little or none of it. I described this aggression to give voice to a reality many teachers have to cope with in worse conditions than my own.

Resistance may be one of the departure points for seeing some difference between U.S. and Brazilian situations. Still, this difference may make the need for a dialogical pedagogy only more urgent here because of the student resistance to traditional methods. I also should say that the dialogical classes I tested are not magical answers to passivity or aggression. They cannot instantly convert alienation and disruption to peace and harmony. The results have been encouraging but mixed. There are some schools where conditions are so bad that more global changes are needed to support the changes made in any single classroom.

Paulo   Why don't you tell me more about the resistance problems in your culture, to make clear what teachers face in the classroom?

Ira   The problem of student sabotage is mostly a problem in high school in the U.S. Next comes junior high school and after that the community colleges. High schools in urban and suburban areas experience student sabotage. I should add that there are many schools that are orderly, maybe too orderly! I visited one such junior high school in Massachusetts, not a sound coming from inside or outside the classrooms, and I had to ask if school was in session that day. But, you can find passive or aggressive student resistance in North Dakota as well as in New York City. I visited a high school in the middle-class suburbs of Long Island, and found disorder and vandalism. At my neighborhood high school in the South Bronx, the library was burned up! Aggression at urban high schools is notorious because the racial aspect is there. The inner cities are increasingly non-white and impoverished while the teacher corps remains mostly white and middle-class. This breeds more resentment in the students.

At elite universities you find both passive withdrawal and active participation in the curriculum, because those rich places have a solid decorum about them. They look very good. So do private schools and the public schools in richer districts. The more elite the school the more it communicates to the students that they are going places, so there is a reason to put up with the curriculum. Playing by the rules in an elite school can pay off in your future. But, in poor school districts and in shabby community colleges, students see their future already in their present, a life of squalor, disregard, going nowhere. The most sensitive observer of students in the 1983 reform wave, Theodore Sizer, found that "social class" was the single most important variable among schools. He wrote after a national tour of high schools, "Tell me about the incomes of your students' families and I'll describe to you your school."[4] Class and race inequality are no secrets to resentful ordinary students. Those who are aggressive say that playing by the rules is a sucker's game. You haven't got much to gain by being good, so why should you behave? This feeling is present in many of my mainstream college students, who see the shabby rooms and know that this education doesn't take you seriously, can't be a serious credential in society, so why should you take it seriously. Added to students' prolonged frustration in high school, the shabby budget college provokes more resentment.

The sad reality is that students are largely alienated, bored and uncooperative, even when they are 'well-behaved.' Who can celebrate their silent boredom or their passivity? Most of my mainstream college students are not aggressive and not cooperative in the classroom. They are waiting for the teacher to speak and do all the work and leave them alone to copy down what should be memorized. Some can respond to a liberating, dialogical class. But, they generally begin passively alienated, and many stay that way until the end.

Transforming Silence and Sabotage: The Limits of Education

Paulo   It's interesting, Ira, to see again how systematic or formal education, in spite of its importance, cannot really be the lever for the transformation of society. We must understand in a dialectical way the relationship between systematic education and social change, the political transformation of society. The problems of school are deeply rooted in the global conditions of society, perhaps the problems of discipline and alienation above all.

While you were talking, I was thinking for example, of how a teacher working several years in the classroom, trying to become a very concrete example to the students of a radical, democratic teacher, after five years can fall into some despair, or can fall into some cynicism. Because, in fact, the two hypotheses of despair and cynicism are constant temptations we receive or to which we are exposed if we struggle with the concrete problems of education.

Precisely because education is *not* the lever for the transformation of society, we are in danger of despair and of cynicism if we limit our struggle to the classroom. What we have to do, I think, from the very beginning of our experience as teachers, is to be critically conscious of the limits of education. That is, to know that education is not the lever, not to expect it to make the great social transformation. We should know that it is possible to accomplish something important in the institutional space of a school or college in order to help the transformation of society. If we understand this limited and connected nature of education, if we understand how formal education relates to the global society without being only the reproducer of dominant ideology and without being also the primary lever of transformation, if we understand our educational practice this way, then we avoid a certain naive optimism which can lead us in the future to a terrible pessimism. By avoiding naive optimism at the beginning we prevent ourselves from falling into despair and cynicism.

I have been teaching since I was 19, when I was still in secondary school, because I started high school late. That was when I was teaching Portuguese syntax. Of course, in the beginning I had my naive optimism which I began to control through my practice. That is, the more I was being a teacher, the more I began to understand what it meant to be a teacher. And now, for example, education is my main front of action but I am still not tempted by despair or cynicism. Because I have the limits clearly in front of me, I helped myself avoid the two temptations. Knowing the limits of education did not lead me to reduce my activity in this area, but instead increased my political goals. But most of all, I increased my political work outside of the schools. I saw the need to act where the levers for transformation do exist. So, this desire to work outside formal education as well as inside, in neighborhoods, for example, did not diminish my desire to educate but only gave me a new direction for it.

Knowing the real limits of formal schooling in society helped me redirect my work. About those limits, I could say concretely that when I am with a group of twenty or forty students, here or in Brazil, discussing some aspect of reality to try to unveil it, even when I am discussing the very process of education, I am not thinking that when I say goodbye to the students I have twenty-five more revolutionaries! No, no! (Laughing) But what we may have after finishing the seminar is an increase in the curiosity of the people. We may have challenged them to become more aware of the contradictions in society. Perhaps some of them may start asking themselves with whom do they stand politically and against whom do they stand. Maybe a few of them will become much more strongly engaged in the process of transformation. This is what *I* can do as a teacher because this is what *education* can do, at the level of our action in public schools and colleges.

Because of these limits, I also try in Brazil to have time to work as an educator and politician outside the institutional or official space of the schools. I try to work inside the social movements, with workers. Sometimes I cannot work directly with groups of workers. So, then, I work with groups of educators who are teaching among the workers. Now, I don't have the quantity of hours to give to this kind of activity that I would like to give.

This does not mean that it is better to stop doing things in the schools. Secondly, it is also important to underline that those who prefer to work inside the space of the schools have to be respected. I say this because sometimes people fall into sectarian positions and say that we should have nothing to do with teachers who work only inside schools. Sectarians think that only they are the true activists or else think that activists should only work outside the schools. No. Educators inside schools do important work and must be respected for contributing to social transformation.

For me, it would not be enough to work only inside the schools. It was never enough for me. I remember that when I worked thirty years ago in Recife, many times I left the university at six or eight o'clock p.m. and went directly to lower-class areas where I had a meeting with forty or fifty working people, sometimes to discuss the nature of education. But, there are those who prefer to be altogether outside, or altogether inside. It's their right.

What is very important to me, Ira, is how *not* to work alone, how to know the others, how to establish relationships so that we could come to a meeting and say I work outside the school where I observe these things, and do any of these realities help you who work inside the school to do transformation better? I would ask, Can what I know from the outside help you tomorrow do something different than what you are doing today? Can what you do inside school help me do the transformation on the outside better?

Ira   Those teachers and activists outside formal education do work closer to the centers of power, the real levers of transformation as you put it. The despair of many teachers now on the inside comes partly from education being a depressed sector of this society. It was marginalized after the radical 60s, to reduce the egalitarian challenge developing on campus. The heady days of protest, experiments, and expansion turned almost overnight into budget cuts, firings, dismal careerism and repressive back-to-basics programs. Teachers who work in schools or colleges for transformation often feel isolated there, wondering what their work amounts to in such a repressed area of the economy. Education was marginalized by the conservative reaction to the 60s precisely because of its political potential. Schooling was brought back inside the limits of establishment ideas.

Paulo   Yes, this is important. Say something more.

Ira   In the 60s, protest movements thrived on campus and to some extent spread into high schools. Many students challenged the Vietnam War, racism, sexism, the official syllabus, and the authoritarian relations of the classroom. These protests in education unsettled the establishment, which responded with a long counter-offensive beginning with Nixon and continuing through the Reagan years. I've been referring to this recent history on and off, Paulo, because it's impossible to understand the current crisis of U.S. education without setting it into the past twenty-five years.

Even the conservative Reagan years have examples of education hosting opposition. The anti-nuclear movement and the anti-intervention movement have campus bases. Prior to the gigantic march at the U.N. in June 1982 in New York, there were campus teach-ins on the arms race held at 151 universities in November 1981. In the fall of 1984, rallies and teach-ins against Reagan's policies in Central America were held on many campuses also. In the spring of 1985, a number of colleges had militant actions against apartheid in South Africa, some with hundreds of arrests and others with weeks of protest encampments. These movements reflect those off-campus, in the environmental, women's and church movements for peace. For now, it may be sensible for any single liberatory teacher to test the possibilities for outside connections. Sometimes the connection can be thought of as an extension of the inquiry begun in class. Sometimes it can be thought of as a parallel politics, separate from classroom experiments, as activities in the school or college as a whole. Sometimes it will be off-campus work, in a community or an organization.

Liberating education in general and the single classroom in particular cannot transform society by themselves. This limit needs to be repeated so that none of us mistake what dialogical learning means. Critical curiosity, some political awareness, democratic participation, habits of intellectual scrutiny, and interest in social change are realistic goals from inside a dialogic course. Further, what a single class can do in connecting to out-of-class politics is limited not simply by watchful administrations or by the standard syllabus, but also by the eccentric group of students in the course. Students in class are a random group of the school population. The students are not a self-selected pro-transformation group looking for a political task. They will acccept liberatory transformation unevenly. Whole groups will reject it. Thus, a teacher's interest in connecting inside to outside is necessarily limited by the students' uneven development and their diverse ideological commitments. So, the teaching process by itself in the classroom cannot remake society. It can evolve critical curiosity. It can develop the commitment of the teacher and some students to the goal of transformation. But, the movements outside are where more people who dream of social change are gathering. A political movement could be described as a place of organized ideas and action where people gather consciously to reconstruct themselves and society. A liberating classroom in a traditional school or college is a place of mixed intentions organized by a dialogic teacher with students who rarely come there thinking to change themselves or their society. Knowing this difference helps avoid euphoria and despair in practicing within the limits of the classroom.

As I was thinking and saying all these things about the limits and potentials of dialogical classrooms, in the back of my mind I kept wondering about your earlier statement. So, I have to go back now and ask you something, Paulo. At the moment you began responding to my reflection on 'the culture of silence' and 'the culture of sabotage' here in North American schools, why were you provoked to discuss the limits of education? Or why education is not the lever for social transformation?

Paulo   Ah, yes, yes, (Laughing) that is a good question. Of course, when I said those things on the limits of education, there were some words behind my reflection which I did not pronounce. Yes, I started from a distant point of the route! (Laughing)

Ira   You flew over the starting point and landed beyond the mountain. Talk about the mountain.

Beyond the Limits of Education

Paulo   I wanted to say in discussing the limits of education that all these kinds of cultural expressions you talked about, such as silence, alienation, sabotage, aggression, have some very, very concrete material reasons in society. And I wanted to add that it is *not* through just our democratic witness that we change these conditions, even though our witness is required as one important force in making the change. Only social conditions can explain the reactions of students in the classroom and these conditions need more than our democratic pedagogy to be changed.

I said 'democratic' in the way we are using it here, the liberatory teacher who makes an invitation to the students for transformation, who teaches in a dialogical way instead of an authoritarian way, who sets an example as a critical student of society. It is not through our witness or our mere example that we change the social realities that create student behavior in the classroom. These realities are rooted in society and make possible the reactions of students in the classroom. Through liberating education we can make some localized changes in the classroom which should not be mistaken for changes in the global society, even though these immediate changes can become factors in a larger transformation.

If it was possible to change reality simply by our witness or example, we would have to think that reality is changed *inside* of our consciousness. Then, it would be very easy to be a liberatory educator! All we would have to do is an intellectual exercise and society would change! No, this is not the question. To change the concrete conditions of reality means a tremendous political practice, which demands mobilization, organization of the people, programs, all these things which are not organized just inside the schools, which cannot be organized just inside a classroom or a school.

Ira   I agree, but, can we discuss education as one institution that helps construct student behavior? Or, should I say that the subsector of education confirms and extends the consciousness being developed generally in mass culture? The official curriculum helps to solidify the uncritical, dependent consciousness being produced through a number of mechanisms in society. The social relations of education are in accord with the hierarchy of society, which Bowles and Gintis referred to as "the correspondence principle."[5] This means that the logic of domination is reproduced in school as in any other institution, so that when we attempt dialogical education we are necessarily contradicting the dominant ideology, politically interfering with school's task of reproducing domination. This is a concrete contribution of the liberatory class to social transformation, I think. Do you agree?

Paulo   Yes. But, I would like to turn the question around, maybe to reverse the question by discussing the global transformation again. I think we have emphasized in these conversations the point that while education is not the lever for social transformation, nevertheless transformation itself is an educational event. Transformation teaches us, shapes and reshapes us. Secondly, we are also convinced that education strongly helps to clarify, to unveil, the conditions we are in. This suggests again what I proposed earlier in our talks, that liberating education must also be thought of as something that goes on outside classrooms in social movements which fight against domination.

Have I made clear why I began with the limits of education? How can we know the reasons for student reactions of silence or sabotage unless we go beyond the limit of education and find the origins and the solutions in the politics of society? How can we change the conditions which disrupt the classroom unless there is a social movement for transformation? Teachers who don't acknowledge the social roots of this problem disarm themselves from understanding their own predicament.

Reading and Resistance: School-words versus Reality

Paulo   When I think more about student resistance and the limits of education, I have the impression that one of the main difficulties is a dichotomy that exists in the educational experience in the States. I am here speaking about the dichotomy between *reading the words and reading the world.* I see this as one of the main obstacles here in America for practicing liberating education, trying to get a critical grasp of the objects under study. What do I mean by the dichotomy between reading the words and reading the world? My impression is that the world of American education, the school, is increasing the separation of the words we read and the world we live in. In such a dichotomy, the world of reading is only the world of the schooling process, a closed world, cut off from the world where we have experiences but do not read about those experiences. This schooling world where we read words that relate less and less to our concrete experiences outside has become more and more specialized in the bad sense of this word. In reading words, school becomes a special place that teaches us to read only school-words, not reality-words. The *other* world, the world of *facts*, the world of *life*, the world in which events are very alive, the world of struggles, the world of discrimination and economic crisis (all these things are there!) do not make contact with students in school through the words that school asks students to read. You can think of this dichotomy as one kind of 'culture of silence' imposed on students. School reading is silent about the world of experience and the world of experience is silenced, without its own critical texts.

Ira   Dialogical education bridges the gap. It connects reading words with reading reality, so the two can speak to each other. It gives student reality a voice in school at last, changing the abstract intellectual idiom of the classroom.

Paulo   Exactly! The school command of words only wants students to describe things but not to understand them. Then, the more you separate description from understanding, the more you control the consciousness of the students. They are kept only at the surface level of reality and do not go beneath it, into a deep critical understanding of what makes their reality what it is.

This kind of critical consciousness in the students would be an ideological challenge to the dominant class. The more this dichotomy between reading words and reading reality is exercised in school, the more we are convinced that our task here in the school or college is only to work on concepts, to work only on texts that speak about concepts. But, to the extent that we are being trained in a strong dichotomy between the *word-world* and the *real-world*, working on concepts written in a text has to mean dichotomizing text from context. And then, more and more we become specialists in reading words without being preoccupied with connecting the reading with a better understanding of the world. In the last analysis, we separate the theoretical context from the concrete context. A dichotomized pedagogy like this reduces the power of intellectual study to help in transforming reality.

If we look at it closely, this dichotomy can become very funny. It makes us more able to *play* with theories, some of them even *good* ones. For example, this is what explains how some very good Marxists have never drunk coffee in the house of a worker! They are very good Marxist theorists, who never had even a small experience in a slum. They are Marxists who know, nevertheless, about discrimination, because they walk the streets, and inside the university they also perceive racism. They are *experts* in Marx. However, because of their isolation from everyday life, Marx experts are not *Marxists*. They can even say that they know Marx but they hate him, because Marx is only a text for specialists who discuss concepts. Do you see? (Laughing) It is very interesting how we can create this kind of intellectual in the dichotomy between reading words and reading reality.

What happens, then, when a young teacher meets for the first time the hypothesis of changing his or her behavior in the classroom? What happens when the young teacher meets the possibility of changing her or his teaching practice? Maybe she or he read some text and thinks for the first time to become a critical educator, a new way of simultaneously reading the word and reading the world. What happens? He or she comes to the classroom with a new conviction, but this new teacher was already shaped into the dichotomy between text and context. Then, it is hard to overcome the old dichotomy and integrate words and world. The teacher has a hard time giving witness in overcoming the rupture of intellectual study from the experience of the world. Dialectically connecting the two which have been separated so far and for so long is opposite to the teacher's official training.

I think we have in this point one of the main differences between Latin America and the States. For me, this is one of the great obstacles to liberating pedagogy here in America. The ideology of the dichotomy is much stronger and more concrete in the States than it is in Brazil. Look, in Brazil, we have those who are against the integration of the word and the world in intellectual study, for certain. Some object to it for sophisticated reasons as specialists in a field and some object to it naively as not what they choose to do in teaching. We have serious people, very good people, who want in the classroom only what they call "great seriousness," which means very academic, conceptual material like Hegel, texts, texts, texts. But their objections to dialogical education where we integrate the text and the context, the word and the world, are not the kind of obstacles you face in the States, where the opposition to such teaching is much stronger: Am I right about this?

Ira   In general, I agree with you. The official curriculum is very imposing here. The traditional texts and pedagogy are very normative. They establish the powerful norms which intimidate teachers, discouraging them from doing something different. The result is either a bookish academic curriculum or a dehumanizing vocational program. Either curriculum is presented as a value-free system where conceptual analysis does not make contact with the real world of students. We have in the official curriculum a strong bias to empiricize and to abstract. Where a course does describe some part of reality in detail, it doesn't offer students a critical unveiling of its politics. Where a course does offer conceptual frameworks, these concepts are abstract, so far from applying to reality that they keep the students unarmed in challenging their culture.

Students withdraw into passive noncompliance or offensive sabotage in response to a disempowering education, this dichotomy of reading from living, of intellectualizing from experiencing. Our hypothesis suggests, then, that domination is more than being ordered around impersonally in school, and more than the social relations of discourse in a transfer-of-knowledge pedagogy. Domination is also the very structure of knowing; concepts are presented irrelevant to reality, descriptions of reality achieve no critical integration, critical thought is separated from living. This dichotomy is the interior dynamic of a pedagogy that disempowers students politically and psychologically.

Year after year, this dichotomy destroys student enthusiasm for knowledge. Students learn to have low expectations for their schooling. Many hear the teacher read off the curriculum for the term and they want to yell out, Oh God, not again! They keep going over the same material from year to year, or get new material presented in dull, abstract ways, in nominally different but emotionally interchangeable courses, alike in their emptiness. The mandated syllabus and standard exams and commercial textbooks preside over this sad waste of such wonderful years in a student's life (and in a teacher's life). No wonder there is a culture of sabotage here. Perhaps teachers in Brazil or Europe work in cultures where student resistance is more controlled. Brazil and Europe have authoritarian education systems also. But, they are more traditional societies than we have here in the States. Thus, there may be more discipline and less aggression in the everyday workings of the institutions. Students may have more cultural restraints on their behavior.

Paulo   At the universities, generally, I don't see in Brazil and did not see in Europe the level of aggression you've spoken about in some American schools. But, this kind of aggression, I've been told, does exist now in high schools in some peripheral areas of Sao Paulo. This aggression exists for social reasons, in Brazil just as in the States. It is not a personal question. That is, some adolescents are so angry with the lack of decent conditions for living that they destroy the schools and they attack the teachers.

Ira   Here, too, unemployment and squalid conditions in school and society alienate adolescents, especially in the inner cities.
    Suppose we apply dialogical learning to this predicament. The new pedagogy will be situated in the dichotomy of the old education which separates reading texts from reading reality. Our teaching will respect the language and the themes of the students, but will challenge them with critical inquiries into the conditions they now sabotage or surrender to passively. The liberatory approach can create conditions for some illumination, some systematic study, but there is no guarantee that dialogics in any particular setting can stop the disorder or the passivity. For sure, a liberating course cannot produce more jobs, or conditions for more stable families, or less racism and sexism, or better housing, a reduced arms race, a more democratic college or even a more appealing school building. Only organized opposition can achieve those goals. What we can say is that the dialogical method contradicts the logic of domination, contradicts the dichotomized curriculum, and challenges the social relations of learning which inhibit democracy and critical thought. This will not change society by itself, of course, but it can aim for a detente in the class war in the classroom. Dialogics offer the hope of a truce between students and the teacher,

to open discussions on the reality enveloping both. I see these as the operating limits for a liberatory teacher in my culture.

Paulo   I think that is sensible. And concerning the student rebellion you talked about, I think one of our tasks, which is so difficult, should be to try to transform the rebellious consciousness into revolutionary consciousness. It's not easy, of course, because there is a fantastic difference of quality between the two, where merely rebellious consciousness and action lead you to act almost by acting, just to demonstrate you are against something which you don't even perceive very well.

Rebellion without critical awareness is almost an explosion of impotence. If you transform it into revolutionary consciousness, you have then a completely different reaction and attitude. It begins to relate tactics to strategy, dialectically. It begins to insert its actions within the real limits and the real possibilities of history, at that moment. Many things become possible from this transformation of rebelliousness.

Ira   We began by discussing if a culture of silence exists in the States or elsewhere in the way it exists in Latin American or Brazilian society. I also asked if students in an affluent democracy need liberation if they don't live in authoritarian cultures common to the Third World. What final reflection do you have in comparing the conditions of the North and the South?

Paulo   Here, you have wealth, power, many big buildings. But, the wealth in the North only disguises great manipulation, domination, in the culture. Americans and Brazilians both live in capitalist societies. Because of this, we both face manipulation and alienation, with ruling elites as privileged minorities who command the whole society. These elites over both nations keep telling us that their private interests are 'national interests.' While they hide their control by naming their interests as national ones, here in the U.S. you live in the headquarters, the metropole of capitalism. In Brazil, we are on the periphery, strongly dependent on the finance centers in the North. Our dependence keeps us poor and this poverty makes the social contradictions very visible everywhere in the streets of Sao Paulo, for example. In the North, power and wealth make it easier to hide the contradictions, the inequalities and the exploitation. The process, though, is similar, one of domination. But, the living cultures surround us with the look of greatly different societies. The opaque conditions of daily life in an affluent culture can cause special confusions in the North, which only make critical illumination harder and more necessary.

Notes

¹ See Pierre Bourdieu and J.C. Passeron, *Reproduction in Education, Society, and Culture* (Sage, Beverly Hills, 1977), for a discussion of "symbolic violence" in the official curriculum. Michael Apple has written about socialization through the official syllabus in terms of "the hidden curriculum." See Apple's *Ideology and Curriculum* (London, 1979), and his essay "The Hidden Curriculum and the Nature of Conflict," *Interchange*, volume 2, number 4, 1971, pp. 27-40.

² A seminal essay on the hidden agenda of mass education, its depressant intentions behind the veneer of opportunity, is Burton Clark's "The Cooling-Out Function in Higher Education," *American Journal of Sociology*, volume 65, May, 1960, pp. 569-576. Clark later reviewed the debate his thesis touched off and he unfortunately endorsed the need for "cooling-out" in a society and job market with limited, hierarchical rewards ("The Cooling-Out Function Revisited," in *New Directions for Community Colleges*, ed. G.B. Vaughan, San Francisco, 1980). See also Murray Milner's treatise on the failure of education to be "the great equalizer," the great mobility machine to level class differences, *The Illusion of Equality* (New York, 1972). Two superb essays on this predicament are Jerome Karabel, "Community Colleges and Social Stratification," *Harvard Educational Review*, volume 42, number 4, November, 1972, pp. 521-561, and Fred Pincus, "The False Promises of Community Colleges: Class Conflict and Vocational Education," *Harvard Educational Review*, volume 50, number 4, August, 1980, pp. 332-361.

³ High-tech is a myth of economic prosperity. Behind the myth of computers as the new golden goose for all of us, there is a reality of low-skill, low-wage, non-unionized jobs. The high-tech explosion has led to 'computer literacy' being a new demand for curriculum. But, down the road, computer science programs will be graduating an over-supply of labor into a saturated, low-wage job market. For a discussion of this depressant effect of high-tech, see two reports by Stanford researchers Henry M. Levin and Russell W. Rumberger, "The Educational Implications of High Technology," IFG Project Report 83-A4, Stanford, Institute for Research on Educational Finance and Governance, 1983, and "Low Skill Future of High Tech," *Technology Review*, volume 86, number 6 (August-September 1983), pp. 18-21. The de-skilling effects of technology on the workforce were discussed in earlier decades by James Bright, "Does Automation Raise Skill Requirements?", *Harvard Business Review*, volume 36, number 4 (July/August), 1958, pp. 85-98, and by Harry Braverman in *Labor and Monopoly Capital* (New York, 1974). Braverman sharply focused on the depression of wages as well as work skills and on the disempowerment of labor thanks to this process. The troubling relationship between education and the job market, where extended schooling graduates more trained personnel than the job market can absorb, is also discussed in Ivar Berg's *Education and Jobs: The Great Training Robbery* (New York, 1970),

and Richard Freeman's *The Over-Educated American* (New York, 1976). Lastly, for a critical look at technology by a computer science professor, see Joan Greenbaum's *In The Name of Efficiency* (Temple, Philadelphia, 1979).
[4] See Theodore Sizer's contribution to the post-1983 school reform crisis, *Horace's Compromise* (Boston, 1984), p. 6, for his comments on "class" in the schools he visited. John Goodlad was also sensitive to the role of social class in education, in his major report of this period, *A Place Called School* (New York, 1983). For a stronger critique in this period, see Fred Pincus, "From Equity to Excellence: The Rebirth of Educational Conservatism," *Social Policy*, volume 14, number 3, Winter, 1984, pp. 50-56. Further criticism of the official view on the education crisis after 1983 can be found in George Leonard, "The Great School Reform Hoax," *Esquire*, April, 1984, pp. 47-56; Andrew Hacker, "The Schools Flunk Out," *The New York Review of Books*, April 12, 1984, pp. 35-40; and Walter Karp, "Why Johnny Can't Think: The Politics of Bad Schooling," *Harper's*, April, 1985, pp. 69-73.
[5] In the 1970s, two classic and comprehensive statements on schools and social inequality appeared: Christopher Jencks' *Inequality* (New York, 1972), and Samuel Bowles and Herbert Gintis' *Schooling in Capitalist America* (New York, 1975).

CHAPTER 6

How Can Liberating Educators Overcome Language Differences With The Students?

Researching Student Language: The Idiom and Starting Point for Dialogue

Ira   We began speaking on the re-formation of the teacher from the transfer-of-knowledge approach to dialogical methods. We went on to talk about initiating transformation among the students, the limits of liberating education as well as the risks, the cultures of silence and sabotage, and how liberating education with its democratic process and its dream of an egalitarian society differs from the official curriculum's support of inequality. What I want to raise in this chapter is the question of language, that is, the idiom in which teachers speak to mainstream students or to a popular constituency.

Teachers ask about the differences between their language and that of the students, which are obstacles to dialogue. Sometimes this is discussed as a conflict between academic and colloquial idioms. Democratic discourse in the classroom is hindered if the teacher and the students cannot communicate well in their separate idioms.

Teachers are educated in colleges where they learn a cultivated language very different from the idioms of the mainstream. The idioms of everyday life are alien to the Standard English, correct usage, special words and extended syntax of intellectuals. This problem is more acute in community colleges, at inner-city schools, and where white educators are teaching non-white students.[1] The language gap between working-class students and their professors is especially large, while people of color often speak several dialects and languages. Latinos speak Spanish; Asians speak a variety of languages; Afro-Haitians speak a French creole. Besides the bi-lingual groups in the U.S., there is also the problem of several varieties of black English, depending on where the black person is from, West Indies to rural South to urban North to Nigeria. You can get some idea of a problem more complex than simply *one* working-class idiom different from the teacher's cultivated voice.

These language problems are also experienced by activists in neighborhoods, offices, factories or shops. We need to know how to construct a language which bridges the gap. Should I say a few things about my experience with this question?

Paulo   Yes, say some things about your teaching and then I will speak on the question also.

Ira   I teach mostly white working students in an urban college. With them, I speak a different idiom than I am speaking now with you. Also, my classroom discourse is not the same as my speech among my teacher-peers, when I sit in seminars or committees or workshops with them. Neither is my classroom speech like the idiom I use in my private life apart from the college. The idiom I speak in my courses evolved after years of listening to students. I should add that I grew up in the working class, so my basic speech was not a cultivated one, something that turned out to be a resource in creating dialogue with nontraditional students.

I went through two universities and through the 60s, so by the time I got back to the mainstream in my Open Admissions English classes, I spoke an intellectual and political idiom very unlike the language of everyday life. But, I still had South Bronx accents in my voice, which gave me a tone close to the students, even if my syntax and vocabulary were different.

In the mainstream classroom, by studying the students' speech, I could pick up phrases and expressions as well as rhythm, tone and body language. I could also get a feel for their conceptual tolerance, that is, at what moment my philosophical voice went beyond their limits of conceptual understanding. I tried to make my sentences approach conversational idiom, in terms of speed, humor, colloquial references, and phrases used by the students. My education here included asking student speakers for explanations when they used expressions I did not know. They were far more reluctant to stop me and ask me to explain my chewy phrases, so I could not count on them understanding what I said simply because I said it out loud in a conversational patter. I had to ask them and to prepare exercises to see if I was communicating. I also asked myself about the social relations of discourse, the politics of verbal exchanges in the classroom, the script for talking we inherit from the traditional curriculum. It's one thing to change lexicon, syntax, style of humor, and cadence of speech, but its another to have the relations of classroom discourse change as well. I've said some things before about how we are socialized into the official classroom script. The teacher speaks in a loud voice and the students speak in a low one. The teacher says most of the words uttered out loud, dominating the hour with her or his subjectivity, limiting the subjectivity of the students. The teacher's didactic voice occupies the classroom with correct usage that surrounds the students and inhibits their utterances, provoking reactions of silence and sabotage. As I mentioned before, the verbal density of an overtrained intellectual can easily silence the verbal expression of undertrained students, especially working-class ones. The didactic lecture voice is a thick medium, unfamiliar in its standard forms, and risky with public humiliation for students who can't perform well in an alien usage. No wonder they shut up, leaving many teachers asking how they can get the students to participate. Studying the teacher's voice and the language of the students is a starting point.

I can only learn my students' idiom, consciousness, key themes, and real cognitive skills if they let me, if I create a classroom discourse where they open up. I can teach effectively only by knowing their levels of thought, skill, and feeling, but I can only research these if they are open to performing. Being open means producing language that reveals what they know in the words they know it. They won't cooperate in teaching *me* unless the classroom treats them as respected human beings in an important project of learning. The verbal milieu of the classsroom is one key to this opening. It lets students know if this class is going to be a repeat of the alienating classes of the past, or if a creative venture is possible. An imposing teacherly voice confirms their cultures of silence or sabotage.

The early weeks of the term are the most important in exercising some restraint on my own voice. I try not to say more than necessary then, to start out with the students saying as much as possible, so I gain access to their idiom and consciousness while they practice active roles in the dialogue. Their words are the raw material I study. I learn how severely and among whom the cultures of silence and sabotage exist. I learn the themes most urgent to this random gathering of students. I also hear expressions from their lexicon which I add to my own developing idiom. I learn levels of cognitive and political development. The more I hear, the more grounded I get in their experience and in their levels of knowing.

Students expect to hear a lot of teacher-talk that doesn't relate to their experience and doesn't mean much, with a teacherly emphasis on the few words worth copying down for the short-answer exam coming up soon. I'd like to desocialize all of us from these expectations. The habits are so old and powerful by the time students reach high school or college that it's hard to convert the socialized silence and get students to respond in extended give-and-take debates. The teacher's verbal habits are even older in the classroom, so her or his own reversal is difficult, too.

Once, a young group of students told me I was speaking in slow motion. They told me I was "real" and didn't talk down to them, but I was putting them to sleep with my long sentences and phrases. So, I speeded up. Most of all, I want my *whole* speech to be worth listening to, because I have to give up the right of the professor to bore students. This is an unwritten law of school inequality: Teachers have the exclusive right in class to go on and on even if everyone is bored. I want students to know that I speak not to bore them, not to exercise control, not to impose knowledge, and not to fill up the hour and earn my salary, but to communicate, to know something with them. I know a lot and say a lot in class. But, I can't let the classroom discourse set my speech on a pedestal.

For me, the dialogic class has been best as a long discussion that finds its themes and motifs. That possible odyssey takes patience on my part. Students don't jump into the discussion for a long time. So, I have to exercise group dynamics to build a momentum of exchanges. I'd like to think of verbal exploration as one in-process test of the dialogical method. If I hear one-phrase short answers coming back to me from the students, I know that critical dialogue isn't working. Still another in-process test for me is if the students address each other in the verbal exchanges. From their old cultures of silence and sabotage, they are no more willing to speak to each other than they are willing to talk to the teacher. If they respond to each other's statements in a serious way, then I see some desocialization is underway, because they recognize their peers as creators of worthy discussion in an intellectual setting. They are overcoming their alienation.

Do you know what many teachers do when facing student silence or one-syllable answers? Teachers start answering their own questions! I observed this several times in a high school I visited and then again in a college program I was evaluating. I also read more examples of this bizarre habit in a report on a New York City high school. To get over the embarrassment of student silence, teachers wind up having a very intelligent conversation with themselves during class, answering out loud the questions they have just spoken out loud. If the transfer-of-knowledge teacher has the answers already worked out in the syllabus, why waste time in getting students to guess? The teacher can answer his or her own questions and get it over with! This is the most angelic moment of traditional pedagogy, because students learn again how the ideal answer, the perfect formulation, is already worked out in the teacher's mind or in the textbook. How could student utterances do it any better? Heaven has already been invented and the paradise of knowledge is complete. If students only keep quiet long enough, they'll force the teacher to say the perfect answer out loud, handing them one more splinter from heaven's gate. Then, of course, the students will copy down or simply ignore the right answer, successfully sabotaging the curriculum's desire to get them to work.

Another discourse habit of teachers is our use of the pronoun "we" when talking to the class. The official syllabus has silenced and distanced students from the teacher, so the teacher creates fake comradery by saying, "We're going to do a paper for next week," or "We're going to cover the French Revolution tomorrow," when the teacher really means, "I'm assigning you some homework for next week. Write a paper on..." In traditional courses, the "we" is pure verbalism, a verbal democracy that hides the absence of real democracy. The lone authority at the front of the room is an "I" in charge of "them." When such a teacher uses the fake "we," the truth is that no "we" has been negotiated. The teacherly "we" can only become an authentic "we" in a dialogical format that respects student participation in the course.

The politics of discourse is key here. So much is at stake in the way we speak in the classroom. It's fair to say that the fate of dialogical education rests in the classroom discourse.

Social Class and Classroom Discourse: Abstract versus Concrete Speech

Paulo   When I think about the language I use and the language the students use when they first come to the university, above all in the students' first year in the university, I have to think again of the dichotomy between reading words and reading the world, between the dance of concepts, a conceptual ballet we learn in the university, and the concrete world that the concepts should be referring to. The distance of the concepts from concreteness is the problem I come back to when thinking of the question of language in the classroom. The concepts should be associated with a concrete reality but they are not, creating a pedagogical problem. When the students come to us in the university, their experience of language is much more the experience of defining the concreteness of their existence, not an experience of dancing with concepts by themselves.

When we think of language as also involved in social classes, we understand the classroom problem more easily. When we compare our syntax with the syntax of workers, for example, no matter if the workers are Americans or Brazilians, we can perceive how class conditions are expressed through language. And we easily see how workers, for instance, have a very direct language as well as living a life that is a very direct one. The concreteness of their language reflects the concreteness of their existence; their language is as concrete as their experience. Sometimes, when I say 'slum' or 'discrimination,' for example, the words leave my mouth without any kind of weight, as if they are light words. When I say them, of course, I feel their deep meaning, but above all I get the meaning much more intellectually, much more through the description of reality and the understanding of it as a concept which, because of my political choice in society, takes me at least near the concreteness but not into it as a reality. But when these same words are pronounced by the people who live in slums and by the people who are discriminated against, the language has weight. It is 20 kilos for each word! (Laughs) It is a very heavy word when it leaves the mouth of a person exactly in the concrete reality of the word. Of course, I am speaking symbolically but you understand what I mean.

The question, for me, is not whether to abolish in our teacher's language words like 'epistemology,' 'cognitive subject,' 'praxis,' 'manipulation,' 'ideology,' 'social classes,' 'transformation,' 'regionalism,' or 'alienation.' No. These concepts are absolutely important for us! They have been shaped through the history of thought. They have meaning. My question is not to deny them, but rather how to use them in such a way that they are put next to concreteness. This is the question. How to diminish the distance between the academic context and the reality from which the students come, the reality which I must know better and better to the extent that I am engaged in some way with a process of changing it.

It also seems important to me, Ira, to emphasize once more that these differences of language or idiom that we are referring to have a political and ideological foundation. The question of power is there, enveloping our idioms and the problems of language even though we don't always perceive this power. The differences of language are not strictly linguistic or pedagogical problems. The dominant class has the power to establish its language as the standard. What we do in a classroom is very influenced by the power of elite standards.

Because of this political preoccupation with language, we have another preoccupation: How to bring conceptual language close to concreteness when working with students in a classroom. The students come to the university and the question of conceptual concreteness becomes a real question in the course. I have this same experience with graduate students in one semester and undergraduates the next term. First of all, at the beginning of our course, I ask them to talk about their lives outside the university. No matter if they are teaching in another school or college, or doing research, or working in a bank. I ask them to talk about what they do and how they do it, about how they speak when they are not in the university. I just ask, Why don't you start talking about what you do, one by one? And I use no watch, no time limits. Through this kind of exercise, I simultaneously begin to get their language and necessarily their themes, which come through their words and their syntax.

University students in Brazil generally come from the middle classes. They are not usually workers or peasants. They belong to the same verbal universe I belong to, but they don't yet have a grasp of the academic treatment of concepts. But if they are coming into the university, they need to learn how to use concepts in the way they are used in the academy. If they don't get such a command of conceptual language, how will they read Marx, for example? And what right do I have to say that they don't have to read Marx because Marx is too difficult for them? How can they read the Structuralists or the Functionalists, which they must read, if they don't learn conceptual language?

I want to develop with students their grasp of conceptual language, but I begin the course with concreteness, with discussion by them of their own experiences. By discussing their concrete lives, as each makes her or his first speech in class, what I must do from a dialogical point of view is to begin making comments on each verbal report. If students speak in the seminar to describe their experience, when they finish, I get two or three points from their exposition, and I go to the blackboard and write them down, asking the student what did he or she mean by them. At this moment, I say to the student that what I am trying to do is to go beyond the concreteness of your language and get to the conceptualization. Little by little, the teacher has to introduce students to academic and theoretical language. Sometimes it is not necessary to introduce it because students already possess it. Then, you just reinforce their command of language. One of the things we must make very clear to the students is that all of us have the right to ask, What do you mean by that? It's no cause for shame if you ask what something means. This is a simple and important lesson.

In diminishing the distance between concepts and reality, in starting from the student understanding of their concreteness as they express it, the issue of language is involved with the act of knowing, the act of gradually illuminating the conceptual meaning of experience. We must start from student perceptions, no matter if they are peasants in informal education or if they are workers or if they are university students. We have to start from their own levels of perceiving reality. This means that we start from their language, not from our language. But starting from their levels of knowledge about reality, we try to go with them to more rigorous levels of knowing and expressing reality.

Ira   I agree about beginning with student perceptions. Let me probe the issue of conflicting idioms in the classroom. We can use more of our conceptual language at elite schools where the students receive some of that idiom from their privileged backgrounds. But when we leave the plush campuses for community colleges or urban public schools or community-based programs, our idiom is a problem. How should we change our speech?

Paulo   This question seems to be of greater importance. There is a big difference I already referred to, between the semantics and syntax that we use in academia as intellectuals and the syntax we hear spoken by ordinary people, the peasants and the working-class. The two idioms are distinct in their forms. At the same time, these differences do not permit us as so-called intellectuals to say that popular speech does not have the capacity for abstraction. Ordinary people do not do the kind of abstraction done by academics like us. Our abstracting makes us more and more distant from the concrete. When common people speak, they try to understand their experiences through parables, metaphors, and stories, which keep them close to the concrete. The stories that they tell are the way they respond to the questions we ask. On the other hand, they tell stories to express themselves in relation to the world, and to give expression to their world. The metaphors and parables substitute for concepts as we use them, with the advantage of being profoundly concrete in comparison to the abstractness of an intellectual's language. The stories deal with the concreteness with which the popular classes know, that is, know in ways organic to their existence. The problem this poses for us as political militants or as political educators working among popular groups is, how can we learn little by little the structure of thought in these groups and how can we fully grasp their metaphors, the role of parables and stories, so that we can translate our abstract concepts into their idiom. It is precisely in this way that we will increase our communication between ourselves and these popular groups. I will repeat again here something I mentioned before: It is not a question of prohibiting the popular groups from reaching one day the same kind of conceptual language that we use. It is a question of understanding how ordinary people through their special and profoundly ethical forms of expression are capable of making explicit the problems in the world. Their language is densely weighted with judgments on their world, captured in stories and parables. We need to see how they are capable of translating our concepts into the concreteness of the popular language.

Ira   Can you talk about how you change your idiom from one situation to another? When you go to Christian base-communities, or to city neighborhoods, do you speak a different language there among peasants, workers, and church activists?

Paulo   If I am working at the university in Brazil, or with a group of North American college students, I use academic language. But when using academic language, if I perceive that the students are having difficulties understanding the meaning of the words, I continue to use the words but I say "That is..." and explain the meaning. For example, if I say "the gnosiological cycle" and I perceive an air of no understanding in the students, I will then say, "That is, the cycle of the act of knowing, the relation between knowing existing knowledge and producing new knowledge." Sometimes I go beyond and discuss the etymology of the word. Because of that, I always suggest special dictionaries for the students to use.

But if I am working or talking with a group of peasants, it is impossible to speak about "the gnosiological cycle." Not because the peasants are unable to understand what the term means; they participate in the knowing process wonderfully. They can understand it as a process they live out, producing knowledge and knowing what you know, which are the two moments of "the gnosiological cycle" I spoke about earlier. Peasants participate in the two moments, knowing and producing knowledge, according to the levels of their intellectual experience. What they cannot understand is the language used to name it.

Suppose I am talking to a group of peasants and it is not a systematic or formal meeting, but I just went there. I would not think of pronouncing these academic words. Nevertheless, if it is necessary during the conversation to talk to them about that process of knowing, I have to speak in their language. I must know from their vocabulary the words I can use to speak about this material. I could ask them, for example, how they learned to harvest what they planted. They would answer, "By doing it." I could then ask them, How do you teach your kids to do it? They could answer, "We bring them with us and they see us doing it." Then, I would say, "Look, this is what I mean, learning some knowledge which really exists now, and can forever be known, this is what I mean when I talk about the cycle of learning. You produce knowledge and can know that you know something." From their experience of teaching their kids or of knowing how to plant and harvest, I try to find examples, a vocabulary to explain my concepts.

Ira   Do you find much difference between speaking to peasants and speaking to workers in the cities?

Paulo   Ah, yes. The language of the workers is more involved with the kind of political struggle they are in. The workers are in a struggle which generally teaches them more than the experience of the peasants teaches them, unless the peasants are also in a very good process of struggle, from which they also learn. Their social learning through political conflict makes workers much more open to understanding the kinds of reflections we do in the university. But even among workers who are more involved in politics than peasants, I don't use the sophisticated academic language. Because of that, I must learn their metaphors and their symbolic language. We have to learn more and more from them the value of metaphors. How is it possible through metaphors to say lots of things that replace the complexity of our academic concepts?

Ira   Can you think of any metaphors that strike you as good replacements for academic language?

Conceptual versus Metaphoric Language: Transforming the Academic Idiom

Paulo   Right now, I could repeat a very interesting metaphor in symbolic language that I used one day in the course here at the University. Once, an intellectual tried to participate in the activities of a group of peasants. He went day after day to them, trying to become a kind of advisor. On the third or fourth day, one of the peasants told him, "Look, my comrade, if you think you come here to teach us how to cut down a tree, it is not necessary, because we already know how to do that. What we need to know from you is whether you will be with us when the tree falls." This is very symbolic language. It is very rich. It is poetic precisely because metaphoric language is poetic.

Also, I would challenge you to reread some of my texts and you will find easily in them the influence of the Brazilian culture on me. Because I use lots of metaphors in the analysis I try to do of reality, some academics say that I do not have rigor. Of course, I use very sophisticated metaphors. I remember one now, that I used in *Pedagogy of the Oppressed* (1970), "untested feasibility." I meant by "untested feasibility" the future which we have to create by transforming today, the present reality. It is something not yet here but a potential, something beyond the "limit-situation" we face now, which must be created by us beyond the limits we discover. And I called that "untested feasibility."

When I went back to Brazil this time in 1980, to live there again permanently, in my first contacts with peasants and workers, I really felt difficulty with my language. I had spent 16 years far from Brazil. I had contact with workers and peasants in different countries of the world, but speaking this kind of English, not my native language, having translations done for me. When I met again with peasants and workers in Brazil, at first I had some difficulties in communicating. But, in the third meeting I began to reconquer my native idiom. I began to feel at home again.

Ira   It's difficult for American teachers to feel at home in the language of working-class students. Our professional training in college and our own class backgrounds separate us from mass culture.

Paulo   We have to learn how to invite the students gradually into the conceptual world, to help them more and more to grasp the meaning of academic conceptualizations. Concerning this question of language with peasants and workers, for example, we can have two ways of being elitist. One way is to impose on them our language as the only valid one. The second way to be elitist is to make a caricature of our own speech. If we diminish our own speech or limit it to copying theirs, we become simplistic instead of being simple. We caricature popular speech when we limit our own speech to theirs.

When you become simplistic in relating to workers or peasants or students in a class, it means that you start from a conviction that they are inferior to you. You act as if they are not able to understand you.

We have to be simple, but simplicity does not mean to caricature the students as simpletons. To be simple is to treat the object of study with seriousness, with radicality, with depth, but in an easy way to be grasped by the others whose intellectual exercise is not the same as ours. Simplistic language reduces the object of study to a characterization of itself. By doing this, you also reduce the audience you are addressing. This is elitism, to diminish the audience you speak to.

Ira   Some teachers in nonelite settings are tempted to talk down to the students. But, students and ordinary people know right away if you are condescending to them. A patronizing teacher talks as if the students are children who can only follow one-syllable words and short sentences, in a sing-song rhythm. Often, classroom talk is dominated by a three-step question-response-evaluation, with the teacher asking a short-answer question and the students giving minimal replies.[2] Such infanitilizing discourse insults students, who respond often with silence or sabotage.

At my working-class college, I learned a strategic dialogue to draw out conceptual rigor from experience. I try to begin courses with my own verbal restraint, so that there is an opening for students to speak. Your round-table of student speeches at the opening of your seminars is similar to the beginning in my own courses. I begin in a very alienated student group, so a concession I have to make is that when students present themselves in the beginning, I can't always question them vigorously then. If I come at them immediately with conceptual questions, it can drive the students into silence, because the verbal environment feels dense, unfamiliar, aggressive, judgmental. As a way of circling in, I ask students to interview each other in groups of two, and find out from each other some details of your lives, and then have your partner make the class report on you. This reduces intimidation and also helps students begin a peer dialogue which encourages them to take each other more seriously. This exercise can also develop habits of public speaking and careful listening.

While I listen to their peer reports, if I hear parables or unusual phrases or similar themes emerging from report to report, I ask questions and pose connections among different speakers. I'm observing their action and interaction through a language exercise here, and make my own interventions cautiously, not pouncing on a theme or a student remark, to give the process a chance to move past student resistance. Students in my classes are wary of teachers, especially their teachers' questions, which they experience as a trap and an embarrassment. The trap is that they can't perform well in the teacher's idiom, and the embarrassment is their hapless guessing for the right answer. Students learn they are safer in silence. Their teachers are always correcting them, so merely opening their mouths risks humiliation again.

Paulo   Yes, I understand the restraints you are referring to. In Brazil, at least in my experience, I do not come across the problem you speak about. If I just say to a 19-year-old in the university, Look, I don't agree with you. Can you tell me again what you think? He or she does so easily. But in your reality, you are right, speaking with restraint. You are starting from the student and not from the teacher.

It's a very interesting challenge, to begin from the student position. When I talk about that, I always give a concrete example to clarify my epistemological point of view, which is: If I am on this side of the street and I want to go to the other side, I have to cross the street. This means that it is absolutely impossible for one to arrive on the other side starting from over there. Every arrival comes from the point from which we started, and the point from which we started never is the one where we arrive! What many teachers and political activists don't perceive is that the *here* of the liberating teacher or militant is the *there* of the students. The political activist and the liberatory teacher have to start from the *here* of the students. We must grant to the students their *there* as the point from which we begin the transformational teaching to arrive *here*.

Ira   Teachers are not trained to leave their *there*. Teachers learn that the 'good' student mimics what the teacher does on her or his side of the street. Mimicry is not what we have in mind with dialogical education.

I want to raise, then, a question for the liberatory educator who also begins on the teacher's side of the street. The metaphor of crossing the street advises teachers to take their critical thought, bodies of knowledge, and academic idiom to the reality of the students. From what you suggested before, this means re-forming our conceptual idiom into stories and concrete examples inserted into student experience. Then, critical transformation becomes a possibility. For me, the problem now is, Where does the process go? Where is the new *there*? Our starting point is situating dialogue in student themes and language; this means dealing with a student reality separate from the teacher's. Bridging that gap is the key to transformation. But, if we do build the language bridge, what is the end-point, the destination, the arrival point? Is it simply returning to the teacher's starting position?

Making the Process Go: The Teacher's Directive Responsibility

Ira   I'm asking if students will move towards the teacher's position or if the dialogical process will mobilize the teacher too. How does the teacher change in the process? Does the teacher move forward also to some new point, thanks to the mutual education of dialogue? My sense is that the teacher becomes more student-centered as he or she makes concrete the abstractions of academic language. The teacher learns how to existentialize philosophy while the students learn how to philosophize experience. If the teacher makes progress away from the conceptual ballet you spoke of earlier, that means the teacher is also being transformed in the process of offering transformative education. The end-point would have to be described, then, as new positions for teacher and students both, new idioms for both.

Am I being ultra-democratic or ultra-existential in posing the question like this? Does it sound as if dialogical education is only a constant becoming? I do recognize that liberatory teachers and activists are models and leaders of transformation. They organize transformation within the historical moments they face. Our side of the street, then, is a more developed dream and political awareness, more advanced than we find on the other side, where students are not yet organized into their own process of transformation. Still, my years of experimenting with dialogical education have changed me as a teacher, intellectual, and activist. Crossing over to the student side of the steet freed me from the traditional language and limits I began with after graduate school. Going to the other side of the street, or rather, taking my dream to the other side of the street, changed me at least as much as the students changed, probably more so.

Paulo   But, even though you are being open to a new thing, you must from the beginning of your action have your dream, have it with some clarity. Because if you are not more or less clear concerning what you would like to create, you fall into what I've called here laissez-faire, pure spontaneity. You lose the objectives of your dream when you become spontaneous. It happens to teachers and to militants who lose touch with their politics.

For me, education is not a happening. As a liberating educator, I am very clear concerning what I want. Nevertheless, I don't manipulate the students. This is what is difficult in our approach. Even though my tomorrow and my there are clear to me, I cannot manipulate the students to bring them with me to my dream. I have to make clear to them what my dream is, and I have to tell them that there are other dreams that I consider *bad!* (Laughing) Do you see? This is the tension we have to experience between being manipulative and being radically democratic. On the one hand, I cannot manipulate. On the other hand, I cannot leave the students by themselves. The opposite of these two possibilities is being radically democratic. That means accepting the directive nature of education. There is a directiveness in education which never allows it to be neutral. We must say to the students how we think and why. My role is not to be silent. I have to convince students of my dreams but not conquer them for my own plans. Even if students have the right to bad dreams, I have the right to say their dreams are bad, reactionary or capitalist or authoritarian.

Ira   The directive responsibility in our pedagogy and in every other demands that the teacher have goals and a point of view, one dream or another, which means the teacher cannot be neutral or casual in the process.

Paulo   Ah, yes! That's a very good thing you said now, can you repeat it for me?

Ira   The teacher is unavoidably responsible for initiating the process and directing the study. Choosing goals makes neutrality impossible. By directing a course of study, by choosing certain books and by asking certain questions, and by the social relations of discourse in the class, every teacher expresses his or her political choice.

Paulo   Yes. Look, Ira, I became so stimulated now from your reflection. This is why every kind of education always has a certain moment which I call 'the inductive moment.' This is the moment in which the educator cannot wait for students to initiate their own forward progress into an idea or an understanding, and the teacher must do it. If students spontaneously keep moving their critical study forward, why not! Applaud them when they do it. But there are moments when students do not start their own development and the educator must begin it.

And do you know what is the difference between a *liberating* educator and a *domesticating* educator concerning this point? It's that while the liberating educator starts assuming the responsibility of being inductive, he or she looks for the process to overcome the inductive moment, in order to transform it into a comradery, that is, a moment undertaken by students themselves and not only by the teacher.

Ira   What defines an inductive moment? The point at which an educator makes an intervention to draw the pieces of knowing to-

gether? Gathering the threads into a whole that poses a critical problem or perception through which the students are invited to go on
to more critical dialogue? If I followed you, the liberating educator
makes the induction in a way that develops the students' own initiative in making their inductions, thus distributing responsibility for
inductive moments.

Paulo   Yes, of course! You have to constantly invite the students
to get the inductive moment into their grasp as soon as possible, so
that they can use it in the course. But, the manipulating, domesticating educator always keeps in his or her *own* hands the induction
of the process. The authoritarian perspective leads such a teacher to
monopolize the inductive function.

Because of this difference in the dialogical and authoritarian methods vis-a-vis the inductive moment, I invite my left comrades to be
democratic. They don't have to be afraid of this word! (Laughs) That
is, of course, we have to be creative but we can't just sit back and
wait for students to put all the knowing together. We have to take
the initiative and set an example for doing it.

'The Inductive Moment' in Critical Discourse

Ira   You've spoken about the importance of concreteness. One
obstacle to the inductive moment is the abstractness of the intellectual's idiom. So, it matters here to go back to your original point about
transforming the language of the teacher so that his or her inductions
avoid being word-ballets.

One routine practice of the classroom has the teacher making a
summary at the end of the class hour. At its best, the summary is
the final inductive moment of the day. But, often it is merely a hur-
ried, final word from the teacher which concludes mechanically what
happened during the previous hour. Another practice is the teacher's
habit of interrupting a speaking student at any moment, to summarize, paraphrase or rephrase the student's speech in correct usage,
formal syntax, or the conceptual vocabulary of the teacher's specialty.
The students are not allowed to interrupt each other or the teacher,
which is a rule of discourse obviously violated by the culture of
sabotage. So, there is a behavioral expectation in class that after a
student speaks the teacher will translate the student utterance into
an official form of language.

These discourse habits stand in the way of provoking dialogue in
the classroom. They make students into persons who cannot interpret

themselves, who must be translated and converted into standard usage, as if they are speaking an exotic tongue. I walk gently when it comes to summarizing or rephrasing student statements in correct usage. I try to synthesize my idiom with student language for the summary, to preserve the integrity of the original remarks. Sometimes, my avoidance of an end-hour summation leads students to demand a concluding word from me. Their demand suggests that what I say will be heard with unfamiliar attention, so I feel more comfortable making a summary then. I still like to invite students to try the summation with me, to exercise their own critical thought. At other moments, I agree to offer a summary if one or two students will try one first. Many students refuse, which requires me to go around the class and find someone with the courage to try. The summation may then become an act of peer-reflection instead of a ceremonial teacher-stamp on the hour's work.

There's another aspect of discourse that I want to raise before hearing your own reflection. This has to do with another kind of 'silence.' At moments in my classes there are silences. Discussion stops for a time. Habitually, I'm responsible for generating more discourse. It is the teacher's directive responsibility to re-focus the study. But, I see here another opportunity to test a desocializing pedagogy. What I mean is that the very routine of a teacher filling the silences conditions students to avoid their own inductions. I try using the silence to provoke the students' active reflection on what to do next. Sometimes I say to the class that I will not always fill the silences, but want them to take on that responsibility also. Students expect teachers to do all the active learning and to have the final word, so even these internal summaries are moments before the class hour ends where I ask them to practice induction instead of leaving all the learning to me.

Paulo   I like very much what you said. I agree with you about how to confront the silence. I agree with your discussion of the task of making the summary. But also I think we should understand these points not as prescriptions for other teachers. For instance, other teachers in other circumstances, and you also in other classes in a different semester, can make summaries, and should make summaries during three, four, five sessions. What do I mean by this? Let us suppose that you start working with a group of students and you perceive that this class for different reasons is more inhibited than others, is farther from assuming some actions quickly, does not yet believe in themselves, in their ability to make summaries. If you more or less perceive that, you are obliged to make summaries in three or four sessions, in order to teach them how to make summaries, as an example to students. Education is above all the giving of examples through actions. Nevertheless, by making the summary, you are not making it only to show the students that you know how to make a summary. It is not a question of the teacher's vanity or pride. No! You are an educator. That is, you are making the summary for teaching them how to make the summary. All these things are absorbed into your dialogical action, as an example of critical activity.

Some teachers think that making a summary is not part of their teaching practice at all. No! It is a legitimate part of the curriculum, as long as his or her perception of curriculum is *not* a prescriptive one. Because of that, then, you would have to call the attention of the students to the specific point of the summary as a moment in their education as to what the task of a summary is. The teacher's own reflection on the summary reveals to students the way of doing it. By doing that, you are putting together your words and your action. That is, you are giving reasons for why the teacher makes the summary.

Ira   You are right about not being prescriptive or mechanical about the summary. The liberatory teacher can do it to demonstrate a critical activity and to challenge the teacher's verbal monopoly of the final word.

Paulo   For example, let us suppose that in the first day of class you begin to make the summary. First of all, you could ask a question to them and to yourself: What does a 'summary' really mean? For what do we make a 'summary' at the end of our discussion? At the moment in which you challenge them to get distance from the very act of making the summary, the summary itself stops being a mere bureacratic moment of the classroom. It becomes transformed into a fundamental part of the act of knowing. Do you see? Then, by asking this kind of reflective question on the act of reflection, you begin to challenge them to assume as quickly as possible the task of also making summaries.

Ira   I agree with you, Paulo, but I see this as a delicate moment because the teacher can easily fall into a routinely narrating voice, rather than provoking student summarizing. The teacher tends to assume ownership of the summation. From traditional pedagogy, from the transfer-of-knowledge, who has the greatest right to possess the conclusion? The teacher, of course. So distributing ownership of the summary from the teacher to the students will be delicate, like transferring a property right, a political power, and an intellectual facility all at once. Just think of the teacher's familiarity in doing summaries and the students' nonpractice of them. There will be a verbal inequality here that matches the political inequality of the traditional curriculum. The self-reflective summary may need a conversational idiom to give students access to it.

Paulo I would like to say something more about the act of making the summary in order to underline the importance of it. It does not mean that I do summaries every day in class. No, but it is a theoretical point important for student comprehension.

In the last analysis, what we do when we try to establish a cognitive or epistemological relationship with the object to be known, when we get it into our hands, grasp it, and begin to ask ourselves about it, what we really begin to do is to take it as a *totality*. We then begin to split it into its constituent parts. This is exactly the moment of analysis we are working for in class, analyzing this or that object, sometimes through the reading of the text, sometimes written by ourselves and sometimes written by another person. Sometimes we try to split the object through the dialogue with the students. In a certain moment, even though we may not have exhausted the process of splitting the object, we try to understand it now in its totality. We try to *retotalize* the totality which we split! This is precisely what we have to do. The moment of summarizing has to do with this effort of retotalizing of the totality we divided into parts. Because of that, making the summary is not just a bureaucratic description of what we said before! It's not just a list of components. It is one of the moments in which we try to know.

Humor in Dialogue

Ira Can we discuss now other qualities of dialogue? Where does humor enter? Where do comedy, conviviality, excitement and emotion fit in? In traditional classrooms, there is a lot of boredom or anxiety. There is also a power struggle in the exchange of language. Does dialogical education offer some humor or joy?

Paulo Yes, of course! And I even used humor a lot in my experiences in Brazil thirty years ago, in adult literacy. I never use irony, but humor, yes. For me, irony reveals a lack of security. Sarcasm betrays an insecurity in the speaker. Humor also unveils reality with such illumination! We should use it because of this.

Ira Would you agree that people who joke with each other find a way to become peers? You relax mostly in society with your equals, not with superiors or subordinates. Power struggles make it hard to joke or to relax. You are always on guard for the ones above or the ones below you. Equals are more able to speak at the same level and let down their defenses, tell funny stories and laugh together. The arrival of a superior closes down the comedy. You become more cautious, less open.

Paulo   But, there is a very strong difference between humor and just laughing. A humorist is not just a smile-maker, someone who makes people laugh. No! Even sometimes, good humor leads you *not* to smile or laugh. But, on the contrary, good humor does not make you laugh as much as it makes you seriously think about the material. Humor is Chaplin. He unveiled all the issues he tried to describe, to live with in the cinema. In the shows, he revealed what was behind the situations. Sometimes, I think there is such a lack of security in some people, that they need to just laugh constantly, need to make jokes. If they did not make a joke in the beginning of their speech, they would not be able to speak, because they are so insecure. This is a mere impression I have, that people who make jokes are trying to conquer the audience. It's almost a kind of self-defense.

For me the question is not to convince people because I can make them laugh. The thing is to know if I can analyze the issues seriously. Nevertheless, if I am able to do this, then I can have humor in doing it. For example, if I can now not be humble, I can say that in last night's meeting with the group of Latin American exiles here in Vancouver, I had humor when I told them about my sometimes difficult adjustments to the new countries I went to after my exile. I never was ironic and I never tried to conquer the audience by only trying to make them laugh. I had humor when I was able to recognize my mistakes in Chile or in Africa, my not knowing the way men are supposed to be friendly in those societies, whether men are supposed to touch or not. In the last analysis, the sense of humor makes you laugh at yourself. This for me is strongly necessary for an educator in the dialogical perspective. Nevertheless, you cannot give courses to make teachers into good humorists!

Ira   Humor is not a mechanical skill you add to dialogical methods like icing on a cake. It has to be part of our character and the learning process. But, I often think that teachers can benefit from acting, voice, dance, and comedy workshops. Not because these creative exercises will make teachers into new men and women, but rather because comic and creative talents are too often ignored. They are not taken seriously as resources for teaching. Perhaps drama workshops or creative writing sessions can bring out latent imagination. Can an uncreative teacher lead a creative class?

I think of group dynamics and discussion-leading as two other skills that liberatory teachers need to develop, in addition to performing skills like comedy and voice. If you think of the emphasis on cognition in the university, you can see the exclusion of humor and emotionality. The result is academic education without joy or inspiration. The classrooms of America are like this, according to the 1983 Goodlad report I mentioned earlier, which saw such an emotional vacancy inside school. Some thirty years ago Jerome Bruner complained of the same dullness when he went around the U.S. observing schools.[3] This chronic dullness in school helps students become anti-intellectual. Their lives outside school are humorous, and comedy is one way they experience their subjectivity. When learning is humorless and emotionless, it denies them two subjective values.

I agree with you, though, that humor is not the same as a cheap laugh, as we say in the States. Humor is richer and more demanding than joking. Clarity about your politics and the methods of dialogical education can help with the security needed to be humorous, but I've observed humorless classes taught by radical teachers who are plenty clear on their politics. They want to stimulate critical curiosity in the students, but their discourse was flat, without comedy and feeling. If students see the teacher bored, emotionless, or anxious, or if students are offered a plodding 'correct' line, it is unlikely they will feel curiosity. They will think intellectual life is a drag.

Subjectivity is engaged by humor and feeling, as well as by a critical idiom that is also colloquial. Humor helps make the learning moment 'real,' a quality that can reverse the artificial school experience. The most likely student contact with academic humor is the witty, entertaining teacher (who competes with the class clown for attention). This is a performing skill of a good lecturer or discussion leader, but a teacher's solo performance is not enough for dialogue. Students have to make humor also from inside their understanding of the thing being studied. I raise this question because I see the emotionally bleached classroom sabotaging the liberatory project. The colorless classroom doesn't satisfy the teacher any more than the students. The teacher also needs some emotional or humorous texture from the course to feed his or her morale.

Facing Racism and Sexism in a Dialogic Class

Ira   I'd like to raise here two specific aspects of language teachers ask about, racism and sexism. These two dimensions are unavoidable in social life and education.

I've observed in my classes that men interrupt women when women are speaking, but women don't interrupt the men. In general, the women are not allowed to finish their speeches if a man wants to speak. Some women insist on their right to finish, but most have been socialized into deferring to a man when he starts talking, even if he interrupts them. When I see this happening and the women don't finish their own statements, I interrupt the man. I tell him that the woman student hasn't finished. I add that both men and women have a right to finish their own speeches without interruption. This is news to the students in the classroom, that men are violating a democratic rule that both men and women have equal rights in discussion. By interfering with an automatic behavior, I try to raise perception of it. Vygotsky emphasized this in his discussion of Piaget's "law of awareness," impeding a routine act develops insight into that act.[4]

Another aspect of sexism is that women students in my classes tend to speak in lower voices than the men and I have to encourage them to elevate their volume. The woman's voice often starts out in a tone that does not command the same attention as a man's voice. I notice this as a political problem of discourse and then draw out female voices for an equal presence in discussion. Women have less opportunity to exercise critical voices in public, so I do some compensating in the classroom by asking the women to extend their remarks when they speak. I'll sustain eye contact a little longer and show no impatience to have them stop in favor of my response. I stop the men from prematurely ending the women's remarks, but I also try to beat the men into the conversation when the woman finishes, to invite her to say more. This sexist problem of discourse co-exists with *thematic* expressions of sexism made in the classroom. Some men routinely say that women have no right to do 'men's' jobs like fireman or truck-driver, that women don't have to earn as much as men for the same work because the man has to bring home the bacon in the family, that sexual violence is amusing, that men have the right to be promiscuous but women don't. I re-present such statements to the class as themes for our critical study. I don't lecture the students making such remarks but begin a dialogue which draws out many reflections from me and the other students.

What I want to raise here is the issue of sexism in the very form of discourse, not only in statements or expressed ideology. I have similar concerns with the question of racism. The non-white minority in my college is unusually silent in the classroom, outnumbered by white peers, in an area with a reputation for tense race relations. So, I make special efforts to encourage non-whites to enter the dialogue and to extend their remarks, as well as addressing race issues and racist remarks when they surface in class. I also bring in stories and articles on this theme. In general, it has been harder for non-whites to exercise their voices in my college than it has been for women.

Do the themes of sexism or racism appear in Brazilian classrooms as problems?

Paulo   Yes, they do. Brazilian society is a very authoritarian one. It has been so for a long time. Racism is strong in Brazil. Saying that we don't have racism in Brazil is either naiveté or shrewdness, but not reality. We are a strong *machista* society, not a Marxist one. For me, racism and machismo are expressions of authoritarianism, also.

One of the new things I noted in my return to Brazil in 1980 was the struggles of the women. That is, the women in Brazil have begun to fight, begun to protest, begun to reject continuing to be objects at the command of men. It does not mean that they already conquered their freedom. At the same time, I could also see on my return how part of the black population of Brazil had begun to become aware also. It began to study Brazilian history in a different way. They now emphasize their contributions as black people to the historical-cultural development of the country. Official history has hidden black contributions to Brazil.

Nevertheless, at least in these past years I am back teaching in Sao Paulo, and walking all over the country of Brazil, and participating in discussions sometimes with 3,000 students, in big rooms and stadiums, I still don't see the kinds of things you talked about in your classrooms, in terms of the way men and women relate, in spite of knowing how machista our culture is. For example, in the seminars I work in at two universities, I never noted a woman being inhibited from talking because a man, a male student, spoke more than her. What I observed is that when some men students tried to impose their male position on the women, the women rejected it immediately! They rejected it strongly! The women put the men in their place. But, this does not mean that the society in Brazil is becoming *less* macha. No. What I am saying is that among the students I don't perceive the men behaving in the way you described.

When you say that you try to stop the male students, I agree with you, but nevertheless you must be careful not to take the responsibility on yourself for making the liberation of the women. The women must make their own liberation, with the contribution of some men who agree with them, who are with them in their struggle. For example, last year I participated in a national TV program in Brazil, a two-hour discussion with six people asking questions. Two on the panel asking questions were women and they asked me about the women's struggle. And I gave an answer which created a serious problem for us, above all in Northeast Brazil!

I said on the TV program, "Look, some years ago a woman asked me the same question in London. And I will tell you now what I said in London some years ago: *I am also a woman!*"

You can imagine what happened then! The telephone calls we received from the Northeast of Brazil, where I was born. I was asked, "Paulo, did you change *so* radically? What happened to you?" But I said 'I am a woman' in a very, very strong way not to be agreeable to the women, no. Not to be demagogic. Not because I thought I could have some leadership in the struggles of the women. I am sure that the women's struggle has to be led by them. But I am sure also that as a man my contribution to the struggle of the women must be accepted by the *critical* women. The *naive* women may say, "No, you have nothing to do with us because you are a man." This is naiveté. If the women are critical, they have to accept our contribution as men, as well as the workers have to accept our contribution as intellectuals, because it is a duty and a right that I have to participate in the transformation of society. Then, if the women must have the main responsibility in their struggle, they have to know that their struggle also belongs to us, that is, to those men who don't accept the machista position in the world.

The same is true of racism. As an apparent white man, because I always say that I am not quite sure of my whiteness, the question is to know if I am really against racism in a radical way. If I am, then I have a duty and a right to fight with black people against racism.

Ira   The dialogical classroom can take racism and sexism as themes for critical study, showing how they divide the people and help the dominant class. It can also analyze the language of sexism and racism as we express them. Further, we can raise awareness of the unequal discourse between the sexes and the races. What I want to ask now is this: Suppose the liberating class studies work, play, education, or food, as themes from daily life, or suppose the liberatory class examines bodies-of-knowledge from biology, history, or literature, all not immediately about race and sex. Does the classroom develop a critical consciousness, a conceptual habit of mind, which by itself interferes with racist and sexist ideology? Is the development of critical thinking *apart from* explicit themes of race and sex by itself a value in the struggle against inequality?

Paulo   It depends, Ira. First of all, I see racism and sexism very much linked to capitalist production. I don't say that they should be reduced only to the question of capitalism. I don't say that racism and sexism can be reduced into class struggle. But, I don't believe in the possibility of overcoming racism and sexism in a capitalistic way of production, in a bourgeois society. Nevertheless, it does not mean that in a socialist society racism and sexism will be overcome automatically.

For me, this is one of the tasks for revolutionaries to accomplish. If we really want to reinvent society, in order for the people to be more and more free, more and more creative, this new society to be created by men *and* women cannot be racist, cannot be sexist. But this is one of the consistencies revolutionaries have to watch out for in their speech and their action. Because of that, we also cannot wait for the revolutionary transformation in order to overcome racism and sexism. We must start now.

Ira   If we say that we can't wait for a new society before we begin transforming racism and sexism, can we also say that dialogical education helps prepare the way for erasing sexist and racist attitudes? Does critical education create conditions for ending racism, sexism, or authoritarianism?

Paulo   I think so. I hope so. We must be very, very critical every time we speak about emancipatory education, liberatory or liberating education. We must repeat always that we are not meaning with these expressions that in the intimacy of a seminar we are transforming the structures of the society. That is, liberating education is one of the things which we must do with other things in order to transform reality. We must avoid being interpreted as if we were thinking that *first* we should educate the people for being free, and *after* we could transform reality. No. We have to do the two simultaneously, as much as possible. Because of that, we must be engaged in political action against the dehumanizing structures of production.

Ira   My sense is that critical dialogue develops intellectual habits which undermine the myths supporting racism, sexism, and the elite control of the economy. I understand critical consciousness as gaining reflective distance on your own thought, action, and society. This distance is a metaphor for separating your consciousness from the dominant ideology socializing us in mass culture, daily life, and school. These are places where we internalize racism, sexism, and such values as self-doubt and love of the rich and powerful, which help wed us to the system.

If education offers some intellectual separation from dominant myths, it can be politically uncomfortable for the ruling elite. Since

the 60s, the authorities have tried to eliminate nontraditional programs for minorities, in women's studies, and in experimental teaching. From their point of view, these words and these courses are
politically challenging. The authorities speak now about 'reclaiming
a legacy,' putting back the traditional subjects through a core curriculum, the official American Heritage as a reaction to the egalitarian
and dissenting themes of the 60s. Alternative learning with or without
mass movements is not harmless politics, from the establishment
point of view, which is some indication that classroom discourse is
a factor in social transformation. Are the authorities over-reacting to
dissident and liberatory education or are they prudent in stopping
critical culture in the schools?

Paulo   I always strongly think that the dominant powers are not
wrong in their plans for education. They know what they are doing.
They are not making mistakes in pursuing their curriculum. In one
of our conversations, I discussed a main task of the ruling elite, or
one of the main tasks proposed by the ruling class for education, or
one of its main expectations from schools. This is precisely the reproduction of the dominant ideology. The reproduction of dominant
ideology depends on its power to make reality opaque. But, immediately, I said there is another task in the space of the schools, which
in spite of the interests of the elite does not depend on them, precisely
the task of *demystifying* the dominant ideology. This task cannot be
accomplished by the system. It cannot be accomplished by those
who agree with the system. This is the task for educators in favor
of a liberating process. They have to do this through different
kinds of educational action; for example, through teaching music or
mathematics, teaching biology or physics or drawing, no matter.
Those who believe in changing reality have to accomplish the transformation.

When elites try to silence some issues, analyzing these themes even
in a naive way can produce some risks. The task for those who are
not the reproducers of the dominant ideology is to discover ways
independently in the curriculum to analyze these issues. If you ask
me, Paulo, how? I don't know. We must know when we are con-
fronting the problem in our situations. And above all for here, I could
not say how because I am not an American. But, in Brazil, I know
how to do that. The democratic opening in Brazil in the last few years
makes it possible to increase critical education. Once again, this dem-
onstrates that education does not shape society but rather global
politics condition what we can do in education.

Notes

[1] An excellent ethnographic study of the language differences between students and teachers is Shirley Brice Heath's *Ways With Words* (Cambridge, 1983). Heath probes the conflicting literacies between Piedmont area schoolchildren and their teachers. She proposes teaching for a situated literacy.

[2] For a treatise on classroom discourse, see Shirley Brice Heath, *Teacher-Talk: Language in the Classroom* (Language in Education: Theory and Practice, 9, Washington, Center for Applied Linguistics, 1978). Heath analyzes the question-response-evaluation routine in elementary education, a discourse pattern that spills over into the upper grades.

[3] John Goodlad, in his eight-year study *A Place Called School* (New York, 1983), found that less than 3 percent of class time showed any emotional tone in the thousand classrooms observed by his research team. Jerome Bruner made a similar discovery on his school tour in the 50s, reported in "Learning and Thinking," *Harvard Educational Review*, Vol. 29, No. 3, Summer, 1959, pp. 184-192. A year later, Bruner published his widely-read volume on the post-Sputnik Wood's Hole curriculum conference, *The Process of Learning*, a document proposing discovery models of pedagogy.

[4] See L. Vygotsky, *Thought and Language* (MIT, 1962) , p. 16, 88-90.

CHAPTER 7

The Dream Of Social Transformation: How Do We Begin?

Starting Out: The Ethics of Transforming Consciousness

Ira   For our last chapter, Paulo, I want to ask how you would begin on Monday morning at a new school or college. What are the first things you would do as a liberating educator? Another issue is our right to begin transforming student consciousness. What gives liberating educators the right to change the consciousness of students? What ethics of transformation justify this pedagogy?

Paulo   About the right to begin the transformation of consciousness, I'll summarize what I said on manipulation, domination, and freedom, and then maybe add a few things. I said that the liberating educator can never manipulate the students and cannot leave the students alone, either. The opposite of manipulation is not laissez-faire, not denying the teacher's directive responsibility for education. The liberating teacher does not manipulate and does not wash his or her hands of the students. He or she assumes a directive role necessary for educating. That directiveness is not a commanding position of 'you must do this, or that,' but is a posture of directing a serious study of some object in which students reflect on the intimacy of how an object exists. I call this position a radical democratic one because it attempts directiveness and freedom at the same time, without authoritarianism by the teacher and without license by the students. This is not domination. Domination is when I say you *must* believe this because I say it. Manipulation is dominating the students. Manipulating culture makes myths about reality. It denies reality, falsifies reality. Manipulation is when I try to convince you that a table is a chair, when the curriculum makes reality opaque, when school and society present the system of monopoly capitalism as 'free enterprise.' In opposition, the liberating class illuminates reality. It unveils the *raison d'etre* for any object of study. The liberating class does not accept the status quo and its myths of freedom. It challenges the students to unveil the actual manipulation and myths in society. In that unveiling, we change our understanding of reality, our perception.

Education always has a directive nature we can't deny. The teacher has a plan, a program, a goal for the study. But there is the directive *liberating* educator on the one hand, and the directive *domesticating* educator on the other. The liberating educator is different from the domesticating one because he or she moves more and more towards a moment in which an atmosphere of comradery is established in class. This does not mean that the teacher is equal to the students or becomes an equal to the students. No. The teacher begins different and ends different. The teacher gives grades and assigns papers to write. The students do not grade the teacher or give the teacher homework assignments! The teacher also must have a critical competence in her or his subject that is different from the students and which the students should insist on. But, here is the central issue: In the liberating classroom, these differences are not antagonistic ones, as they are in the authoritarian classroom. The liberating difference is a tension which the teacher tries to overcome by a democratic attitude to his or her directiveness.

The directive nature of a liberating course is not properly in the educator but in the practice of education itself, while the dominating educator keeps in his or her hands the objectives of education, the contents of education, and the very power of directiveness in education. All these things are monopolized by the dominating educator, and something more, the very choice of the educatees about their education. Liberating educators do not keep the students controlled in their hands. I always try to relate to the students as cognitive subjects, as persons who are with me, engaged in a process of knowing something with me. The liberating educator is with the students instead of doing things for the students. In this mutual act of knowing, we have rationality and we have passion. And this is what I am.

I am an impassioned educator, because I don't understand how to be alive without passion.

As teachers, we have something to offer, and we must be clear about our own offering, our competence and directiveness. But the offering is not a paternal one. It's not a gesture of angelic giving by the teacher. In the liberating perspective, we really have nothing to give. We give something to the students only when we exchange something with them. This is a dialectical relationship instead of a manipulative one. Do you see? This question of manipulation is very interesting to me, especially when I am asked about it in North America. In the culture here, in the daily life, there is great manipulation. There are many messages and directions for what you should be doing, what you should buy, what you should believe. Also, the culture here has many, many myths about freedom and happiness and about the rest of the world, which also you hear every day. "The American Way of Life" for example, is a political idea often presented as the only good one for the world. Another myth is that the special mission of America is to teach the whole world how to be free. I know that there are good aspects of life here and also good dimensions of American democracy. But, when such myths become global crusades, then they are instruments for manipulation. I think maybe people are so sensitive to the question of manipulation here because there is already so much of it.

From another aspect, there is also the fear of freedom, which Erich Fromm studied so well.[1] A liberating educator challenges people to know their actual freedom, their real power. As a result, people may feel manipulated when asked to reflect on such a difficult subject, because it is something they do not want to think about or they want to deny, their fear of becoming free, taking responsibility for their freedom.

Ira   I agree with you about the fear of freedom and the sensitivity to manipulation here in the U.S. It may come from the pervasive domination in my culture, which constantly uses the words 'freedom' and 'liberty' in daily life. The mass media are everywhere and are tightly controlled by the dominant elite. Also, education is a mass experience now all the way through college. So, the official curriculum is one more mechanism for attempting domestication on a grand scale.

Liberatory education challenges domination by illuminating reality for what it is, a culture where people have the power to confront manipulation. This critical pedagogy invites people to know what is hidden from us and to know how we cooperate in denying our own freedom. A liberatory class can also unveil the limits of domination in a society where the system presents itself as invulnerable. Many people, especially in an affluent society like the U.S., may refuse such an invitation and consider it manipulation merely to be challenged by such questions.

Can we concretely discuss our liberatory challenge in terms of racism and sexism?

The Right To Challenge Inequality and Domination

Paulo   Yes. What is the right of the educator to challenge racist or sexist positions of the students? Maybe I should just say one thing. The educator has the right to disagree. It is precisely because the teacher is in disagreement with the young racist men or women that the educator challenges them. This is the question. Because I am a teacher, I am not obliged to give the illusion that I am in agreement with the students.

There is a strong ideological dimension to this question of challenging and transforming the consciousness of students. The dominant ideology makes its presence in the classroom partly felt by trying to convince the teacher that he or she must be neutral in order to respect the students. This kind of neutrality is a false respect for students. On the contrary, the more I say nothing about agreeing or not agreeing out of respect for the others, the more I am leaving the dominant ideology in peace!

Ira   The ideology of the 'neutral' teacher fits in, then, with support for the status quo, because society itself is not benign. Consciousness is not a blank page; school and society are not neutral fields of social equals. Not acknowledging or not challenging inequality in society is to cooperate in hiding reality, hiding conditions that would weaken dominant ideology. The teacher who pretends that reality is not problematic thus reduces the students' own power to perceive and to act on social issues. An opaque reality disempowers people, by holding a screen in front of what they need to see to begin transformation. 'Neutral' teaching is another name for an opaque curriculum, and an opaque curriculum is another name for a domesticating education.

Paulo   Yes! In the liberating perspective, the teacher has the right but also the duty to challenge the status quo, especially in the questions of domination by sex, race, or class. What the dialogical educator does not have is the right to impose on the others his or her position.

But the liberating teacher can never stay silent on social questions, can never wash his or her hands of them.

There is another thing also, Ira, about which I would like to make a comment, just to be more rigorous. When you asked whether the educator in our political perspective should have the right to challenge the consciousness of the students in order to change it, I think that it's important for us to clarify a little bit again this question, because of our possible reader's understanding of our discussion.

Of course, by challenging the students we are thinking to give some little contribution to the possibility for them to change their way of understanding reality. But, we must know, or at least we must make clear here, we are not falling into an idealistic position where consciousness changes inside of itself through an intellectual game in a seminar. We change our understanding and our consciousness to the extent we are illuminated in real conflicts in history. Liberating education can change our understanding of reality. But this is not the same thing as changing reality itself. No. Only political action in society can make social transformation, not critical study in the classroom. The structures of society, like the capitalist mode of production, have to be changed for society to be transformed.

For example, if you want to understand better the exploitation of the workers, you can do this rigorously in the classroom. You can study how production is organized under capitalism. But in order to change this object of study, for better social relationships in production, you have to change completely the structure of society. At the level of the classroom only, you can achieve much better understanding of this issue without changing it as a reality.

Ira   If capitalism cannot be changed as a social structure inside the classroom, can we say that capitalist ideology is either reproduced or not reproduced there, in the students' consciousness? School is one of several agencies to reproduce dominant ideology. One force of the classroom can be its interfering with the consciousness needed to support exploitation and inequality. In complex societies like mine, this can have a consequential effect. The failure of the schools to reproduce business culture and work discipline has been a crisis for the establishment since the 60s. In the 80s, a parade of commissions has passed by in the official attempt to figure out what's gone wrong in the schools.[2]

Also, real social conflicts are played out in the classroom, between people of color and white people, between men and women, between authoritarian teaching and student sabotage, between ideologies of class and ones of egalitarianism. These problems are the open sores of society which the dominant curriculum ignores. A critical study of these issues contradicts the reproduction of dominated consciousness.

Paulo   Yes, the authoritarian relations of production are inside the schools.

Ira   In some ways, the classroom is protected from the worst effects of race, sex, and class domination in the larger society, so it is a zone of intellectual combat, not physical attack, where opaqueness and domination can be examined. But, still, you are right. Social change will be made by organized opposition outside the classroom, against the political and economic structures which control education. Critical courses are part of that social conflict, but they alone cannot win.

Paulo   The issue of social conflict is absolutely important here. In the last analysis, conflict is the midwife of consciousness.

Ira   Conflict does create the conditions for transformation. Paulo, you've spoken about the right and the duty of the liberating teacher to undertake the transformation of student consciousness, but I think we should add that it's wrong to view it as a professorial conspiracy against the students. For one thing, the teacher is also re-formed to some degree. The teacher is not in a position where he or she thinks, What should I do to the students next?

Paulo   (Laughing) Yes, that's good.

Opening the Dialogue: Invitation, Not Manipulation

Ira   The charge of 'liberatory' manipulation is weak when I think of my classroom experiences over the last fifteen years. I find myself more changed by the students than I've been able to change them! The students set limits for the kind of liberating process I offer. It should be no suprise that students have the power to resist any learning process. Even when they accept the dialogical class, their situations, their themes, their idioms, and their pace of development influence where the course goes. Teachers know how artful students can be in the power relations of the classroom. Students know how to manipulate teachers. They possess strategies for keeping authority at bay. It is a kind of elitism to see the students as weak, passive, or vulnerable, or open to any kind of devious stratagem of clever intellectuals. The reality at my college is that students are shrewd and feisty.

With student alienation as the given of mass schooling, this brings me back to my opening question, how to begin teaching in the real conditions we face on Monday morning, to change disabling education to a transformative process. This is a question I hear often from teachers: How do we begin?

Paulo   Those who accept the task of social transformation have a dream but they also have such a quantity of obstacles in front of them. As I said before, the teachers who support the status quo are swimming with the current, but the ones who challenge domination are swimming against the current. Diving into this water means risking punishment from the powers that are in power. Because of this, the liberating educator has to create in herself or himself some virtues, some qualities which are not gifts from God or even given to them from reading books, even though reading books is important. The liberating educator has to create by creating, in the very practice of teaching itself, learning the concrete limits for his or her action, getting clear on the possibilities, not too much behind our limits of necessary fear and not too far ahead.

On the other hand, the establishment forces us to live with much more fear than is necessary to survive. The gain for the establishment is pushing us too far behind the limits of our fear. By making us more afraid than is necessary, the establishment makes us stop short of the real possibilities now for transformation. This leaves a certain open political space we should occupy but don't. In order to expand the space we have for challenging domination, we first have to occupy the full space there is now. The government does not want us to occupy the space that really exists because it wants to keep us back from expanding the space. So, we may choose to go only one or two meters ahead when in fact there is a kilometer open to us.

With this introduction on discovering the real space for transformation, maybe I can speak more on how to begin teaching by telling a story about a liberating educator and some Spanish workers in Frankfurt, Germany. It was for me an example of an educator beginning by *doing with* the students instead of *doing for*. That is, the teacher was also a subject in the learning process. He learned in practice what was possible.

I was invited many years ago to Frankfurt by a group of left people. This group was composed of Christian left and Marxist left people. Up to that time, they were fighting among themselves. They had trouble staying together. They were intolerant of each other. Nevertheless, they agreed to meet together because of me, so I was an excuse, a pretext for them to do some work together, something good. And I went.

They wanted to discuss politics and education in the process of mobilizing the working class. They invited a Spanish worker to join our group. We were one worker and fifteen intellectuals! It was a very interesting combination. I needed a translation between them and me, because I don't understand German (only when they say "Paulo"!). But the Spanish worker spoke fluently in German. In the coffee break, the worker came to me and spoke in Spanish, and told me his story.

He said, "Paulo, one year ago, a group of five Spanish workers including me thought to organize a politics course for Spanish workers in exile. Then we met and did exactly what you educators *really* do. *We* organized the contents of the course because *we* knew what the others should know, and ought to know, like *you*." He was telling this to me humorously. He went on to say that they began to invite their colleagues, their peers. All of their fellow Spanish workers said to the five organizers, "You are crazy! I did not come to Germany to follow any course of politics. I am here to get money, and one day to go back to Spain to buy a little house. I don't want even to hear about politics."

Then, the worker telling me the story said, "We met again together to analyze our failures." I asked him if they stopped their project after their first attempt failed. He answered "No. We thought to make some research. But, not like you." It's very interesting the way he understood the problem. And he said, "The five of us in different factories began to ask our peers about what they like to do, what are their expectations in being in Germany besides getting money. Two days after that, we met again to make our evaluation of what we heard from them. The first thing, their first preference was to drink beer in German bars!"

It's so interesting to understand this expectation psychoanalytically. In the last analysis, the German workers discriminated strongly against the foreign workers. They viewed the foreigners as if they were animals. And one of the things the Spanish workers felt unconsciously would give them a different relation to the German workers would be to join them in the moment they were drinking. This would also be a way for them to be respected, to do something that the Germans liked to do. Certainly, it is a myth, an impossible dream, but it is very concrete. The Spanish worker who made the research told me that they eliminated this expectation from their teaching plans because they could not work directly on getting Spanish workers drinking with Germans in the German bars.

They found that a second expectation or taste was to play cards. The Spanish worker-educator then said to me, "Paulo, we five teachers became experts in all the kinds of card games. We learned them and when we were ready we began to go each Saturday, each of us, to the house of one worker, where we met five others, so we met twenty-five Spanish workers a week. When I was playing cards, sometimes without looking at their eyes" (he was such a psychologist!) "I took my card, put it on the table, and said, 'Did you know what happened last week in Madrid?'" (fantastic, no?) "Then, one of them asked me, 'What happened?' And I said, still without looking at them, that a group of workers were put in jail for attempting a strike to get better salaries. There was a total silence after I said that. I also was silent. Why?" (This man was fantastic, one of my educators without knowing it, maybe one of five or six very good educators I have had in situations like this.) "Why should I break down this silence? It had a reason, because I was introducing a very, very painful issue, a political one. We continued to play. Later, another card, another question, another silence. When we finished, they wanted to talk more."

This was for me a wonderful example of how to begin. The teacher learned how to read reality, changing his practice from what he learned in practice. It also showed how the educator did not separate research from teaching. That traditional dichotomy says that the researcher is not an educator and the educator is not a researcher. It is very destructive. Research is more and more divided into specialties where a deeper knowledge of the part does not teach you more about the totality, where the person doing research is a 'scientist' or 'theorist' who does not dirty his or her hands in reality, while the teacher does not research the conditions for education.

The Spanish worker-teacher was both a theorist and a practitioner. He got information on a part and related it to the larger problem of education. His research also revealed the mimetism of dominated consciousness, how the dominated want to copy the dominant. That is, before the dominated experience themselves in the struggle to overcome the feeling of inferiority, they are mimetic of the powerful. They have a strong desire to drink like the Germans with the Germans in the German bars.

Ira This story reminds me of the Italian worker in the movie *Bread and Chocolate* who wants so much to drink with the Swiss-Germans in their own bars, he even dyes his hair blonde!

Paulo We saw that film in Geneva, the very place it happened, the strong feeling of inferiority there, a fantastic story.

Ira The Frankfurt story is about racism, but also about how teachers situate themselves in the conditions of their students, to begin dialogue. They brought everything they needed to the class except the knowledge that counted, the consciousness and expectations of their students. To gain that knowledge, they began a grounded research into their students' culture.

Besides grounded research, what else would you do to begin liberatory education? In an earlier conversation, you mentioned the 'ideological map' or profile of the institution. This is research into the political terrain you are operating on, the groups, authorities, issues, and structure. What else would you say to yourself as you begin?

A Practical Agenda For Day One

Paulo   First of all, we should be clear that our work, our activities as an educator, will not be enough to change the world. This for me is the first thing, not to idealize the educational task. But, at the same time, it is necessary to recognize that by doing something inside the space of the school we can make some good contributions. We need to have more or less clear the limits we have as educators. Going far beyond the limits can frighten the people we want to change reality with. For example, in working among fundamentalist peasants, it can sound like a terrible thing if you announce that we must radically change our reality. They believe that God makes all things, so their difficult situation is only a test by God of their love for Him. This legacy is a concrete reality, a limit, *a destiny*, in their point of view. If you speak about changing destination, you make it sound as if the revolution is against God, and not against capitalism. The liberating educators or cadres lack competence when they make such a tactical error. They did not know the limits of the situation; they did not carefully research their terrain.

Secondly, and necessarily, I would need to improve my humility vis-a-vis the students by working with them, not as a tactic but as a necessity. What do I mean by this? Of course, I need to be sure that I have some knowledge, that I know something. If I don't know, I cannot be a teacher. But, what I have to know is that even though I possibly know something more than the students who come to work with me, they also are able to know, and they already know many things when they meet me in class. I will want to find ways for the students to show in class what they know.

Thirdly, I must be clear that I need to reknow what I think I know, to the extent that the educatees know with me and among themselves. I have also to be clear that the starting point for them to experience some knowable object which I propose cannot be my understanding of the object and the reality. It means the teachers must have some indications about how the students are understanding their reality different from the teachers' reality. Also, I need to know what are some of their main expectations by coming to this class. Why did they come to work with me this semester? What are their main dreams? These things help me understand the levels of their perception, their language, the difficulties they are having in understanding academic language. These first moments allow me to understand what kinds of difficulties they are having in reading texts. This is necessary for me to help them, but my task is not only to help them, to speak to them, but to speak with them.

Fourthly, I also have to be more or less critical concerning how our society is working. I need critical understanding of the very ways the society works, in order for me to understand how the education I am involved in works in the global context and in the context of the classroom. In the last analysis, we change ourselves to the extent we become engaged in the process of social change. In the intimacy of social movements for transformation, we find a very dynamic moment of change. To separate the global dynamics of social change from our educational practice is a mistake.

One issue in reknowing what the teacher knows, especially in the connection of education to power in society, has to do with the ideology of 'aptitude' and 'aptitude' tests. A good book to read here is the one you mentioned before by Bisseret, *Ideology, Class Language and Education*.[3] She described very well the crisis of the bourgeoisie after it took power from the aristocracy. The notion of noble birth as a sign of achievement was replaced by an ideology of making your own destiny without regard to birth. But, how could the bourgeoisie then justify keeping workers in their place? How could they explain that under capitalism workers did not go as far as the elite? They invented the idea of 'aptitude.' And science was there immediately to help out! Science invented tests to prove 'aptitude.' Unfortunately, children from the working-class do not seem to show 'aptitude.' I am suspicious of 'aptitude.' To begin as a liberating educator, I could reflect on the students and my thoughts, and ask what I think about 'aptitude.'

Another thing, we intellectuals should examine the nature of our own idiom. The challenge to liberating educators is to transform the abstract speech we inherit from our training in the bourgeois academy. This takes some courage to reinvent our idiom while still being rigorous and critical. That is, the new language of a radically democratic society will not be the "word-ballets" of an abstract intelligentsia, and will not be the language of an acritical working class either. Another idiom must emerge as part of the historical process of revolutionary transformation. Finding that idiom requires intellectuals to break with the elitism of their training and with the discourse that currently guarantees them prestige or rewards in the academy.

Also, we must work to have some good classroom experiences in reading texts, which is something the teacher should consider at the beginning. We must continue to study books as another way of reading the world, in addition to reading the world without going through books. How can reading books give the students contact with the reality of the country, not just their immediate reality? This requires studying books and newspapers, listening to television and radio, listening to people talking in the streets. The teacher needs to know how to read the reality of the students through texts as well as through the reality itself. Reality is not a *positum*, fixed and complete, waiting for the teacher to bring it to the students like a package, like a piece of meat. No! Reality is a becoming, not a standing still.

As an example of reading a changing reality, I could speak about a man from Brazil, a young, fantastic leader, a worker who is the President of the Workers Party, known also in the States, Lula, the famous Lula. He studied only a few years in primary school, but for me he is one of the best readers of Brazilian reality today, without having made any university studies, not even high school. But, he is experiencing himself strongly in a political practice as president of the party, understanding more and more the situation of Brazil. It is beautiful to see how he answers the questions asked him on television programs, how he debates other politicians, how he discusses issues with so-called intellectuals at some moments, and with very good intellectuals who work in the same party or in other parties. He feels secure vis-a-vis the moment of history in the country.

The other day I talked with Lula after a television conversation where a very good intellectual said to him, "Lula, it is a surprise for me, because I know you do not have time to read, but still you speak very seriously about the historical moment of Brazil, especially the situation today." Then, Lula said, "I really *don't* read." I said to him after that I disagreed with him. I said, "Lula, you are for me one of the best readers of Brazil today, but not readers of the *word*, readers of the *world*. That is, you are reading the history we are making every day. You are understanding it, grasping it to the extent that you are making it also. Please, don't say any more that you are not reading. You can say that you are not yet reading books. But you are reading history."

I think then that this is something that we also have to try as teachers preparing for the classroom. This is not to diminish the indispensable academic experience, but to diminish the distance which was established between reading words and reading the world. This means giving examples to the students which call their attention from time to time to the kind of reflection we are doing, how we are using words when we try to grasp an object.

To do this, with careful attention to the words spoken in the analysis, the teacher has to be full of respect for what the students say. For example, for a teacher starting out in a class, there is no such thing as stupid questions from students and there is no such thing as *the* answer from the teacher. All the questions deserve to be answered, and we maybe never have *the* answer, but possibily one of the answers. We must avoid dogmatism and disrespect.

Ira   The habit of taking student statements seriously needs cultivation by teachers under pressure to 'cover the syllabus' while teaching large classes. Too many classes with too many students and a long official syllabus make it hard for teachers to attend to any student's words or needs. Also, student remarks will often be in halting, nonstandard idioms, so the mere form of their expression can easily provoke teacher impatience. Even more, liberatory teachers will hear expressions of sexism, racism, obsessive concern with 'communism,' impatience with serious intellectual study, and mimetic love of the rich and powerful. Negative consciousness has to surface, or be allowed to surface, or be provoked to the surface, if the teacher is to get authentic information on the levels of student thought. Racist and sexist remarks have to be drawn out as legitimate objects of study, as authentic parts of student consciousness. How can you study anything kept silent?

Paulo   Yes, all questions must be permitted, but one thing that is impossible for a 'democratic' educator is to permit aggression in students to go beyond some limits. It is impossible to allow a student to demolish a room and to order a teacher to get out. There must be limits on behavior. What a teacher cannot do is to use limits to silence students just because students think differently from the teacher.

Ira   In my college, students are very shrewd, 'cagey' in colloquial idiom. They sit tight in the beginning of a course and try to 'psych out' the teacher's politics. If their own ideology is different from the teacher's, many students at my college tend to keep quiet, play it cool, and coast through the war zone. If they speak, they will fashion their words inside the vocabulary of the teacher's politics. When they write papers, they also try to copy the teacher's ideology, to get a good grade. You see? These students begin expecting lower grades for disagreeing with the teacher, or put another way, they 'get by' through agreeing with the boss, the teacher. What I try in this situation, in the beginning of the term, is to demonstrate that there is no punishment for disagreeing with me, and also there is no reward for simply agreeing with me. I do this in several ways. In class, I react blankly to any student who mimics my ideas in his or her own voice. I do not model approval of mimicry. Then, I raise questions about my very own position, phrased by the student, to challenge their manipulation of me for a grade. If students write papers mimicking my ideas, I do the same thing, but in written response on their essays, asking leading questions about the ideology they 'psyched out.' I don't give automatic As to the mimic-papers and my written questions urge the student to reason out the issues in depth, next time. From the reverse point of view, if a student writes a paper or makes a statement antagonistic to my views, I don't pounce on him or her in a one-to-one debate. Instead, I reproduce the paper for class reading and discussion, or re-present the statement as a problem-theme for our inquiry.

Because students know how to mimic their teacher's ideology to get a good grade, this is another reason why some verbal restraint on my part in the early weeks is important. By saying less, I provoke more authentic student ideology, because I give the students less of my ideology to fashion fake agreements around. I wish I could do this more successfully than I do. I often get too enthusiastic about something I heard in class or about a reading I bring in, or a reading a student offers to the group, and I talk more than I should, giving students a lot of material on my point of view. Or else I come to class one day too tired to listen carefully, or not yet stimulated by student statements, so I talk too much. Sometimes this sparks the students' own excitement, and other times I get papers simply copying my words.

When I begin a semester, I review the traditional school script and remind myself how teachers and students are socialized to behave in the dominant curriculum. I also try to read what my students read, listen to the radio, see TV and go to pop movies, like you suggested before, Paulo, to study their reality, a mass culture I grew up in but one now different from my own.

Imagination in Dialogue: Making the Future Possible

Ira   Let's finish our talks by discussing intuition and imagination. You speak often about our political 'dream.' But, the dialogical method emphasizes critical thinking, historical knowledge, and social inquiry. I'd like to speak now about imagination in terms of taking our 'dream' of transformation to reality in our actions. How are imagination and intuition resources for liberating education?

In a society like mine, vast resources are available to the establishment for myth-making: radio, TV, newspapers and magazines, schools, pro sports, rock music, staged spectacles like political campaigns. The dominant culture possesses many tools to shape the way people think about the past, present, and future. In this culture war over consciousness, people's imaginations are supervised as one control on their exercise of political power. The present order of society can extend its hierarchy into the future as long as it dominates the political process, including political imagination. Our project of social transformation involves anticipating a society different from the one we have now. To prevent this, mass culture surrounds consciousness with myths and images that crowd out the ability to imagine alternatives, to anticipate a history different from the one we live in now. Expecting the current system to go on forever is a kind of mass despair useful to the elite who now have power.

In schooling, the opaque, official curriculum not only hides reality but it also blocks dissident imagination. We see the future in terms of present relations, the structures limiting us, the values already immersing us. To rescue imagination and intuition, to exercise them as opposition resources for conceiving and making change, liberating pedagogy needs to stimulate alternative thinking. This can offer students some distance from the enveloping messages and images of mass culture.

Critical thinking needs imagination where students and teachers practice anticipating a new social reality. Imagination can be exercised as a resource to expel dominant ideology and to open up some space in consciousness for transcendent thinking. I've asked students to be imaginative generally in the courses I teach. Our social inquiries regularly include a moment called "reconstruction," where I ask students to imagine alternatives to the social problem they have investigated, as a model of future solutions. The class that goes farthest in this has been the Utopia one, not surprisingly. Utopia is a theme available for designing courses in a number of departments.

Paulo   Yes, but I think that imagination, guessing, intuition, cannot be dichotomized from critical thinking. That is, intuition for me is almost guessing. It's something where my feelings challenge me in order to foresee. It's something that tells me there is something over there. Or, there is something coming. I think, Ira, the more we are able to improve in ourselves our sensibility, the more we will be able to know rigorously.

Nevertheless, we cannot stop at the level of intuition. We have to treat the object of the intuition with rigor. This is also one of the tasks of those intellectuals whose choice is social transformation, to exercise rigor on political intuitions, not by offering regular seminars, but rather inside the everyday experience of a political party. Intellectuals, working people, and leaders of political movements all have knowledge as well as intuition. They need to share the different things they know and intuit. What they know and what they intuit are not exactly the same. One way intellectuals can help social movements is by making available special knowledge they possess as experts in a field.

Intellectuals can offer scientific information on the capitalist system of production. Look, in some ways, workers and working-class leaders know how the system works. They know this very well at the level of sensibility. The workers know they are 'objects' of exploitation, that their labor power is being exploited, taken from them. What is necessary now, is just to go beyond the sensibility of the fact, in order to get the *raison d'etre* for the facts. Intuition is absolutely indispensable for me in this process of knowing, as long as we don't stop at that level, but go beyond. It is as if we got on the bus of intuition but at some moment in the road have to get on a different vehicle to go farther.

In some respect, through imagination you can see ahead also, like with intuition. Now, we can go to the Utopian aspect, for those who are 'out of place!' (Laughing) For me, being a 'prophet' does not mean to be a crazy man with a dirty beard, or to be a crazy woman. It means to be strongly in the present, to have your feet firmly planted on the ground, in such a way that foreseeing the future becomes a normal thing. You know the present so well, you can imagine a possible future of transformation. Imagination at this level is side-by-side with dreams. At this moment, I can tell you and the possible readers of our book a story which touched me a lot when I heard it, about anticipating history.

Some years ago, I was in Bissau, and I was talking with people who had worked very near Amilcar Cabral during the revolutionary struggle there. At one moment, a woman I spoke with said to me, "Paulo, one time I was in a group of militants at a meeting with Comrade Cabral, in Guinea-Conakry. Cabral was talking to us and trying to make an evaluation of the on-going liberation movement. After one hour of discussion, after making clear some points, he suddenly closed his eyes, and said to us, 'Now, let me dream.' And then he began to talk with his eyes closed. He talked about what should be in Guinea-Bissau after independence. But he went even towards some details of the organization of the country, of the bureaucracy, of education, of the people, while the others were silently listening. After thirty or forty minutes of speaking like this, in a dream, he finished and one of the militants risked asking him a question. He asked, 'Comrade Cabral, is it not a dream?' Cabral opened his eyes, looked at him, smiled, and said, 'Yes, it is a dream, a possible dream.' And he finished the meeting by saying, 'How poor is the revolution that doesn't dream.' "

This is imagination. This is the possibility to go beyond tomorrow without being naively idealistic. This is Utopianism as a dialectical relationship between denouncing the present and announcing the future. To anticipate tomorrow by dreaming today. The question is as Cabral said, Is the dream a possible one or not? If it is less possible, the question for us is how to make it more possible.

Notes

[1] See Erich Fromm's *Escape From Freedom* (New York, 1941), *Man For Himself* (New York, 1947), and *Beyond the Chains of Illusion: My Encounter With Marx and Freud* (New York, 1962).

[2] On the great school reform crisis launched from the establishment in 1983 in the U.S., see footnote [1] in the "Foreword."

[3] Noelle Bisseret, *Ideology, Class Language, and Education* (Boston, 1979).

BIBLIOGRAPHY

SELECTED BIBLIOGRAPHY: Resources for Transformation

Ada, Alma Flor, and de Olave, Maria del Pilar, *Hagamos Caminos: A Bilingual Reading and Language Development Series*, Addison-Wesley, Reading, Massachusetts, 1985.

Adams, Frank, with Horton, Myles, *Unearthing Seeds of Fire: The Idea of Highlander*, Blair, Winston-Salem, North Carolina, 1975.

Apple, Michael W., *Ideology and Curriculum*, Routledge and Kegan Paul, London, 1979.

———, *Cultural and Economic Reproduction in Education*, Routledge and Kegan Paul, London, 1982.

Aronowitz, S., and Giroux, H., *Education Under Siege*, Bergin and Garvey, South Hadley, Massachusetts, 1985.

Ashton-Warner, Sylvia, *Teacher*, (first edition 1963), Bantam, New York, 1979.

Auerbach, Elsa Roberts, and Burgess, Denise, "The Hidden Curriculum of Survivial ESL," *TESOL Quarterly*, volume 19, number 3, September, 1985, pp. 475-495.

Avrich, Paul, *The Modern School Movement: Anarchism and Education in the United States*, Princeton University Press, New Jersey, 1980.

Bastian, A., Fruchter, N., Gittell, M., Greer, C., and Haskins, K., *Choosing Equality: The Case for Democratic Schooling*, Temple, Philadelphia, 1986.

Berlak, A., and Berlak, H., *Dilemmas of Schooling: Teaching and Social Change*, Methuen, New York, 1981.

Berthoff, Ann, *The Making of Meaning*, Boynton-Cook, Montclair, New Jersey, 1981.

Bisseret, Noelle, *Education, Class Language and Ideology*, Routledge and Kegan Paul, Boston, 1979.

Bourdieu, P., and Passeron, J.C., *Reproduction in Education, Society and Culture*, Sage, Beverly Hills, 1977.

Bowles, S., and Gintis, H., *Schooling in Capitalist America*, Basic Books, New York, 1976.

Brown, Cynthia, *Literacy in 30 Hours: Paulo Freire's Process in Northeast Brazil*, Alternate Schools Network, Chicago, 1975.

Carnoy, M., *Education as Cultural Imperialism*, McKay, New York, 1974.

———, and Levin, H., *Schooling and Work in the Democratic State*, Stanford University Press, California, 1985.

Collins, Dennis, *Paulo Freire: His Life, Thought and Work*, Paulist Press, New York, 1977.

Cuban, Larry, "Policy and Research Dilemmas in the Teaching of Reasoning: Unplanned Designs," *Review of Educational Research*, Volume 54, Number 4, Winter, 1984, pp. 655-681.

Dewey, John, *Democracy and Education*, (first edition 1916), Free Press, New York, 1966.

———, *Experience and Education*, (first edition 1938) , Macmillan, New York, 1963.

Donald, James, "How Illiteracy Became a Problem and Literacy Stopped Being One," *Journal of Education*, Volume 165, Number 1, Winter, 1983, pp. 35-52.

Elsasser, Nan, and John-Steiner, Vera, "An Interactionist Approach to Advancing Literacy," *Harvard Educational Review*, volume 47, number 3, August, 1977, pp. 355-369.

Finlay, Linda Shaw, and Faith, Valerie, "Illiteracy and Alienation in American Colleges: Is Paulo Freire's Pedagogy Relevant?," *The Radical Teacher*, number 16, December, 1979, pp. 28-37.

Fiore, Kyle, and Elsasser, Nan, "'Strangers No More': A Liberatory Literacy Curriculum," *College English*, volume 44, number 3, February, 1982, pp. 115-128.

Fisher, Berenice, "What is Feminist Pedagogy?," *The Radical Teacher*, number 18 (no date), pp. 20-24.

Frankenstein, Marilyn, "Critical Mathematics Education: An Application of Paulo Freire's Epistemology," *Journal of Education*, volume 165, number 4, 1983, pp. 315-339.

Freire, Paulo, *Pedagogy of the Oppressed*, Continuum, New York, 1970.

———, *Education for Critical Consciousness*, Continuum, New York, 1973.

———, *Pedagogy-in-Process*, Continuum, New York, 1978.

———, *The Politics of Education*, Bergin and Garvey, South Hadley, Massachusetts, 1985.

Giroux, H., "Writing and Critical Thinking in the Social Studies," *Curriculum Inquiry*, volume 8, number 4, 1978, pp. 291-310.

———, *Theory and Resistance in Education*, Bergin and Garvey, South Hadley, Massachusetts, 1983.

Goodlad, John I., *A Place Called School*, McGraw-Hill, New York, 1983.

Greene, Maxine, *Landscapes of Learning*, Teachers College, New York, 1978.

Gross, Ronald, and Gross, Beatrice, eds., *The Great School Debate: Which Way For American Education?*, Simon and Schuster, New York, 1985.

Grumet, Madeleine R., "In Search of Theatre: Ritual, Confrontation, and The Suspense of Form," *Journal of Education*, Winter, 1980, pp. 93-110.

Heath, S.B., *Ways With Words: Language, Life, and Work in Communities and Classrooms*, Cambridge, New York, 1983.

Hirshon, Sheryl, with Butler, Judy, *And Also Teach Them To Read: The National Literacy Crusade of Nicaragua*, Lawrence Hill and Company, Westport, Connecticut, 1983.

Hoggart, Richard, *The Uses of Literacy: Aspects of Working-class Life*, Chatto, Windus, London, 1957.

Hunter, Carman St. John, and Harman, David, *Adult Illiteracy in America*, McGraw-Hill, New York, 1979.

Illich, Ivan, *Deschooling Society*, Harper and Row, New York, 1972.

Jencks, Christopher, et.al., *Inequality*, Basic Books, New York, 1972.

Katz, Michael B., *Class, Bureaucracy and Schools: The Illusion of Educational Change in America*, Praeger, New York, 1971.

Kohl, Herb, *Basic Skills*, Bantam, New York, 1984.

————, *The Open Classroom*, New York Review Books, New York, 1969.

Kozol, Jonathan, *Free Schools*, Houghton-Mifflin, Boston, 1972.

————, *Children of the Revolution: A Yankee Teacher in the Cuban Schools*, Delta Press, New York, 1980.

————, *Illiterate America*, Doubleday, New York, 1985.

Levin, Henry M., "Why Isn't Educational Research More Useful?," *Prospects*, Volume 8, Number 2, 1978, pp. 157-166.

————, "The Identity Crisis in Educational Planning," *Harvard Educational Review*, volume 51, number 1, February, 1981, pp. 85-93.

————, and Rumberger, Russell W., "The Educational Implications of High Technology," Project Report 83-A4, Institute for Research on Educational Finance and Governance, Stanford University, February, 1983.

Mackie, J., ed., *Literacy and Revolution: The Pedagogy of Paulo Freire*, Continuum, New York, 1981.

McFadden, John, *Consciousness and Social Change: The Pedagogy of Paulo Freire*, Ph.D. Dissertation, School of Education, California State University, Sacramento, 1975.

Miller, Valerie, *Between Struggle and Hope: The Nicaraguan Literacy Crusade*, Westview, Boulder, Colorado, 1985.

Moriarty, Pia, *Codifications in Freire's Pedagogy: A North American Application*, M A Dissertation in Adult Education, San Francisco State University, 1985.

————, and Wallerstein, Nina, "Student/Teacher/Learner: A Freire Approach to ABE/ESL," *Adult Literacy and Basic Education*, Fall, 1979.

Noble, Phyllis, *Formation of Freirian Facilitators*, Latino Institute, Chicago, 1983.

Ohmann, Richard, *English in America*, Oxford, New York, 1976.

————, "Literacy, Technology, and Monopoly Capital," *College English*, Volume 47, Number 7, November, 1985, pp. 675-689.

————, "Where Did Mass Culture Come From? The Case of Magazines," *Berkshire Review*, Volume 16, 1981, pp. 85-101.

Ollman, Bertell, and Norton, Theodore, eds., *Studies in Socialist Pedagogy*, Monthly Review, New York, 1977.

Pincus, Fred, "The False Promises of Community Colleges: Class Confict and Vocational Education," *Harvard Educational Review*, August, 1980, pp. 332-361.

————, "From Equity to Excellence: The Rebirth of Educational Conservatism," *Social Policy*, Winter, 1984, pp.11-15.

Schniedewind, Nancy, "Feminist Values: Guidelines for Teaching Methodology," *The Radical Teacher*, number 18 (no date), pp. 25-28.

————, and Davidson, Ellen, *Open Minds to Equality*, Prentice-Hall, New Jersey, 1984.

Schoolboys of Barbiana, *Letter to a Teacher*, Vintage, New York, 1971.

Shor, Ira, *Critical Teaching and Everyday Life*, University of Chicago Press (3rd Printing), Chicago, 1987.

————, *Culture Wars: School and Society in the Conservative Restoration, 1969-1984*, Routledge and Kegan Paul, Methuen Press, New York, 1986.

Spring, Joel, *Education and the Rise of the Corporate State*, Beacon, Boston, 1972.

Wallerstein, Nina, *Language and Culture in Conflict: Problem-Posing in the ESL Classroom*, Addison-Wesley, New Jersey, 1984.

Willis, Paul, *Learning to Labor: How Working Class Kids Get Working Class Jobs*, Columbia University Press, New York, 1981.

Wirth, Arthur, *Productive Work—In Industry and Schools: Becoming Persons Again*, University Press, Maryland, 1983.

Vygotsky, L., *Thought and Language*, MIT Press, Cambridge, (first edition 1962), 1977.

Zimmet, Nancy, "More Than The Basics: Teaching Critical Reading in High School," *Radical Teacher*, No. 20 (no date), pp. 11-13.

Index

Machismo, 165
Manipulation, 171, 172, 173–174, 176
Mass movements. *See* Social movements
Me-decade, 115
Memorizing, 86
Metaphors, 150, 152–153 (*See also* Language)
Mimicry, 117–118, 155, 179, 184
Modern School Movement, 35
Motivation, 4–7, 32, 104; intrinsic, 23; of
   knowing, 8; profile of, 6
Movements. *See* Social movements
Myths, 82; dominant ideology and, 55, 168; in
   Germany, 178; making of, 185; symbolic
   violence, 123; of United States of America,
   173; value-free learning, 12–14, 174

New School Movement, 35

Official curriculum. *See* Traditional curriculum
Official ideology. *See* Dominant ideology
Opaque curriculum. *See* Traditional
   curriculum
Open Admissions, 19, 21, 22, 59–60, 144

Parallel classroom, 10
Parallel education, 10
Parallel pedagogies, 44
Passive education. *See* Traditional curriculum
The Pedagogy of the Oppressed (Freire), 39, 61,
   122, 153
Physics course, 107–110, 116
Political movement, 133 (*See also* Social
   movements)
Politics, 12–13; education and, 8, 10, 31, 33,
   45–46, 61; social transformation and, 34–35
Power, 13, 22, 31–32, 34, 35, 43, 73, 76; in
   classroom, 93, 162, 176; language and,
   148–149 (*See also* Society)
Progressive School Movement, 35, 109
Prophet, 186
Protest movements. *See* Social movements
Public education system, 76

Other Books of Interest from *Bergin & Garvey*

LITERACY: READING THE WORD & THE WORLD
PAULO FREIRE & DONALDO MACEDO
Foreword by Ann Berthoff
Introduction by Henry A. Giroux
Critical Studies in Education Series
224 Pages

EDUCATION UNDER SIEGE
The Conservative, Liberal & Radical Debate Over Schooling
STANLEY ARONOWITZ & HENRY GIROUX
Critical Studies in Education Series
256 Pages

CRITICAL PEDAGOGY & CULTURAL POWER
DAVID LIVINGSTONE & CONTRIBUTORS
Introduction by Henry A. Giroux & Paulo Freire
Critical Studies in Education Series
368 Pages

WOMEN TEACHING FOR CHANGE
Gender, Class & Power
KATHLEEN WEILER
Introduction by Henry A. Giroux & Paulo Freire
Critical Studies in Education Series
240 Pages

THE POLITICS OF EDUCATION
Culture, Power & Liberation
With a Dialogue on Contemporary Issues
PAULO FREIRE
Introduction by Henry A. Giroux
Translated by Donaldo Macedo
Critical Studies in Education Series
240 Pages

THEORY & RESISTANCE IN EDUCATION
A Pedagogy for the Opposition
HENRY A. GIROUX
Foreword by Paulo Freire
Introduction by Stanley Aronowitz
Critical Perspectives in Social Theory Series
304 Pages

BOYS & GIRLS AT PLAY
The Development of Sex Roles
EVELYN GOODENOUGH PITCHER & LYN HICKEY SCHULTZ
Foreword by David Elkind
224 Pages